Believing & Obeying Jesus Christ:

The Urbana 79 Compendium

Edited by
John W. Alexander

InterVarsity Press
Downers Grove
Illinois 60515

InterVarsity Press is the book-publishing division of Inter-Varsity Christian Fellowship, a student movement active on campus at hundreds of universities, colleges and schools of nursing. For information about local and regional activities, write IVCF, 233 Langdon St., Madison, WI 53703.

Distributed in Canada through InterVarsity Press, 1875 Leslie St., Unit 10, Don Mills, Ontario M3B 2M5, Canada.

Acknowledgment is made to the following for permission to reprint copyrighted material: All Scripture quotations, unless otherwise indicated, are from the New American Standard Bible, © The Lockman Foundation 1960, 1962, 1963, 1968, 1971, 1972, 1973, 1975, 1977. All Scripture quotations marked RSV are from the Revised Standard Version of the Bible, copyrighted 1946, 1952, © 1971, 1973. All Scripture quotations marked NIV are from the New International Version of the Bible, copyright ©New York International Bible Society, 1973, 1978. The poem on pp. 177-78 is "Make Me Thy Fuel" from Toward Jerusalem by Amy Carmichael. Taken from copyrighted material used by permission of the Christian Literature Crusade, Fort Washington, Pa. 19034, and by SPCK, London.

ISBN 0-87784-728-2
Library of Congress Catalog Card Number: 79-3633

Printed in the United States of America

10	9	8	7	6	5	4	3	2	1	
89	88	87	86	85	84	83	82	81	80	

Contents

FOREWORD

The 12th Inter-Varsity Student Missions Convention is now history. You hold in your hands the messages given there by God's own people that moved thousands of intelligent, eager students to proclaim that they are ready to follow Jesus Christ overseas as missionaries.

As we enter the decade of the 1980s we are accompanied by a great wave of students stepping forth from Urbana 79 into God's waiting world. What are billions of people waiting for but to hear the gospel of our Lord Jesus Christ, which is the power unto salvation and which will change their very lives?

We have a great message to share. Our whole world's population could be reached for God's glory by the dedicated service of the thousands of students who said "yes" to Christ's Great Commission at Urbana 79. As you read through this book, your heart is bound to be stirred again and again by the challenge set forth by the speakers at Urbana 79.

Thousands of students' lives were changed during those days. For what purpose? Indeed, to go forth into a needy world to share with others that Jesus Christ is a wonderful Savior who died for their sins. May your hearts be blessed so that you, too, will desire to join the ranks of those who are pointed toward the waiting mission fields of our world.

John E. Kyle

PREFACE

The year was 1979. For five days, December 27-31, nearly 17,000 people occupied the entire campus of the University of Illinois in Urbana for the 12th national missions convention sponsored by Inter-Varsity Christian Fellowship of the United States and Canada.

The single overriding purpose of Urbana 79 was to glorify the Lord Jesus Christ by helping students in seeking God's place for them in world missions and thus to serve the church in strengthening its ministry.

Within that primary purpose the convention had three major objectives:

1. To help each student consider seriously what the Bible says about God's eternal and unchangeable plans for the world-wide proclamation and demonstration of the gospel of Jesus Christ.

2. To help each student consider seriously the situation in

the world today as the church of Jesus Christ proclaims and demonstrates the message of redemption.

3. To help each student consider seriously what these two things mean, individually and corporately, in seeking God's will for his or her life in the context of the body of Christ and his or her relationship to the world, both on campus and beyond.

Over 19,000 people preregistered for the convention. Of the 16,800 who arrived on the scene, there were 15,000 students, 800 missionaries, 300 pastors, 500 Inter-Varsity staff members including volunteers and 200 other friends.

These were trying days on the world scene. In Iran the terrorists were in their second month of holding fifty Americans hostage in the embassy in Teheran; the Ayatollah Khomeini had vowed to keep them captive until world opinion forced the Shah to return home from exile and face trial before the Iranian people. Armies of the Soviet Union were in the process of invading and taking control of the government in Afghanistan. The Middle East seethed with turmoil over the displaced Palestinians. Persecution and near-genocide had exterminated millions of persons in Cambodia, Laos and Vietnam. One wondered if God were setting the stage for Armageddon.

At Urbana 79 we were aware of the turmoil and prayed that God's will would prevail in the affairs of men. The convention aimed to help students discern God's will as to how he wanted them involved in the witness for Christ in such a world.

The theme of the convention was "that all nations might believe and obey Jesus Christ." Bible study phases of the convention focused on Paul's Letter to the Romans. Each day's schedule commenced with time for a private morning watch (quiet time) in which delegates were encouraged to use a series of studies (prepared by Yvonne Vinkemulder) in Romans 6—8.

From 8:00-9:00 each morning the delegates were in small group Bible studies averaging from eight to ten members. Dispersed throughout the university, these 1,600 small groups were each led by a student or staff member who had been prepared specifically for these daily ministries. All of these small groups worked their way through studies based on Romans 12—15.

From 10:00 until 11:00 each morning the delegates filled the huge Assembly Hall for an hour of daily Bible exposition by John R. W. Stott (from All Souls Anglican Church in London) on the first five chapters of Romans. From 11:00 until noon the assembly sang, prayed and listened to messages from missionaries from diverse ministries: rural missions, inner-city missions, mission boards, independent mission work, etc.

Afternoons were free with a host of options. The university Armory was open for delegates to confer with missionaries stationed at scores of booths blanketing the enormous Armory floor. Workshops, seminars and discussions led by missionaries were dispersed throughout classrooms and lecture halls from one end of the campus to the other.

Each evening from 7:00 to 9:00 delegates again jammed the Assembly Hall to sing, pray and hear messages from missionaries and mission leaders. The day closed with the small groups meeting once again, this time for sharing and prayer.

There were specialized Bible study groups during the 8:00 to 9:00 a.m. hour for pastors (chaired by James Reapsome of *Christianity Today* and addressed each morning by Gordon MacDonald of Grace Chapel, Lexington, Massachusetts). Another session, for missionaries, was led by Donald Patterson of First Presbyterian Church, Jackson, Mississippi.

Each day the excellent multi-media presentations by Inter-Varsity's TWENTYONEHUNDRED PRODUCTIONS powerfully presented, through music and visuals as well as the spoken word, key issues facing us in missions.

What were the results? God alone can answer that question in full, but a few results are known even as this volume goes to press. Around 200 delegates indicated they had received Christ during the convention. About 8,000 submitted signed decision cards indicating their readiness to serve as missionaries if God should call them. Numerous mission agencies said they had received an overwhelming response from students who submitted names and addresses and asked for assistance in discerning opportunities for mission service. An offering of over $500,000 was taken the evening of December 30 to support worldwide student witness. Another offering for famine relief in Cambodia exceeded $60,000. Most of the delegates also fasted during the noon meal of December 29, enabling the University of Illinois food service to refund $20,000 which was divided up into four gifts of $5,000 and awarded to four agencies engaged in poverty relief.

God worked during Urbana 79. In the words of one student, "I met God in a new way at Urbana, and I'll never be the same again."

May Jesus Christ be praised! May his message be proclaimed around the world so that all nations might believe and obey Jesus Christ!

John W. Alexander

Part I

Introduction

1
Why Are We Here?

John W. Alexander

Welcome to Urbana 79. We are here and God is here.

It's a joy being with you at the start of this convention. Right at the outset let us remind ourselves that we are assembled here in the name of Christ Jesus. It is our desire that he will have the pre-eminence in everything that we think, in all that we say and all that we do.

At a time when the world around us seems to be careening toward Armageddon, when there is so much tension and friction, so many people hungry and hurting, so much hopelessness and despair, we who are in the body of Christ come with a word of hope, because Jesus Christ is indeed the hope of this troubled world. He is the light to the darkness and it is our earnest desire that everybody have a chance to hear about him, have a chance to meet him, have a chance to be saved and transferred out of the kingdom of darkness into his kingdom of light.

That is why we have chosen as the theme of this convention

"that all nations might believe and obey Jesus Christ." And if
they are to believe him, they must hear about him first. And so
we are intent. We plan. We pray that the message will be sent
and that they will hear.

It is my conviction that there is no better way for us to start
this convention than to bow our hearts, confess our sins, be
cleansed by his Spirit and be forgiven. The prayer I will ask you
all to pray with me is an old one. It is a prayer of confession from
The Book of Common Prayer (Anglican) which many of our fore-
fathers in the faith have prayed in almost every country of the
world and over a span of time exceeding four hundred years:

Delegates: *Almighty and most merciful Father, we have erred
and strayed from Thy ways like lost sheep. We have followed
too much the devices and desires of our own hearts. We have
offended against Thy holy laws. We have left undone those
things which we ought to have done, and we have done those
things which we ought not to have done. And there is no
health in us. But Thou, O Lord, have mercy upon us, miserable offenders. Spare Thou those, O God, who confess their
faults. Restore Thou those who are penitent, according to Thy
promises declared unto mankind in Christ Jesus our Lord.
And grant, most merciful Father, for His sake that we may
hereafter live a godly, righteous, and sober life to the glory of
Thy holy name. Amen.*

Alexander: *Our heavenly Father, you have heard our confession of our sin and of our sins. Now we thank you for pro-
viding a remedy for sin, a provision through Jesus Christ:
what He did at Calvary through His atoning death, and
through His mighty resurrection. We thank you for crediting
to our account as repentant sinners the holy righteousness of
our Savior Jesus Christ. We thank you for the Holy Spirit and
His convicting power which has drawn us to Christ, has
quickened us who were dead in trespasses and sins and has
given us new life, eternal life through Jesus Christ our Lord.
Amen*

And now let us direct our attention to a basic question, namely,
why are we here? There are different ways of answering a question like that. Let me suggest that we are here because we are

unified by five basic convictions. And I would like to identify each of these five very briefly.

First, we believe that God is at work in spite of the terrible chaos and hostilities that exist that we hear about. We believe that God is in the process of drawing a host of people to Christ, people of all ages and classes and races and kindreds and languages and tribes—men and women who will respond to Christ for transfer out of the kingdom of darkness into the kingdom of light. That is one conviction that unifies us here tonight. That is one reason we are here.

Second, we believe that Jesus Christ is the focal point of God's great plan. Indeed, we believe that it was through Christ that the earth was created, the world came into being, and that it is through him it is held together by a cohesive action that keeps it from disintegrating. And in everything he, Christ Jesus, is to have pre-eminence.

There is a third belief that unites us. We believe in the Holy Spirit, the One who convicts men of sin, stirs within them a sense of need, of spiritual hunger and then draws them with great magnetic power to Christ himself across that line which separates darkness from light.

Let me suggest a fourth belief that unites us. We believe that God has spoken to his people through the prophets, through Jesus Christ when he walked this earth, through the Holy Spirit and through the writers of the Old and New Testaments. In other words, we believe that the Bible is the definitive, infallible, inerrant revelation of God's truth to mankind. We believe the Bible to be the light unto our feet and the lamp for our pathway. We believe the Scriptures to be the touchstone by which all other writing is to be evaluated. To the best of our ability we desire to think biblically, to speak biblically, to live biblically.

There is a fifth conviction that unites us and can be a fifth reason as to why we are here. That is because we believe in the church. As God's Spirit gives people new life in Christ, he makes them one with all who believe. And all of these persons constitute the church irrespective of sex, race, language, nationality, ethnic background, abilities. If Jesus Christ is their Savior and Lord, then they are part of the church.

Those are five convictions, five basic premises upon which
this convention has been planned—indeed five good reasons
why you and I are here.

But let me close these brief comments by answering the question, "why are we here?" in terms of what we expect to get out of
it. And here let me suggest four aims, objectives or aspirations.

The first is this: to help every one of us consider seriously
what the Bible says about God's eternal and unchangeable plan
for the worldwide proclamation and demonstration of the gospel. In other words, we begin with God and seek his will.

Our second aim is this: to consider seriously the situation in
this world. When we leave here in five days each of us, I trust,
will know more about what this world is like, particularly as it
is viewed from the eyes of people from other nations who serve
overseas. We will learn about the situation of the world today
as the church of Christ proclaims and demonstrates the message
of redemption.

The third objective is this: to help each of us consider seriously what these first two objectives mean, individually and corporately, in seeking God's will for our lives in the context of the
body of Christ and our relationship to the world.

The fourth and final aim for those of us who are students and
return from here to a campus is that we will be better spearheads
for God's Spirit and that we will impart a missionary vision and
concern to fellow Christians, for it is on that campus that God
has placed us.

I pray that every one of us will find these next five days a great
time of drawing closer to Christ Jesus and of fulfilling those
purposes for this Urbana 79.

2
What's Next?

Ronald G. Mitchell

A great many students who sign up to participate in an Urbana missionary convention do not necessarily feel a personal call from God to become foreign missionaries. Those of us attending for the first time have heard about how inspiring and challenging the convention is from others who have attended before. And of course we want to check out for ourselves what our I-V staff members keep telling us about this state university campus becoming "holy ground" for a few days. There is also for many of us that very basic issue regarding world mission: "Will I meet my life partner here?" This was my own situation as a student going to Urbana in 1970.

Through an Urbana experience missionary stereotypes can be changed. Those who have not kept up with foreign missions discover the great things that God is doing around the world. You cannot walk away from Urbana holding the popular and widespread view of missionaries as some kind of twentieth-century anachronism.

At Urbana 1970, black Christian students were able to come together to deal with their own particular concerns. One workshop we had brought out the many great contributions of black Americans to foreign missions in the past and also in the present.

In these ways Urbana helped me. But it was not until a number of years later that God led me to consider foreign missionary work for myself. As I left Urbana 70, my main concern was still the inner city of New York where I grew up.

New York City is a place where young people can easily grow up without ever being confronted personally with the good news of Jesus Christ. It is a place where there are too few people actively involved in evangelism. It is a place where to be a committed Christian can be a very lonely struggle.

Beyond all the cultural attractions, there is a side of New York that many tourists know nothing about. It is rat-infested neighborhoods where the buildings look as if they have been bombed out like post-World War 2 Germany. It is street gangs and drug pushers. It is hopelessness and despair. It is a place where it seems that people have no time for each other or God.

While growing up in such an environment, I became convinced that things around me could be different. Like many of my peers, I also was swept up with the social consciousness of the sixties. So I committed myself to working for social change.

At the time my commitment was based on romantic idealism. It didn't take long, though, to see that "chasing windmills" has very little effect on society's deeply entrenched evils. Also, how can one change the world when that person's own life needs changing? However, God worked in my life through the witness of Christians and my searching the Scriptures to show me that only through Jesus Christ could both my life *and* the society be changed.

I met others within Inter-Varsity in New York who shared my concern for the whole gospel. And we were challenged to show the college world around us that Christianity related not only to what professors taught in the classrooms, but also to the issues of Black Power, the Vietnam War and the rapid social changes taking place. We were being missionaries in our Jerusalem.

In Acts 1:8 we find Jesus, just before his ascension, outlining to his disciples their call to mission. He tells them, "You shall receive power when the Holy Spirit has come upon you; and you shall be My witnesses both in Jerusalem, and in all Judea and Samaria, and even to the remotest part of the earth." Each Christian has his or her own particular Jerusalem, Judea, Samaria and ends of the earth. Your college campus may be a large part of the Jerusalem which God has called you to. But our concern for missions should never end with our Jerusalem.

After I had finished college, the vision for an inner-city work that encompassed both evangelism and social concern remained with me. As a student, I had done part-time work in community organization and social service. This was with secular organizations. In such a position, there is great opportunity for person-to-person evangelism and also for learning from non-Christians about social action. But the Lord showed me that Christian social concern is not just a carbon copy of the concern of non-Christians. As we fight the evils of the world, we realize that we are dealing with principalities and powers and spiritual forces in high places. Christian social concern, therefore, is unique.

Not long after I graduated God opened the door that enabled me to work toward such a vision. I became a social worker for an inner-city church. Here I not only encountered my Judea, but also my Samaria. God led me into work with young people who were drug addicts and criminals. These were the people we were told to stay away from when I was growing up. We called them "the bad boys."

This work proved to be a real lesson in missions. I was different from them and they knew it. I had never taken drugs or served time in "the joint." But in order to be used of God I had to become sensitive to their own world and experiences. I had to do a lot of listening.

Within or close to each of our communities and campuses there are "Samarias." Our Samaria is those people who are looked down upon by our social group. It is people we do not want to identify too closely with because of what other people might say. Samaria is those on the other side of the tracks.

Before we rush off to the ends of the earth in concern for missions, we need to check out that we are not avoiding our Samaria. It is very unfortunate that a great many organizations and churches involved in foreign missions have completely neglected the Samaria of the inner cities here in the United States. There are mission boards which sponsor work in Africa and Latin America, yet they have by-passed black communities such as Harlem and Hispanic communities such as the South Bronx.

Our concern for mission is distorted if we by-pass our Jerusalem, Judea and Samaria for the ends of the earth. Therefore, if you're thinking about going into foreign missions, become a missionary where you are first. Then, plan on taking time for involvement in cross-cultural Christian witness such as through inner-city work.

But God does not want us to leave out the "ends of the earth" no matter how many needs we see around us. Urbana can greatly help us to realize this. But my own case ended up with God using more than an Urbana convention in order for me to consider going into foreign missions.

Active in the same church and young adult fellowship as I was a young woman from Sierra Leone, West Africa. I became very attracted to her, but after she completed her studies she returned home. However, as we continued to correspond, we knew that God was bringing us together. Quite independently of each other, we both also saw God calling me to serve in Sierra Leone.

It was a real struggle to consider leaving New York City. But soon doors opened in such a way as to confirm that it was truly the Lord's will. As it turned out, I did not meet my wife at Urbana, but through my wife I met my own Urbana!

Today, there are different varieties and styles of missionary service. Many are called to pioneer work among people in places where there are not any Christians. And indeed, the need for more people in such work is very great. On the other hand, others are called to work alongside young national churches as what some call "partners in mission." In Sierra Leone I served in youth and young adult work with a national church which had been autonomous for only a few years.

According to one survey, sixty-five per cent of Sierra Leone's total population is under twenty-five years of age. A great many of these young people are leaving the rural areas and are coming to the rapidly growing towns and cities. In these towns and cities, tremendous social problems are developing. These social problems are all new challenges for the churches in Sierra Leone. God used me to share my background and experience in these areas.

I expected many problems and tensions in my work as a foreign missionary. But there were also some I did not anticipate. Although financially I received "little" as a missionary, nonetheless, I found myself materially richer than the vast majority of those around me. In his book *Odd Man Out?* Donald Banks describes a missionary serving in West Africa who saw himself, paradoxically, as a "poor" rich man. That was what I felt like.

The material poverty of the Third World is hard to ignore when you have to relate to it everyday. One day as I was returning home by car, there were a group of children walking toward me carrying buckets of water on their heads. Many of them hardly had any clothes on. One girl I could see was embarrassed by my passing because she didn't have any clothes on at all. But as I turned the corner to my house, I became embarrassed as the words of Jesus came to me: "I was naked and you didn't clothe me." Was I now to answer, "Lord, when did I see you naked?"

Maybe some of us have never encountered children so poor that they are actually naked. World mission means that we are aware of the poverty, suffering and spiritual needs of people everywhere as if they are living right next door to us.

There cannot be a dichotomy between the sensitivity of those who go overseas and those who do not. Therefore, how we as Christians distinguish ourselves here in the United States from the general culture, which is consumed by materialism, has everything in the world to do with world missions. All Christians are called to a missionary lifestyle.

God's work in missions is a two-way street. Not only can

African Christians be blessed by us, but we also can be blessed by African Christians. Christianity in Africa is expanding at a very rapid rate, and there is a remarkable richness and vitality in the faith and worship of many African Christians. In African Christianity for the most part, we do not find a dichotomy between evangelism and social concern. This is because traditionally in African society, religion and life are inseparable. Also, African Christians are beginning to take a leading role in world missions.

Just before returning home on furlough, I was very blessed to have visited a Sierra Leonean pastor who is now 107 years of age. Everyone calls him "Grandfather Caulker." He lives in a village in an area where the church is very alive and growing rapidly. Grandfather Caulker had started the Christian work in that area in 1910 when he was sent out as a missionary from another part of Sierra Leone.

At that meeting, although not able to move around much, Grandfather Caulker was still very much alive mentally and spiritually. He prayed as one who had walked very closely with the Lord for a great number of years. His life is an amazing testimony of missionary sacrifice. He stands in the tradition of many who have given their lives for the sake of the gospel.

And now, what's next for us here at Urbana?

At Urbana we face the difficult yet exciting issue of how world mission is to be shaped in the coming years. In traditional African society there is a very strong connection between those who have gone before and those living now. Therefore, Urbana is us standing before a great cloud of witnesses, before those like Grandfather Caulker.

Urbana is us standing before a world filled with great physical, social and spiritual needs—a world in need of the love of Jesus Christ.

Urbana is each of us standing before the One who has called us to mission in Jerusalem, Judea, Samaria and to the ends of the earth, asking him: "For me, Lord, . . . what's next?"

Part II

The Messenger and God: Romans 1—5

3
God's
Gospel

John R. W. Stott

Paul's letter to the Romans is a kind of Christian manifesto. It is
the fullest, plainest, grandest statement of the gospel to be found
anywhere in the New Testament. Its message is not that "man
is born free but everywhere he is in chains" (as Rousseau put it)
but that "man is born in sin and slavery, and everywhere is in
chains, but Jesus Christ came to set him free." For here is good
news of freedom—freedom from the cramping bondage of guilt
and self-centeredness which destroy us as human beings. Once
grasp this good news, in your mind and in your experience, and
you will want to share it with the world. Nobody will be able to
silence you.

The sixteenth-century Reformers understood well the vital
importance of this letter. Luther called it "the clearest gospel of
all." Calvin said that "if a man understands it, he has a sure road
opened for him to the understanding of the whole Scripture."
And William Tyndale, the father of English Bible translators,

described it as "the principal and most excellent part of the New Testament, and most pure *euangelion,* that is to say, glad tidings . . . , and also a light and a way in unto the whole Scripture." In his view every Christian should learn it by heart. "The more it is studied," he wrote, "the easier it is; the more it is chewed, the pleasanter it is" (Prologue to Romans in his 1534 English New Testament).

Our task is to study only the letter's first four and a half chapters, but, as we do so, I think we shall come to agree with those Reformers. For we shall discover in these chapters a systematic statement of the main truths of the gospel. Here is fundamental teaching about man—sinful, guilty and inexcusable—about God —revealing his wrath against sin and revealing his mercy in the gospel—about Jesus Christ—seed of David and Son of God, who died for our sins and was raised in triumph from the dead—and about the new community of believers, both Jews and Gentiles, who, having been accepted by God in and through Jesus Christ alone, enjoy an altogether new life characterized by peace with God, a standing in his grace and a joyful expectation of his final glory.

The truths which God has revealed in these chapters are enough to stretch our minds, liberate our consciences, set our hearts on fire and open our lips in praise and testimony. May God himself speak to us through his own Word, and give us grace to listen and respond!

Analysis of Romans 1—5
As a simple analysis of the chapters we shall be studying, I suggest the following:

1. *God's Gospel* (1:1-17). Paul introduces himself as an apostle, summarizes the good news and tells his Roman readers why he is so eager to share it with them.

2. *God's Judgment* (1:18—3:20). Nobody can receive the good news of salvation who has not first heard the bad news of judgment. Only against this dark background does the gospel shine with full brightness. Paul's argument in these chapters is that all human beings have some knowledge of God and of goodness, ignorant pagans as well as favored Jews, the depraved as well as

the refined, but that no human being has ever lived up to his knowledge. All of us have gone against the truth we have known, and therefore all of us stand before God guilty and without excuse.

3. *God's Righteousness* (3:21—4:25). In 3:21-31 Paul explains what he calls "the righteousness of God," that is, God's righteous way of putting the unrighteous right with himself. In a single word we call this act of God "justification." Paul elaborates the source from which it comes (God's grace), the basis on which it rests (Christ's death) and the means by which it is received (faith alone, without works). And then in chapter 4 he illustrates these principles from the life of Abraham.

4. *God's People* (5:1-11). The main verbs of the first 11 verses of chapter 5 are all in the first person plural. "We have peace with God" (v. 1). "We have obtained our introduction . . . into this grace in which we stand" and "we exult in hope of the glory of God" (v. 2). "We also exult in our tribulations" (v. 3). Above all, "We . . . exult in God through our Lord Jesus Christ, through whom we have now received the reconciliation" (v. 11). Who is this *we*? It is God's people. It is the new community which God is creating through Christ. Paul associates himself with his readers and with all other believers throughout time and space, and he describes the great blessings which God has given us through Christ. They are "peace," "grace," "hope," "tribulation," "love" and "joy." They are all the fruits of our justification, the universal privileges of the people of God.

God's Gospel: Romans 1:1-17

Paul has never been in Rome. For ten years he has given himself to the evangelization of four Roman provinces on both sides of the Aegean Sea—Galatia (on his first missionary journey), Macedonia and Achaia (on his second missionary journey) and Asia, based on its capital Ephesus (on his third missionary journey). Now he considers his work in this whole area completed. There is, he writes, "no further place for me in these regions" (15:23). So his eyes are on more distant horizons. It is probably the winter of A.D. 56-57. He is spending three months in Corinth. His immediate plan is to go to Jerusalem in order to hand over the money he has been collecting from the Gentile Christians of Greece to the Jewish Christians of Judea. But after this he is determined to visit Rome. For how could the apostle to the Gentiles possibly neglect the Gentile world's capital city? And from there he hopes to push on still further to Spain, the western extremity of the Empire. He tells his Roman readers about these plans in 15:22-29 (cf. Acts 19:21). But already in the letter's first chapter he announces his desire to visit them, and, because they do not know one another personally, he introduces himself and his message much more fully than usual.

Our first study I have entitled "God's Gospel" since the noun *euangelion* ("gospel") or the verb *euangelizesthai* ("preach the gospel") occurs four times. It divides itself naturally into three sections each of which seems to have a key text:

1. Paul and the gospel (1-5). Verse 1: "an apostle, set apart for the gospel of God."

2. Paul and the Romans (6-13). Verse 15: "I am eager to preach the gospel to you also who are in Rome."

3. Paul and evangelism (14-17). Verse 16: "I am not ashamed of the gospel."

Paul and the Gospel (1:1-5)

It is always intriguing to see how Paul introduces himself at the beginning of his letters. Here he combines two designations, one of great humility and the other of great authority. First, he is "a bond-servant of Christ Jesus," for Jesus Christ has bought him and owns him, and he is entirely at his Lord's disposal, as we are also. Second, he is "called as an apostle," for the risen Lord's appearance to him on the Damascus Road led not only to his conversion but also to his special commissioning as an apostle, by which he was added to the Twelve and in particular appointed "the apostle to the Gentiles." He had not appointed himself to this privileged position, he says, but rather been "called" to it by Christ.

As an apostle, he has been "set apart for the gospel of God." Anders Nygren in his *Commentary on Romans* reminds us that the Greek verb for "set apart" has "the same root meaning as Pharisee," and he goes on to suggest that the apostle is drawing a deliberate contrast: "Paul, who had set himself apart for the law, is set apart by God for the gospel." Thus, the new age or new aeon has dawned, for "the gospel is the great new reality which God has now brought to us" (pp. 45-46). Certainly, it was the peculiar responsibility of Christ's apostles to receive, to formulate, to guard and to teach the gospel, or, as Charles Cranfield puts it, "to serve the gospel by an authoritative and normative proclamation of it" (p. 53). This Paul goes on immediately to do, giving us a summary of the gospel for which he had been set apart. He concentrates on six aspects of it.

1. *Its Origin.* The Christian good news is "the gospel of God" (v. 1). He conceived it. He determined and arranged that there should be a gospel for the world, by sending his Son to be the good news and by sending his Spirit to empower heralds to proclaim it. It is his gospel. Paul and the other apostles did not invent it; God revealed it to them.

This is the first and basic conviction which all of us need. What we have to share with others is not a ragbag of human speculations. It is not one more human religion which takes its place alongside all the other religions of mankind. No, it is "the gospel of God," God's good news for a lost world. Without this there can be no evangelism, no world mission.

2. *Its Attestation.* "The gospel of God" is a message "which He promised aforehand through His prophets in the holy Scriptures" (v. 2). Although he revealed it to the apostles, what he revealed to them was no novelty for he had already "promised" it "through his prophets." The apostles insist on this strongly. In this very chapter (v. 17), Paul quotes a text from the prophet Habakkuk in which the great doctrine of justification by faith is affirmed. In 3:21 he declares that the good news of justification which has been revealed in the gospel was nevertheless "witnessed by the Law and the Prophets." The apostles were clear about this from the beginning. Soon after Pentecost Peter could say, "All the prophets who have spoken, from Samuel and his successors onward, also announced these days" (Acts 3:24). Paul in his speeches took up the same theme. He claimed that he was "stating nothing but what the Prophets and Moses said was going to take place" (Acts 26:22). In particular, it was "accord-

ing to the Scriptures" that Christ died, and "according to the
Scriptures" that he was raised (1 Cor. 15:3-4).

So the apostles were no innovators. Nor are we. Evangelical
Christians are deeply concerned to be biblical Christians, to go
back to the beginnings and to keep evaluating the subsequent
traditions of the churches in the light of the original revelation
of God. Moreover, in so doing, we must not set the Old and New
Testaments in opposition to each other. To be sure, the Old
Testament was anticipation, while the New Testament is fulfillment, for what God taught through his apostles he had "promised beforehand through his prophets." But they do not conflict,
for both preach the gospel. The gospel has a double attestation,
namely the Old Testament and the New Testament. Both bear
witness to Jesus Christ, which is what Paul comes to now.

3. *Its Substance.* Verse 2 is really a parenthesis. If we omit
it and bring verses 1 and 3 together, this is what we read: "set
apart for the gospel of God . . . concerning His Son." The gospel
of God concerns the Son of God. The good news is about Jesus,
his unique person and work. Here Paul concentrates on who
Jesus is; he will have more to tell us later about what he has
done. In verses 3 and 4 he describes Jesus by two balancing expressions. On the one hand, he "was born of the seed of David
according to the flesh," while on the other he "was declared
with power to be the Son of God by the resurrection from the
dead, according to the Spirit of holiness."

These statements about Jesus are packed tight with theology,
and the commentators write pages and pages in their attempts
to unpack them. We shall have to be content with the main
emphasis, which is plain. There are contrasts between what
Jesus was "born" to be and what he was "declared" to be; between what he was "according to the flesh" and what he was
"according to the Spirit of holiness"; between the "seed [de-
scendant] of David" and the "Son of God"; between the weakness implicit in his birth and in his "flesh," and the "power"
displayed in his resurrection and by the Holy Spirit. This person, Paul began by affirming was God's "Son" (v. 3). But the
eternal Son of God first "was born" in lowliness, becoming a
real human being and so veiling his divine glory, and then by

the resurrection he was publicly and powerfully declared to be the Son of God he always had been. It is this person, seed of David and Son of God, Paul goes on, who is "Jesus Christ our Lord" (v. 4).

We could spend days and even weeks meditating on the profound implications of these verses. For here are references, direct or indirect, to the birth, death, resurrection and reign (on David's throne) of Jesus Christ. Here is also a statement of both his humiliation and his exaltation. Here is a claim that he is both fully human and fully divine, his human descent traced from David and his divine sonship demonstrated by the resurrection. And here is the further claim that he is both a historical and a contemporary figure, since the very same person who was once born, killed and raised is today "our Lord," the Master who owns us as his bondservants, rules our lives and appoints us to his service.

4. *Its Scope.* Its scope is all the nations. In verse 5 Paul reverts to the commission which he has received from the Lord Jesus. He calls it "grace and apostleship," which probably means "the undeserved privilege of being an apostle." Moreover, his particular apostleship was to be exercised "among all the Gentiles," that is, all the nations.

Thus the apostle's perspective was as broad as it was long. He set the gospel in the largest possible context. Not only had it been promised for centuries of human history, but it also embraces all the nations of the earth, including the inhabitants of the world's capital city, to whom he refers in verses 6 and 7.

Now Paul was a Jew, and had previously been a bigoted, narrow-minded Pharisee. In spite of the Old Testament teaching that in the messianic age the Gentiles would be included within the redeeming purpose of God, he had despised them as unclean, as "dogs." So let us mark well his emancipation from racial prejudice. He retained his patriotic love for his own people and longed passionately for their salvation (9:1-5; 10:1). But now he loved the Gentiles also and longed for their salvation.

What about us? We too need to be delivered by Christ from all our pride and prejudice—both racial and national—since nobody is beyond the scope of God's love, and God's gospel is for all the nations, indiscriminately.

5. *Its Purpose.* The purpose of proclaiming God's gospel to all the Gentiles, Paul writes, is "to bring about the obedience of faith." He uses the same expression in 16:26. It forms the basis of the Urbana 79 slogan "that all nations might believe and obey Jesus Christ."

"The obedience of faith" is the apostle's definition of the response which the gospel should evoke. It is a particularly important expression coming (as it does) at the beginning and end of the Letter to the Romans. For in Romans Paul outlines more fully than in any of his other letters the good news that God justifies sinners only by his grace (his free and unmerited favor), only through faith (trust in Christ, without any works of our own). Already in verses 16 and 17 the principle of *sola fide* ("by faith alone") is underlined four times. Yet here in verse 5 our response to the gospel is not termed "faith" but "the obedience of faith." How can this be explained?

Clearly Paul is not contradicting himself. Some commentators are always ready to say that Paul was muddleheaded and confused and did not know his own mind. But that assumption is entirely gratuitous. Paul was an exceptionally clear thinker, illumined by the Spirit of God. We must give him credit for logical consistency. We may be quite sure that he does not destroy his own message by declaring here (what he denies elsewhere) that salvation is by faith plus moral obedience. No, he is referring to "the obedience of *faith*," not "the obedience of *law*." He means that a true and living faith in Jesus both includes within itself an element of submission and leads inevitably to a life of obedience.

"By faith Abraham . . . obeyed" we read in Hebrews 11:8. By faith we obey too. The proper response to the gospel is indeed "faith," but the meaning of "faith" is determined by the Person who is its object. He is "Jesus Christ our Lord" (v. 4) or "the Lord Jesus Christ" (v. 7). It is therefore impossible to accept Jesus Christ as Savior without simultaneously surrendering to him as Lord. For he is one Person (our Lord and Savior) and "faith" is an act of total commitment to him, in other words, "the obedience of faith," or "faith-obedience."

6. *Its Goal*. God's gospel, promised in the Old Testament and centering on Christ, is to be preached to all the nations to bring about their faith-obedience. Why? What is our ultimate goal in spreading the good news and seeking to persuade people to respond to it? It is "for His name's sake" (v. 5). The "name" of Christ stands for Christ himself, everything he is and everything he has done, and the exalted rank accorded to him on account of who he is and what he has done. Later, in his letter to the Philippians, Paul will write that God has "highly exalted" Jesus and "bestowed on Him the name which is above every name, that at the name of Jesus every knee should bow ... and that every tongue should confess that Jesus Christ is Lord, to the glory of God the Father" (2:9-11). If it is God the Father's purpose that every knee and every tongue should acknowledge the supremacy of Jesus, it should be our purpose too. We should be "jealous" for the honor of Christ's name, troubled when it remains unknown, hurt when it is ignored, indignant when it is blasphemed and all the time anxious that it should be given the honor and the glory which are due to it.

This is the highest missionary motivation. It is neither obedience to the Great Commission, nor love for perishing sinners (right and strong as these incentives are), but rather zeal for the glory of Christ. Some missionary endeavor has been a thinly disguised form of imperialism; that is, a hunger for the prestige of our country or our church or our organization or ourselves. Only one imperialism is Christian, and that is concern for Christ's empire or kingdom. "For the sake of his name" is the missionary goal which causes all unworthy motives to wither and die.

Here, then, are six fundamental truths about the gospel. Its origin is God the Father and its substance is Jesus Christ his Son. For the good news is "the gospel of God ... concerning His Son." Its attestation is in all the Scriptures, the united testimony of the prophets and the apostles, and its scope is all the nations of the earth. Our immediate purpose in preaching it is to bring people to the obedience of faith, but our ultimate goal is to glorify the name of Jesus Christ.

Or, to sum up these six truths by six prepositions, we may say that the good news is the gospel *of* God, *about* Christ, *accord-*

ing to the Scriptures, for the nations, unto the obedience of faith and for the sake of his name.

Paul and the Romans (1:6-13)

Having described himself and his gospel, Paul now describes his readers, the members of the Christian community in Rome. He uses some rich expressions to indicate what they are and should be. The most striking thing about these expressions is that the verbs are in the passive voice. According to verse 7 the Roman Christians are "beloved of God," while according to verses 6 and 7 they are "called of Jesus Christ" and "called as saints." Similarly, if we are Christians, this is why. Primarily, it is not because we decided for Christ (though we did, and freely) but because God set his love upon us and called us to himself by his grace. God's decision for us antedates our decision for him. His loving call liberated us to respond and to come to him. In consequence, we belong to him, which is what the word *saints* means. By his calling we are members of the holy people of God. So Paul cannot wish for his readers any higher blessing than that they should continue to enjoy the "grace . . . and peace from God our Father and the Lord Jesus Christ" which they have already begun to receive (v. 7).

After this greeting, which speaks so eloquently of God's attitude toward them, Paul goes on to tell them of his own feelings towards them.

1. *He thanks God for them all* (v. 8), particularly because the news of their faith "is being proclaimed throughout the whole world." Paul had not himself been responsible for bringing the gospel to Rome or for planting the church there. But this did not inhibit him from thanksgiving that Rome had been evangelized. The existence of a believing community in the capital had become known throughout the empire. It was a cause for much gratitude and praise.

2. *He prays for them* (vv. 9-10). Mind you, he does not know them personally. But this does not stop him praying for them. "Unceasingly" and "always" he mentions them in his prayers. Nor is his statement merely a pious platitude. No, God himself, whom he serves in his spirit, and who knows the secrets of his

heart, is his witness that what he writes is true (v. 9). His prayers for them doubtless cover many topics, but above all he asks God that "perhaps now at last," if it be his will, he may succeed in coming to them. Notice in passing the humble phraseology which Paul employs (the "if" and "perhaps" and "by the will of God"). Prayer is not a convenient device for bending God's will to ours; it is the divinely appointed way of bending our will to his.

Paul's prayer was answered, and in the affirmative. His wish to visit Rome was granted, though neither at the time nor in the manner that he had envisaged. It is a sobering thought that he arrived there some three years later not as a free men, but as a prisoner, awaiting trial by the emperor to whom he had appealed.

3. *He longs to see them* (11-12). Moreover, he is quite explicit about the reasons for his desire to visit them. To begin with, he hopes to "impart some spiritual gift" to them. His expression is deliberately vague. He does not specify what *charisma* he has in mind. Since he is an apostle, it seems most natural to suppose that he is referring to his teaching. Or perhaps it is "encouragement" that he has in mind, since this is what he goes on to mention in verse 12 and *paraklēsis* ("encouragement") is one of the *charismata* he lists later in 12:8. Although the nature of the gift may be uncertain, its purpose is not. It would be to strengthen them, "that you may be established."

His reason for wanting to visit them is not only to impart something to them, however. In genuine humility he desires to receive something from them as well. He knows what reciprocal encouragement can be derived from Christian fellowship, and although himself an apostle, he is not too proud to acknowledge his need of it. He looks forward to this strengthening, "each of us by the other's faith, both yours and mine" (v. 12). Happy is the modern missionary who goes to another country and culture in the same spirit of humble receptivity—anxious to receive as well as to give, anxious to learn as well as to teach. Paul longs to visit the Christians in Rome.

4. *He has often planned to come to them,* he adds (v. 13). He wants them to know this, although thus far he has been pre-

vented, perhaps simply because he has been too busy elsewhere. He gives now a third reason for wishing to visit them. Beyond the strengthening of the church and the mutual encouragement, he has an evangelistic purpose. He wants to "obtain some fruit" or "reap some harvest" (RSV) among them, just as he has done "among the rest of the Gentiles." It was surely appropriate that the apostle to the Gentiles should hope to do some reaping in the capital of the world.

Paul and Evangelism (1:14-17)

Having told his Roman readers of his desire to "reap some harvest" among them, he goes on to make three statements—plain, personal and positive—of his anxiety to preach the gospel in Rome as elsewhere: (1) "I am under obligation both to Greeks and to barbarians" (v. 14); (2) "I am eager to preach the gospel" (v. 15); and (3) "I am not ashamed of the gospel" (v. 16). These affirmations are immediately arresting because they are in direct antithesis to much of the mood of the contemporary church.

Many modern church members regard themselves as being under no obligation to evangelize. On the contrary, if they engage in evangelism at all, they are very pleased with themselves. They consider that they are conferring a favor upon God. To Paul, however, evangelism was a debt, not a charity.

Next, the contemporary attitude to evangelism is characterized rather by reluctance than by enthusiasm, whereas Paul could say that he was "eager" to share the gospel with others.

Third, Paul could declare that he was "not ashamed of the gospel," whereas our great trouble is that many of us are ashamed of it, often as blushingly ashamed as if we were adolescents.

So the contrast between Paul and some modern church members is complete. We say, "I am under no obligation; I'm not at all eager; in fact I'm rather ashamed." Paul said, "I am under obligation; I am eager; for I am not ashamed."

Now remember, Paul had as many reasons to feel embarrassed as we have. Rome was the capital of the world. People spoke of Rome with awe. It was the symbol of imperial pride and military power. Everybody hoped to visit Rome once in his lifetime, to look and stare and wonder. But who was this fellow Paul who wanted to visit Rome not as a tourist, but as an evangelist? who believed he had a message which Rome needed to hear? and who expected Rome to listen to him? What folly and presumption was this?

According to tradition Paul was small in size, plain in appearance, awkward in manner and contemptible in speech. He had been weakened and even disfigured by illness. He belonged to a despised minority movement within a despised people. That is, he was a Christian Jew. His message was foolishness to intellectuals and a stumbling block to the self-righteous. What then could he hope to accomplish against the proud might of imperial Rome? Wouldn't he be wiser to stay away? Or if he must visit Rome, would he not be prudent to keep his big mouth shut —lest he be laughed out of court and hustled out of town? Evidently Paul did not think so. "I am under obligation," he writes; "I am eager . . . I am not ashamed."

Let's investigate the origins of this apostolic eagerness, so that we may come to share it. It is not difficult to discover them because he states the reasons clearly. He writes, "I am under obligation. . . . Thus . . . I am eager. . . . For I am not ashamed of the gospel, for it is the power of God. . . ." His affirmations are linked to one another in a chain of cause and effect. Negatively, he is not ashamed of the gospel. Positively, he is eager to proclaim it. Why? For two reasons. First, because it is a debt to humanity, which he must discharge. Second, because it is the power of God unto salvation to everyone who believes.

1. *The gospel is a debt to humanity.* It is true that most English versions prefer the expression "I am under obligation" (v. 14). But the old King James' version was quite correct to translate it "I am debtor." For this is what the Greek word *opheiletēs* means. It was used of somebody who had incurred financial debts.

Now there are two ways of getting into debt to somebody. One is to borrow money *from* him. The other is to be given money *for* him by somebody else. For example, if I were to borrow a thousand dollars from you, I would be in your debt until I repaid it. Equally, if a friend of yours in London had given me a thou-

sand dollars to bring to you, I would also be in your debt until
I handed it to you. In the second case it is your friend in London
who has put me in your debt by entrusting me with money for
you.

It is in this second sense that Paul knew he was in debt. He
had not borrowed anything from the citizens of Rome which
he had to repay. But Jesus Christ had entrusted him with the
gospel for the Gentile world. Indeed, several times in his letters
he uses this very expression. He describes himself as "entrusted
with the gospel" (Gal. 2:7; 1 Thess. 2:4; 1 Tim. 1:11; Tit. 1:3;
cf. 1 Cor. 9:17). So it was Jesus who had made him a debtor. And
being in debt, he was anxious to discharge his obligation. Moreover, it was a universal debt. As apostle to the Gentiles, he had
a particular responsibility to the Gentile world, "both to Greeks
and to barbarians, both to the wise and to the foolish" (v. 14).
J. B. Phillips has captured the feel of this statement by translating it "from cultured Greek to ignorant savage."

In a similar way we today are debtors to the world. Has the
message of Christ come to us? Has God opened our eyes to see
the truth as it is in Jesus? Then we cannot possibly keep the
gospel to ourselves. We cannot enjoy a monopoly of it. Good
news is news to share, whether it is good news in the family (like
an engagement or a birth), or good news of an invention or a dis-
covery (like penicillin or a cure for cancer) or the good news of
Jesus Christ. Moreover, our debt (not as individuals but as the
whole church) is universal. Much missionary work has concentrated on peasants in rural areas, while city dwellers, and especially the intelligentsia, have been overlooked. In other countries it is the middle classes who have been reached, while the
industrial masses and the urban poor have been neglected. We
have no liberty to circumscribe the Christian mission. The debt
in which Jesus Christ has placed his church is to all people of
all cultures in all countries.

Such was Paul's first incentive. He was eager because he was
in debt. It is dishonorable to leave a debt unpaid. We should be
as eager to discharge our debt, as Paul was to discharge his.

2. *The gospel is the power of God.* The apostle now develops
a different argument. "I am eager to preach the gospel," he says,

"because I am not ashamed of it. And I am not ashamed of it because it is the power of God for salvation to everyone who believes, to the Jew first and also to the Greek" (v. 16).

The apostle's negative assertion "I am not ashamed of the gospel" is rather surprising, is it not? The very suggestion that Paul could have felt ashamed of the gospel sounds ridiculous. But it is not. I once heard Professor James Stewart of Edinburgh preach on this text. He made the perceptive comment that "there is no sense in declaring that you are not ashamed of something unless you have been tempted to feel ashamed of it." And Paul had without doubt been so tempted. For he knew the message of the cross was a stumbling block to human pride. We experience the same temptation. Did not Jesus himself warn us not to be ashamed of him and of his words (Mk. 8:38)? He anticipated that we would be tempted to do so.

How then did Paul, and how shall we, overcome this temptation? Only by remembering that the gospel of which we are tempted to feel ashamed (because people despise and ridicule it for its weakness) is nonetheless God's power to save sinners. And we know this because we have experienced it ourselves. The gospel has brought us into a new, a right relationship with God. Our sins have been forgiven. Already we have passed out of condemnation into acceptance. God is now our Father. He has adopted us into his family. We are his children. How can we be ashamed of the good news by which God's power accomplishes such a transformation?

The reason why the gospel is God's power for salvation to believers, Paul goes on to explain in verse 17, is that in it "the righteousness of God is revealed from faith to faith." This expression "the righteousness of God" is crucial for our understanding of the gospel, and much ink has flowed in attempts to elucidate it. Is "the righteousness of God" a divine attribute (our God is a righteous God)? Or is it a divine activity (God coming to vindicate his people)? Or is it a divine gift (God bestowing a righteous status upon sinners)? All three positions have been held, and the most satisfactory solution to the problem is to combine all three.

In Romans "the righteousness of God" is his way of justi-

fying sinners, by which he both demonstrates his own righteousness and gives it to us. It is his righteous way of declaring
the unrighteous righteous. He puts us in the right with him,
without thereby putting himself in the wrong. He accepts us as
righteous in his sight, while at the same time declaring and not
compromising his own righteousness. He does it through Christ,
the righteous one who died for the unrighteous, as he will explain later; and he does it "by faith," that is, when we put our
trust in him or cry to him for mercy. Indeed, what God does for
us he does "from faith to faith" (v. 17) which seems to mean "by
faith from first to last" (NIV).

Moreover, this good news of a free justification God had
affirmed centuries previously to his prophet Habakkuk in the
words "the righteous man shall live by faith." Or more probably,
as in the NASB margin, and as commentators like Nygren, Bruce
and Cranfield argue, the epigram should rather be rendered,
"He who is righteous by faith shall live," or "He who through
faith is righteous shall live." Nygren argues that the structure
of the letter demands this translation, since Romans 1—4 explain how a sinner becomes "righteous through faith," while
Romans 5—8 declare how he "shall live."[1]

It was the enlightenment of Martin Luther to see this truth
which sparked off the sixteenth-century Reformation. For a
year, from November 1515 to September 1516, Luther expound-
ed the Letter to the Romans to his students at Wittenberg University. As he prepared his lectures, the centrality of justification
became apparent to him.

> I greatly longed to understand Paul's Epistle to the Romans
> and nothing stood in the way but that one expression, "the
> righteousness of God," because I took it to mean that right-
> eousness whereby God is righteous and deals righteously in
> punishing the unrighteous.... Night and day I pondered
> until ... I grasped the truth that the righteousness of God is
> that righteousness whereby, through grace and sheer mercy,
> he justifies us by faith. Thereupon I felt myself to be reborn
> and to have gone through open doors into paradise. The
> whole of Scripture took on a new meaning, and whereas be-
> fore "the righteousness of God" had filled me with hate, now

it became inexpressibly sweet in greater love. This passage of Paul became to me a gateway to heaven.[2]

To sum up, then, what was the secret of Paul's "eagerness" to preach the gospel? It arose from his recognition that the gospel is both an unpaid debt to humanity and the saving power of God. The first gave him a sense of obligation (he had been put in trust with the gospel), and the second a sense of conviction (if the gospel had saved him, it could also save others). Still today the gospel is both a debt to discharge and a power to experience. We need to meditate on these truths, until in our hearts the light shines and the fire burns. Then and then only shall we be able to say with Paul, "I am not ashamed. . . . I am under obligation. . . . So I am eager to share the gospel with the world."

4
God's Judgment
John R. W. Stott

Nothing keeps people away from Christ more than their inability to see their need of him, or their unwillingness to admit it. As Jesus himself put it, "It is not those who are healthy who need a physician, but those who are sick; I did not come to call the righteous, but sinners" (Mk. 2:17). He did not imply by this that there are some people so righteous that they do not need his salvation, but only that some think they are. In that condition of self-righteousness they will never come to Christ. Just as we go to the doctor only when we admit we are ill, so we will go to Christ only when we admit that we are guilty sinners.

It is this plain principle which lies behind the long passage we are to study today. Paul's purpose in it is to lay the "charge," as he puts it in 3:9, that "both Jews and Greeks are all under sin." He does more than bring an accusation; he marshalls the evidence against us, proves our guilt and secures a conviction. All men and women, without a single and solitary exception, from both the Jewish and the Gentile worlds, are sinful, guilty and without excuse before God. Already they are under his wrath and condemnation.

The way Paul demonstrates the universality of sin and guilt is to divide the human race into several sections and arraign them one by one. His procedure in each case is the same. He reminds them of their knowledge of God and of goodness. He then confronts them with the uncomfortable fact that they have not lived up to their knowledge. On the contrary, they have either deliberately suppressed it or at least contradicted it by continuing to live in unrighteousness. Therefore, they are guilty, inexcusably guilty, before God. Nobody can plead innocence, because nobody can plead ignorance. That is the thrust of Paul's argument throughout this passage. Commentators are not agreed as to precisely which sections of mankind Paul is addressing. I can only share with you my own conclusion, after weighing the alternatives.

First, (in 1:18-32) he describes the depraved Gentile world in its idolatry, immorality and antisocial behavior.

Second, (in 2:1-16) he addresses critical moralists, whether Gentile or Jewish, who profess high ethical standards and, in condemning others, condemn themselves.

Third, (in 2:17—3:8) he turns to self-righteous Jews, who boast of their knowledge of God's will through the Law but do not keep it.

Fourth, (in 3:9-20) he encompasses the whole human race.

Whichever segment of humanity Paul is addressing, his message is substantially the same. "You know the righteous requirements of God," he says. "Yet you have persisted in unrighteousness. You are guilty before God. You have no excuse. And you have no hope either—apart from the grace of God who justifies those who believe in Jesus." Paul does not lose sight of this "righteousness of God." Indeed, it is the only possible context within which he could dare to expose the squalor of human unrighteousness. In 1:17 he has said that God's righteousness is revealed in the gospel. In 3:21 he repeats his statement: "but now ... the righteousness of God has been manifested." It is in between these two affirmations of our gracious

God's justifying righteousness that he sandwiches his terrible exposure of our unrighteousness (1:18—3:20).

The Depraved Gentile World (1:18-32)

Right at the beginning of our long text the apostle develops his argument with relentless logic. In particular, let us look at verses 16-20, in which he refers in succession to the power of God (v. 16), the righteousness of God (v. 17), the wrath of God (v. 18) and the glory of God in creation (vv. 19-20). Each statement he makes is linked to the preceding one by the Greek conjunction *gar*, meaning "for" or "because." Perhaps I could clarify the stages of his argument by engaging him in dialog.

"I am not ashamed of the gospel," Paul says.

"Why not, Paul?"

"Because it is the power of God for salvation to everyone who believes" (v. 16).

"How so, Paul?"

"Because in it the righteousness of God [God's way of justifying sinners] is revealed" (v. 17).

"But why is this necessary, Paul?"

"Because the wrath of God is revealed from heaven against the unrighteousness of men who suppress the truth in unrighteousness" (v. 18).

"But how have people suppressed the truth, Paul?"

"Because the glory of God, 'His eternal power and divine nature,' is clearly seen in the created world, so that they are without excuse" (vv. 19-20).

It really is essential for us to grasp these successive allusions to God's power, righteousness, wrath and glory. The reason why the gospel is God's power for salvation is that it reveals God's righteousness (or way of justifying the unrighteous). The reason why the gospel reveals God's righteousness is that God's wrath is already revealed against the unrighteous. And the reason why God's wrath is revealed against the unrighteous is that they suppress the truth, his glory revealed to them in his creation. Thus Paul affirms a fourfold self-revelation of God, which we can now put in the opposite order:

First, God reveals his glory (power and deity) in creation.

Second, God reveals his *wrath* against the sin of those who suppress this knowledge.

Third, God reveals his *righteousness* toward sinners (his way of justifying them by faith) in the gospel.

Fourth, God reveals his *power* by saving those who believe.

Our text for today begins with verse 18, which declares that "the wrath of God is revealed from heaven." Three questions immediately arise in our minds. First, what is meant by "the wrath of God?" Does God really get angry? If so, second, with whom does he get angry, and against whom is his anger revealed? And third, how is his anger "revealed"? What kind of disclosure is Paul referring to?

First, then, what is "the wrath of God"? It should not be necessary for me to assure you that the God of the Bible never loses his temper or gets mad at people. There is nothing irrational or passionate, nothing capricious or malicious, nothing spiteful or vindictive about his wrath. No, the wrath of God is his righteous reaction to evil, his implacable hostility to it, his refusal to condone it, and his just judgment upon it. Anders Nygren calls it "his holy displeasure at sin,"[3] and Charles Cranfield writes that it is "no nightmare of an indiscriminate, uncontrolled, irrational fury, but the wrath of the holy and merciful God."[4]

We are now ready to put our second question. Against what is God's wrath directed? "Against all ungodliness and unrighteousness of men, who suppress the truth in unrighteousness" (v. 18). It will be observed that the word *unrighteousness* occurs twice, and that it is interpreted in terms of "ungodliness" on the one hand and of "suppressing the truth" on the other. The essence of human sin is, in fact, that it is a rejection of both God and truth. We sinners prefer our own way to the way of God and the way of truth. So we are prepared to defy God and stifle the truth in order to continue in unrighteousness.

It is the open-eyed willfulness of this rebellion which Paul emphasizes, for the rebels are far from being ignorant of what they are doing. They know what is "knowable" about God, since he has himself shown it to them (v. 19). Ever "since the creation of the world" God's "invisible attributes," his "eternal power and divine nature," have been clearly visible and intelligible in his works. Just as an artist reveals himself by what he draws or paints, or by his music or sculpture, so the Divine Artist has revealed himself in his creation. As is written in the Old Testament, "The heavens are telling of the glory of God," and again "The whole earth is full of His glory" (Ps. 19:1; Is. 6:3).

After the great fire of London in 1666 St. Paul's Cathedral was rebuilt by Sir Christopher Wren. He is buried in the cathedral crypt, and his tomb bears a Latin inscription which means "if you seek his monument, look around you. So too, if you seek God look around you at the things he has made." Creation is a visible disclosure of the invisible reality of God. So all human beings have some knowledge of God. We must not misunderstand this, however. Their knowledge of God does not mean that they do not need the gospel. For their knowledge of God does not save them. On the contrary, it condemns them because they have suppressed it.

Therefore, "they are without excuse" (v. 20). Or "there is therefore no possible defense for their conduct" (NEB). In particular, all forms of idolatry are inexcusable. "Even though they knew God [not of course as reconciled sinners know him in Christ, but as all people can know him in creation], they did not honor Him as God, or give thanks." Instead, "they became futile in their speculations, and their foolish heart was darkened. Professing to be wise, they became fools" (vv. 21-22). Of this folly their idolatry was the chief evidence. For they "exchanged the glory of the incorruptible God for an image" in the form of some corruptible creature, whether man, bird, beast or reptile. Verse 25 sums up the essence of their folly. They worship "the creature rather than the Creator" and so exchange "the truth of God for a lie," literally "the lie," since all false worship like idolatry is the supreme lie perpetrated by the father of lies, the devil.

As Paul defines the object of God's wrath, namely the unrighteousness of those who reject him and stifle his truth, his emphasis is plain. It is not only ludicrous to suppose that the Creator could be represented by an image of one of his creatures; it is also inexcusable, being a contradiction of the knowledge God has given them. They should have known better. They *did* know better. But they suppressed their knowledge. The modern idolatries of materialistic secularism, although the images they substitute for God are more sophisticated, are no different in principle. For they are a deliberate denial of the Transcendent Reality which (who) they know exists and claims their allegiance.

Our third question about God's wrath concerns how it is "revealed from heaven against all . . . unrighteousness" as Paul declares it to be in verse 18. To be sure, his wrath will be revealed in the judgment of the last day (2:5). There is such a thing as "the wrath to come" (1 Thess. 1:10). But Paul uses a present tense to indicate that he is referring to a contemporary disclosure of God's wrath. Already God is revealing his wrath in society. Most commentators seem to agree that he explains what he means by the terrible refrain he uses three times in verses 24, 26 and 28, saying, "Therefore God gave them over." Each time the Greek preposition eis is added, to indicate what it is to which God in his holy wrath abandons those who reject him and his truth. In general, he abandons them to themselves, to their own willful selfishness. But Paul particularizes.

First, (v. 24), "God gave them over" to immorality, to dishonoring their bodies. There is nothing more selfish than lust for another human body, outside of the beauty of the marriage relationship.

Second, (v. 26), "God gave them over" to what Paul calls "degrading passions," or what we would call "sexual perversion." He specifies lesbian practices in verse 26 and male homosexual intercourse in verse 27, both of which he condemns as replacing "the natural function for that which is unnatural." In other words, homosexual behavior is a perversion, because it is against "nature," against God's created order and purpose. God's created order from the beginning of Genesis right through the Bible is heterosexual marriage.

Third, (v. 28), "God gave them over" to "a depraved mind," leading to every conceivable form of antisocial conduct. Twenty-one examples are given in verses 29-31, including greed, envy, murder, strife, deceit, malice, slander and arrogance, the lack of respect for parents, and the lack of trustworthiness, love and mercy. It is a horrible list. It describes the breakdown of human community. And Paul adds the final indictment that these people not only practice such things but also encourage others to do so, in spite of their knowledge of God's ordinance that "such things are worthy of death."

Indeed, please notice that each time the refrain comes (namely, "God gave them over"), the reason for his judicial action is repeated; they have stifled their knowledge. Thus the cause and the effect of God's wrath are kept together.

First, "even though they knew God, they did not honor Him.... Therefore God gave them over...." (vv. 21, 24).

Second, "they exchanged the truth of God for a lie.... For this reason God gave them over...." (vv. 25-26).

Third, "just as they did not see fit to acknowledge God any longer, God gave them over...." (v. 28).

It is when human beings rebel against God's self-revelation that he gives them up to the consequences of their rebellion. His wrath is revealed against their ungodliness not in summary acts of judgment but in a process of moral and social degeneration. Standards disappear, absolutes are renounced and society disintegrates. Paul saw it in the contemporary Greco-Roman world, and we seem to be witnessing something similar in the permissive Western society of our own day. The rejection of God is always followed by idolatry in some form or other, and a corrupt mind leads to corrupt behavior. This is a revelation of the wrath of God, the outworking of his judgment on human sin.

The Critical Moralists (2:1-16)
Paul turns now from that part of the ancient world characterized by shameless immorality to another, very different section of it marked by a very self-conscious moralism. Far from approving, even applauding, lawless behavior (1:32), these people deplore and condemn it (2:1-3). Who are they?

Some commentators, although noting that Paul does not address the Jews by name until verse 17, nevertheless believe that it is Jewish moralists whom he has in mind from the beginning of the chapter. They point out the parallels between these verses and chapters 11-15 of the Jewish Book of Wisdom. But we must not overlook the fact that the apostle styles the one he is now addressing as just a human being, "every man of you" (v. 1), and "O man" (v. 3) without specifying any racial, national, cultural or religious background. He seems therefore to be confronting the general phenomenon of human moralism, of people with highly developed faculties of moral criticism, whether Jewish or Gentile.

He certainly does not exclude Gentiles from his description here, any more than he would exclude Jewish idolaters from his description at the end of chapter 1. This interpretation (that the group of people called "critical moralists" includes both Jews and Gentiles) is borne out by verses 9-11. In both verses 9 and 10 he repeats the phrase "the Jew first and also ... the Greek," and then adds the statement in verse 11 that "there is no partiality with God"—in judgment any more than in salvation (1:16). He develops this further in verses 12-16, emphasizing that Jews who have the law and Gentiles who do not, nevertheless both know it and will both be judged by their disobedience to it.

Moralist and *moralizer* are the words which F. F. Bruce uses to identify the people Paul now addresses.[5] Of Jewish moralists there were many, ever ready to criticize Gentiles for their misconduct. Gentile moralists were scarcer. As an example, Professor Bruce suggests, "Paul's illustrious contemporary Seneca, the Stoic moralist, the tutor of Nero."[6]

Although Paul is now speaking to moralists rather than the openly immoral, his basic argument remains the same. Both groups have a certain "knowledge," both contradict it in their behavior and both are therefore "without excuse." He uses the same Greek word of the moralizers in 2:1, as he did of the flagrantly immoral in 1:20. They are *anapologētos*, inexcusable. Yet there is a certain difference between them in the kind of knowledge Paul says they have. According to 1:20 it is a knowledge of God's eternal power and divine nature"; according to 2:2 it is a knowledge of the holy "judgment of God." Not that one section of humanity has one kind of knowledge and a second section another kind. This is clear from 1:32 where the first group are also said to know God's holiness and judgment. Paul is simply stressing each kind of knowledge in its appropriate context.

But all of us have both kinds of knowledge. Because we know God as Creator, there is no excuse for our idolatry; because we know him as Judge, there is no excuse for our disobedience. The Gentiles stand condemned because of the general revelation he has given them outwardly in creation and inwardly in conscience. The Jews also stand condemned because of the special revelation which God has given them in Scripture. God's judgment falls not on the ignorant but on the knowledgeable. Universal moral knowledge and universal moral rebellion have resulted in universal moral culpability.

Coming now to a more detailed study of the early verses of chapter 2, we must notice the careful analysis which the apostle makes of all moralists, including us, who have a God-given understanding both that there is a distinction between right and wrong, and that wrongdoing deserves punishment.

First, Paul exposes our hypocrisy (vv. 1-3) in doing ourselves the very things for which we condemn others. He uncovers a strange human foible, of which we are all aware from experience and observation. It is the tendency to be critical of everybody except ourselves. We are as harsh in our judgment of others as we are lenient towards ourselves. We enjoy working ourselves up into a state of self-righteous indignation over the disgraceful behavior of other people, while somehow the very same behavior does not seem half so serious when it is ours rather than theirs. We even gain a vicarious satisfaction from condemning in others the very faults which we excuse in ourselves. Freud called this moral gymnastic "projection," but another Jewish scholar, Paul, described it long before Freud was born. It is a quirk of fallen human nature, enabling us to retain our moral sense without losing our moral self-respect. We do it by applying our standards to other people instead of to ourselves. The device is simple, slick and sick.

Paul's argument is that this practice leaves us without excuse. If our critical faculties are so well developed that we become experts in the moral evaluation of others, we cannot possibly plead ignorance of moral issues. On the contrary, in judging others (v. 1) we thereby condemn ourselves who do the very same things. We know, whether from the biblical law or from

our created moral sense, the justice of God's judgment (v. 2).
How then can we suppose that when we play God and make
our judgments, we can escape his (v. 3)? This is the hypocrisy
of a double standard—high for others, low for ourselves.

Second, in verses 4 and 5, Paul draws attention to our *im-
penitence*. Sometimes, he says, we take refuge in a theological
argument (for theology can be put to many uses, bad as well as
good), namely, that in "the riches of His kindness and forbearance and patience" God will condone our sin. But such trust
in God's patience is not faith; it is presumption. His kindness
is not intended to give us an excuse for sinning, but rather to
lead us to repentance. If it does not, then because of our "stub-
bornness and unrepentant heart" we are "storing up" something
for ourselves—not the treasure of eternal salvation, as Paul's
"storage" metaphor might have led his readers to expect, but
"wrath," God's holy wrath, on the fearful "day of wrath" on
which his "righteous judgment" will be revealed.

Third, in verses 6-11, Paul refers to our *works* and emphasizes
the indispensable necessity of good works if we are to escape the
judgment of God. Verse 6 states the inflexible principle, laid
down in the Old Testament (e.g., Ps. 62:12; Prov. 24:12) which
Paul echoes here, and which was repeated again and again by
Jesus and his apostles (e.g., Mt. 16:27; 1 Cor. 3:8; 2 Cor. 5:10;
Rev. 2:23; 20:12; 22:12), namely, that God "will render to everybody [Jew and Gentile, immoral and moralist, Christian and
non-Christian] according to his deeds."

Some readers are immediately up in arms. "Paul cannot
possibly mean this," they say. "Has he taken leave of his senses?
Does he begin by affirming that salvation is by faith, and then
destroy his own gospel by affirming that it is by good works after
all?" Others try to restrict the application of Paul's statement to
unbelievers, adding that of course Christians are not judged by
their works. But Paul is neither contradicting himself nor allud-
ing to the judgment of unbelievers alone. He is describing God's
universal principle of judgment, that although his justification is by faith alone, his judgment will be according to our
works.

The reason for this is not hard to find. We have to remember that the day of judgment will be a public occasion. Its purpose will be less to determine God's judgment than to declare it and to vindicate it publicly. The divine process of judgment (the separation between the saved and the lost) is going on *secretly* all the time; on that day its consequences will be made *public*. On the "day of wrath," as we have already noted from verse 5 there is to be a *"revelation* of the righteous judgment of God." Such a public occasion, on which a public verdict will be given and a public sentence passed, will require public and verifiable evidence to support them. The only available public evidence will be our works, what we have done (or not done) and what we have been seen to do. True, God will judge "the secrets of men" (verse 16) but either these will be secret deeds which will then be made public, or, if secret thoughts, corresponding deeds will be produced in evidence. For the only way to demonstrate the presence or absence of saving faith in our hearts is to bear witness to the presence or absence of good works of love in our lives.

As both Paul and James emphasize, a saving faith issues in good works; if it does not, it is bogus (for example, Gal. 5:6; Jas. 2:14-26). I may claim to believe. But if I do not obey him and express my faith in obedience and good works of love, then my claim to believe is spurious.

Verses 7-10 enlarge on this. The final destinies of mankind are described on the one hand as "eternal life" (v. 7) or "glory and honor and peace" (v. 10), and on the other as "wrath and indignation" (v. 8) or "tribulation and distress" (v. 9). The "deeds," on the basis of which the divine judgment will be pronounced, are in verses 9 and 10 termed simply "doing evil" and "doing good." But in verses 7 and 8 they are elaborated. According to verse 7 those who will receive eternal life are "those who by perseverance in doing good seek for glory and honor and immortality." That is, they have a spiritual ambition and an eternal perspective, and they persevere in acts of kindness. Those who will fall under God's wrath, however, are described as "those who are selfishly ambitious and do not obey the truth but obey unrighteousness" (v. 8). That is, their ambitions are self-centered rather than godly, and they suppress the

truth they know in order to follow evil. It is in such deeds that
the secrets of human hearts are revealed.

Further, this applies to every human being, whether Jew or
Greek, as he repeats in verses 9 and 10, irrespective of race and
culture, because God shows no partiality (v. 11). He "will render
to every man according to his deeds" (v. 6) with the strictest
impartiality.

This general principle of God's impartial judgment according
to works Paul now applies in particular to Jews and Gentiles
(vv. 12-16). They differ from each other in that Jews possess the
Mosaic Law, while Gentiles do not. Yet there is no distinction
between them either in the sin they have committed, or in the
guilt they have incurred, or in the judgment they will receive—
unless of course they cry to God for mercy. For "all who have
sinned" (repeated twice in v. 12) will fall under judgment,
whether they have sinned "without the Law" or "under the
Law," since (v. 13) it is not the "hearers" but only the "doers" of
the law who can be justified. And no human being, Jew or
Gentile, has ever obeyed God's law perfectly. So there is no
possibility of salvation along that road.

There is such a thing as partial obedience, however. Even
Gentiles, although they do not possess God's law (a fact which is
stated twice in this verse), sometimes "do instinctively the
things of the Law" (v. 14). This adverb, which the NASB renders
"instinctively," means literally "by nature." It means that God
has created them self-conscious moral beings, on account of
which they "are a law to themselves," or "they are their own
law" (NEB). Although they do not have the law in their hands
(as the Jews do), they nevertheless show by their behavior that
they have it in their hearts. For God himself has written it there
(v. 15), not in the special new covenant sense that the Holy
Spirit has regenerated them (Jer. 31:33) but in the general sense
that God their maker has given them a moral instinct by creation. Moreover, their conscience (which is here distinguished
from their "hearts") also bears its witness, "their thoughts alter-
nately accusing or else defending them." Here their hearts, their
conscience and their thoughts are pictured as joining in a kind
of internal moral debate.

Do not misunderstand this. Paul is saying neither that the Gentiles always know what is right, nor that they always do it, still less that they can earn salvation by doing it. He is saying rather that on those occasions when they fulfill the requirements of God's law (which everybody does sometimes), they give evidence that they know it by nature.

This teaching has great importance. It declares that the same moral law which God has revealed in Scripture he has also stamped on human nature. He has in fact written his law twice, once on stone tablets and once on human hearts. In consequence, the moral law is not an alien system, which it is unnatural to expect human beings to obey. The opposite is the case. God's moral law perfectly fits us, because it is the law of our own created being. There is a fundamental correspondence between God's law in the Bible and God's law in our hearts. Hence we can discover our authentic humanness only in obeying it. If we disobey it, we contradict not only what we know to be right, but we are contradicting our own human being. To do this is to be without sense, as well as without excuse. (Incidentally, it is good to remember this in evangelism. Say to yourself when you are witnessing to somebody, say secretly in your heart, "His or her conscience is on my side.")

Let me add at this point an implication of what Paul is teaching, even though he does not himself draw it out. It concerns evangelism. It is important to remember, whenever we are sharing the gospel with other people, that their conscience is on our side. True, the conscience of fallen human beings is often mistaken (it needs to be educated by the Word of God) and often sleepy (it needs to be awakened by the Spirit of God). True also, some people deny that they have any sense of sin, insisting at the same time that everything is relative now, for there are no moral absolutes anymore. Do not believe them, I beg you. For by creation God still endows all human beings with a moral sense, which our inherited fallenness has distorted but not destroyed. Unless and until people so violate and smother their conscience as to "cauterize" it (a word Paul uses in 1 Tim. 4:2) or render it insensitive, it continues to trouble them. They know they are sinful and guilty, however much they may protest the contrary.

Let us remember this. For the gospel speaks to people only in that condition; it has no message for those who think they are righteous.

Self-righteous Jews (2:17—3:8)

In verse 17, however much he may already have had Jews in mind, Paul now addresses them by name: "But if you bear the name 'Jew.'..." He anticipates their objections to what he has written.

"Surely," some Jewish readers will be retorting, "you can't lump us with Gentile outsiders? Surely, Paul, you must admit that our situation as Jews is entirely different? Have you forgotten that *we* have the Law, the revelation of God, and circumcision, the sign of the covenant of God? Are you saying that we Jews, with God's Law and God's covenant, are no better off than those Gentiles who have neither? Aren't you forgetting the privileges which God himself has given us and which surely will shield us from his judgment?"

That Paul envisages such objections is evident. For he alludes to the law in verses 17-24 and to circumcision in verses 25-29, and insists that neither gives to Jews an immunity to the judgment of God.

As for the law, Paul gives a full description of Jewish self-righteousness. You "rely upon the Law, and boast in God," he says (v. 17). As a result, you "know His will, and approve the things that are essential," for you are well "instructed out of the Law" (v. 18). And being thus instructed yourself, you go on to instruct others. You are confident that you are "a guide to the blind, a light to those who are in darkness, a corrector of the foolish, a teacher of the immature"—all because in the law you have "the embodiment of knowledge and of the truth" (vv. 19-20. This is what God's law is. Paul does not deny it.

Paul's complaint is not about their knowledge, but about their performance. "You, therefore, who teach another, do you not teach yourself?" (v. 21). All this moral knowledge of yours does not exempt you from God's judgment; it rather invites it. For the greater our privileges, the greater are our responsibilities (cf. Amos 3:2). Just as *judging* others brings us under greater condemnation (vv. 1-3), so does *teaching* others. As James puts it in his letter, "Let not many of you become teachers, my brethren, knowing that as such we shall incur a stricter judgment" (3:1). If we judge others, we should be able to judge ourselves, and if we teach others, we should be able to teach ourselves. It should be obvious that, if we set ourselves up as either a judge or a teacher of others, we cannot claim to live in ignorance of moral issues ourselves.

In verses 21 and 22, Paul mentions the commandments against theft, adultery and idolatry, and accuses Jewish moralists of preaching these prohibitions but not practicing what they preach. They "boast in the Law" and at the same time break it (v. 23). Their hypocrisy dishonors God and, as the prophets kept saying in Old Testament days, "the name of God is blasphemed among the Gentiles" because of them (v. 24; see Is. 52:5; Ezek. 36:20, 23).

If their law-knowledge did not exempt them from God's judgment, neither did their circumcision. True, it was the God-given sign of his covenant of grace, in which he promised to be their God and to make them his people. Yet circumcision was no magical ceremony, offering permanent insurance against divine judgment. The covenant sign of circumcision committed God's people to keep the covenant and obey the law. It was valuable, therefore, only to those who proved themselves to be God's people (which their circumcision declared them to be) by their obedience (v. 25). If they broke the law, however, their circumcision would be equivalent to uncircumcision. Their circumcision did not make them what their disobedience proved they were not. So then, the opposite is also true (vv. 26-27). That is, among the uncircumcised, obedience is equivalent to circumcision, and such a person will condemn those who have both the law and circumcision but break the law.

This leads to a tremendous statement in verses 28 and 29, already adumbrated by prophets like Jeremiah, and of course underlined by Jesus, that inward reality is far more important in God's sight than outward ceremony. The real Jew is one inwardly not outwardly, and true circumcision is in the heart not the body, "by the Spirit and not by the letter." One might say

exactly the same of the real Christian and of true baptism. The
outward and visible sign is of great value only if it bears witness
to the inward and spiritual grace received. Such a person, in
whom the Spirit of God is at work, receives "his praise" (which
is the meaning of the word *Judah* from which *Jew* is derived
[cf. Gen. 29:35 and 49:8]) "not from men, but from God."

It is not difficult to imagine that Jewish people would either
listen to such teaching with incredulity, or feel utterly squashed
by it. Paul expresses the questions they would inevitably ask:
"Then what advantage has the Jew? Or what is the benefit of
circumcision?" (3:1). Paul has already answered these questions. From the point of view of merit, or of their efficacy to protect them from judgment, the law and circumcision had no value
and were of no advantage. But this does not mean that they were
worthless. On the contrary, they were great blessings which
God bestowed on his covenant people. In particular his people
"were entrusted with the oracles of God" (v. 2). To be appointed
the trustees of God's special revelation was an immense privilege. It did not make them immune to his judgment if they
proved unfaithful, however.

This will have raised further questions in Jewish minds, now
about the character of God, especially about his faithfulness
and his justice. Would not his judgment on Israel contradict
both these? Paul emphatically denies it. First, God's faithfulness
is not nullified by Israel's unfaithfulness (vv. 3-4). For even if
every human being were found to be a liar, God himself is
always true, as the Scripture says (Paul gives a free translation
of Psalm 51:4). Second, God's justice is equally unstained. An
imaginary objector argues like this: "If our injustice the better
displays God's justice (v. 5), and if our falsehood the better displays his truth (v. 7), if (that is) our sin promotes God's glory by
setting forth his perfection in bolder relief, why should God
complain and judge us? Why should we not rather 'do evil that
good may come' (as some slanderers accused Paul of teaching)?"
(v. 8). Their very suggestion filled the apostle with horror. It
deserved no serious refutation. "Their condemnation is just"
(v. 8), he says. God is going to judge the world (v. 6); how could
he possibly be guilty of injustice?

The Whole Human Race (3:9-20)

Paul is approaching the conclusion of his argument. He has exposed the blatant unrighteousness of much of the ancient Gentile world (1:18-32), the hypocritical righteousness of moralizers and the legal self-righteousness of the Jews who yet break God's moral law. Is there then no benefit at all in being a Jew? Paul asks this question twice, and gives apparently opposite answers.

Question: "Then what advantage has the Jew?" (v. 1).

Answer: "Great in every respect" (v. 2).

Question: "What then? Are we Jews any better off?" (v. 9 RSV, NEB).

Answer: "No, not at all."

It sounds as if Paul is directly contradicting himself. First, he says there is great advantage in being a Jew, and then he says there is none. How can we resolve this seeming discrepancy? By realizing that the "advantage" which the Jews possessed must be understood in terms of *privilege* (that God had entrusted his revelation to them), and not in terms of *favoritism* (that God would exempt them from judgment). That kind of advantage they certainly did not have. For, as the apostle continues, "We have already charged that both Jews and Greeks are all under sin" (v. 9), that is, "under the power of sin" (RSV, NEB). Sin is almost personified. It is a tyrant which holds all mankind imprisoned in guilt and under judgment.

This fact Paul goes on to support from Scripture. He gives a catena of six Old Testament quotations, five from the Psalms (14:1-3; 5:9; 140:3; 10:7; 36:1) and one from Isaiah (59:7-8), which all in their different ways bear witness to the universality of human sin and guilt. Two features of this biblical portrait of mankind are particularly noteworthy.

First, it teaches the *ungodliness* of sin. For example, "There is none who seeks for God" (v. 11) and "There is no fear of God before their eyes" (v. 18). This is more than an assertion that sin is due to ungodliness, that is, that it is because "all have turned aside" from God (v. 12), that "there is none who does good." Mind you, this is true. It is when people fear God that they renounce evil, and conversely when they renounce God that they plunge recklessly into evil. But the Scripture goes beyond this and identifies the very essence of sin as ungodliness, as we saw in 1:18. Sin is the revolt of the self against God. It is the dethronement of God and the enthronement of self. Sin is "getting rid of the Lord God" and proclaiming our own sovereignty. Ultimately, sin is "self-deification."[7]

Second, these Old Testament quotations teach the *pervasiveness* of sin. Sin affects every part of us, every human faculty and function. There seems to be a deliberate listing of these. Our "throat is an open grave" (v. 13) full of corruption and infection, our tongues deceive and our lips spread poison. Our "mouth is full of cursing and bitterness" (v. 14). Our "feet are swift to shed blood" (v. 15), scattering "destruction and misery" in our paths (v. 16), instead of walking "the path of peace" (v. 17). We do not keep God "before our eyes" or reverence him (v. 18). Here then is mention of our throat, tongue, lips and mouth, of our feet and our eyes. All these organs are in rebellion against God.

This is the biblical doctrine of "total depravity," which is much misunderstood. It has never meant that all human beings are as depraved as they could possibly be. Such a notion is manifestly absurd and untrue. We are not all drunkards, thieves, adulterers and murderers. No, the "totality" of our corruption refers to its extent (affecting *every* part of us), not to its degree (depraving every part of us *absolutely*). It means, to quote J. I. Packer, "not that at every point man is as bad as he could be, but that at no point is he as good as he should be."

Now that Paul has quoted these six texts of Old Testament Scripture, it is natural to inquire to whom they apply. The Jew might argue that, of course, they describe Gentile sinners. He would be right. They do. But this does not complete their application. "Now we know," Paul continues in verse 19, "that what the Law says ['the Law' here covering the whole Old Testament], it speaks to those who are under the Law." In other words, these texts describe Jews as well as Gentiles. They are God's portrait of all mankind. Their purpose is to stop every mouth, to silence every excuse and to make the whole world accountable to God. The words "that every mouth may be closed,"

comments Charles Cranfield, "evoke the picture of the defen-
dant in court, who, given the opportunity to speak in his own
defence, is speechless because of the weight of the evidence
which has been brought against him."[8] This is the point to
which Paul has been steadily moving. The idolatrous and immoral Gentiles are "without excuse" (1:20). All critical moralists, whether Jews or Gentiles, are also "without excuse" (2:1).
In fact, all the inhabitants of "all the world" (3:19), without any
exception, are inexcusable. By his expression "accountable to
God" Paul is probably portraying us, says Charles Cranfield, as
"men standing at God's bar, their guilt proven beyond all possibility of doubt, awaiting God's sentence of condemnation."[9]

The reason is that we have all known God's law and have all
disregarded it. That is why "by the works of the Law no flesh
will be justified in His sight." For what the law brings us is "the
knowledge of sin," not its remission. As Luther often said, its
function is not to justify but to terrify, and so to drive us to
Christ.[10]

How should we respond to this devastating portrayal of universal human sin and guilt?

First, we must make it as certain as we can that we have ourselves fled from the just judgment of God upon our sins to the
only refuge there is, Jesus Christ, who died in our place. We have
no merit to plead, no excuse to make. We stand condemned and
speechless. But God himself in Christ on the cross has borne
our condemnation. For this reason only we can be justified, if we
take refuge in Jesus.

Second, we simply cannot keep this good news to ourselves.
All around us are men and women who know enough about
God's glory and holiness to make their rejection of him and of
his law inexcusable. They stand condemned. Their only hope of
justification is in Christ. So let us boldly speak to them of him.
Their mouth is closed in guilt; let our mouth be opened in testimony!

5
God's Righteousness

John R. W. Stott

All men and women of every race and culture—the ungodly, the moral and the religious—have sinned against their knowledge, are therefore guilty before God and have brought upon themselves his holy wrath. They are without excuse and, if left to themselves, without hope. That was the theme of 1:18—3:20, our text for yesterday. The picture was gloomy enough to plunge any sensitive person into deep depression, and even despair. Indeed, as Luther said at the beginning of his "scholia" or commentary on Romans, "The chief purpose of this letter is to break down, to pluck up and to destroy all wisdom and righteousness of the flesh."[11] "There is none righteous, not even one," the apostle concluded. "All have turned aside." In consequence, "every mouth" has been stopped, and "all the world" has become "accountable to God." There was no ray of light, no flicker of hope, no prospect of salvation. There seemed nothing for us to do but wait speechless for the final pronouncement and execution of the divine sentence of death.

"But now," Paul suddenly breaks in with verse 21, God has intervened with a fresh revelation of himself as the Savior of sinners. After the long and starless night the sun has risen again, a new day has dawned and the heavens are flooded with light. For "now ... the righteousness of God has been manifested ... the righteousness of God through faith." Paul's words are an immediately recognizable echo of what he wrote in 1:17, before he launched into his lengthy excursus on the human rebellion. In both passages (1:17 and 3:21-22) he is proclaiming the good news of God's action in justifying sinners, not because of any merit of their own but because of Christ in whom they put their trust. So Paul's devastating exposure of universal guilt must be read in the light of the gospel which precedes and follows it.

The contrast between the two is dramatic. Over against both the unrighteousness and the self-righteousness of man he sets the righteousness of God. Over against God's wrath revealed from heaven he sets God's righteousness revealed in the gospel. Over against our works, which at best are a pitifully inadequate response to the demands of the law, he sets the atoning work of Jesus Christ, which can be appropriated by faith only. Over against man's guilt, he sets God's grace.

Paul expounds the essence of the Christian good news in only six verses (3:21-26). Charles Cranfield rightly calls this brief section "the centre and heart" of the letter, and adds that "it reads like a solemn proclamation."[12] Yet it is crammed full of profound theology, and contains a number of difficult technical terms. So we must work hard to understand it, and cry to the Lord for the illumination of his Spirit. For here are priceless treasures of truth for those who persevere in seeking them.

The key expression of the whole paragraph (vv. 21-31) is "the righteousness of God," which now for the first time is linked with the cognate verb to "justify," or to "declare righteous." Each occurs four times, the noun (dikaiosunē) in verses 21, 22, 25 and 26, and the verb (dikaioō) in verses 24, 26, 28 and 30. Moreover, the two belong essentially together. God's "righteousness," as we saw in our first exposition, is a combination of his righteous character, his justifying initiative and his gift of righteousness. The expression "the righteousness of God" is God's righteous way of "righteousing" the unrighteous. It is his justification of sinners.

Now justification is a legal verdict, the opposite of condemnation. When a judge condemns someone, he declares him guilty; when he justifies someone, he declares him innocent or righteous. Yet when God justifies us, he does more than declare us righteous; he actually bestows on us a righteous standing in his sight. "The righteousness of God" is identical with what elsewhere Paul terms "the righteousness from God"—a righteousness he gives to those who believe in Jesus (e.g., Phil. 3:9; 1 Cor. 1:30).

The sixteenth-century Reformers clearly understood the centrality of the doctrine of justification by faith alone. Martin Luther wrote of it: "This is the truth of the gospel; it is also the principal article of all Christian doctrine, wherein the knowledge of all godliness consisteth."[13]

Thomas Cranmer, the first reformed Archbishop of Canterbury, wrote about justification by God's grace:

This faith the holy Scripture teacheth: this is the strong rock and foundation of Christian religion: this doctrine all old and ancient authors of Christ's Church do approve: this doctrine advanceth and setteth forth the true glory of Christ, and beateth down the vain glory of man: this whosoever denieth is not to be counted for a true Christian man, nor for a setter-forth of Christ's glory, but for an adversary of Christ and His gospel, and for a setter-forth of men's vainglory.[14]

The entire text which runs from Romans 3:21—4:25 concerns "the righteousness of God" or "God's justifying grace." We will consider it under the following divisions:

First, the manifestation of God's justifying grace (3:21-26). Here Paul unfolds the gospel of justification through Christ by faith.

Second, the implications of God's justifying grace (3:27-31). Here Paul answers three objections from an imaginary Jewish critic.

Third, an illustration of God's justifying grace (4:1-25). Here Paul shows that Abraham was himself justified by faith and is

therefore the spiritual father of all Christian believers, whether
Gentiles or Jews.

The Manifestation of God's Justifying Grace (3:21-26)

Paul writes in Romans 3:21-23, "But now apart from the Law the
righteousness of God has been manifested, being witnessed
by the Law and the Prophets; even the righteousness of God
through faith in Jesus Christ for all those who believe; for there
is no distinction; for all have sinned and fall short of the glory of
God."

Paul speaks of a "manifestation" of God's righteousness, that
is, of his justifying grace. The perfect tense here ("has been manifested") probably refers to the historical events of Christ's death
and resurrection, and the present tense in 1:17 ("is revealed") to
the contemporary preaching of the gospel. The God who once
made known his saving plan in Christ continues to make it
known today whenever the good news of Christ is proclaimed.

This manifestation of God's justifying grace, Paul says, has
been made "apart from the Law," for it does not depend at all on
obedience to the law, but only on faith in Christ. At the same
time, it is "witnessed by the Law and the Prophets," for throughout the Old Testament the same doctrine of justification by faith
is taught. As for the prophets, Paul has already cited Habakkuk
(1:17). As for the Law (by which he seems here to mean the rest
of the Old Testament, especially the Pentateuch), he is about to
cite the example of Abraham (chapter 4). There is a vital continuity of teaching on this matter between Old and New Testaments.

In verse 22 Paul enlarges on what he means by "the righteousness of God," emphasizing particularly that it is "through faith
in Jesus Christ" and is therefore enjoyed by "all those who believe." He stresses the availability of salvation for "*all* those
who believe" because, as he goes on immediately to add, "there
is no distinction, for *all* have sinned [a summary of past history]
and fall short [still in the present] of the glory of God," which is
God's ideal exhibited in Christ. All human beings are unrighteous, so God's righteousness is for all who believe. Already in
these two verses the main aspects of God's justification have

been adumbrated—its source, its ground and its means: (1) the
source of our justification is God and his grace; it is "the righteousness *of God*"; (2) the *ground* of our justification is Christ and
his cross; it is "through faith in *Jesus Christ*"; (3) the *means* of
our justification is faith alone without works; it is "*through faith
. . . for all who believe.*"

The remaining verses of the paragraph fill in the details of
this outline, and clothe this skeleton with flesh.

1. *The source of our justification is God and his grace.* Justification is the revealing of *God's* righteousness, and God's
righteousness begins with his gracious, saving initiative. It is
God to the rescue, God coming in Christ to put the unrighteous
right with himself. It is absolutely fundamental to the biblical
doctrine of salvation that the whole initiative from beginning to
end is the Father's. No formulation can claim to be true to Scripture which takes the initiative from the Father and attributes it
instead to us or even to Christ.

The initiative is certainly not ours. For two chapters Paul
has been ramming home to us our sin and guilt, our helpless-
ness and hopelessness. That is why God has now manifested his
righteousness "apart from the Law." This statement will have
sounded shocking to Jewish ears, for what is righteousness but
conformity to the law? Paul's answer is that there is another
righteousness, which is not ours but God's, not our achievement
but his gift, based not on law but on faith.

Next, the initiative is not Christ's either. To be sure, he came
voluntarily, and gave himself for us freely. Yet his initiative was
a response to his Father's: "Lo, I come to do your will," he said.
Therefore, we must never describe the work of Christ in such a
way as to imply any reluctance on the part of the Father.

For the initiative came from the Father himself. The contrast
between verse 20 and verse 24 makes this plain beyond dispute.
According to verse 20, "by the works of the Law no flesh will
be justified in His sight." According to verse 24, we are "justified as a gift by His grace." Justification is a gift of God's sheer
grace, not a reward for any merit or works of ours. For God's
"grace" is his spontaneous generosity, his free and unmerited
favor, his gracious kindness to the undeserving. Grace is God

loving, God stooping, God coming, God giving.

2. *The ground of our justification is Christ and his cross.*
Granted that God justifies sinners "as a gift by His grace," on
what ground does he do so? How is it possible for a righteous
God to pronounce the unrighteous righteous? For that is certainly what he does. No phrase in Romans expresses the paradox of
his action more strikingly than that in 4:5, which declares that
he "justifies the ungodly." It is a fantastic assertion. In the Law
of Moses God repeatedly told the Jewish judges that they must
"justify the righteous and condemn the wicked" (for example,
Deut. 25:1).

But of course! That should go without saying. A righteous
man must be pronounced righteous, and a wicked man wicked.
What more obvious principle of justice could you enunciate?
In consequence, a solemn woe is pronounced against magis-
trates who "justify the wicked for a bribe" (Is. 5:23), and it is
written in Proverbs 17:15 that "he who justifies the wicked, and
he who condemns the righteous,/ Both of them alike are an
abomination to the LORD."

But of course, we say again, that is self-evident. Such perver-
sions of justice would be bound to be an abomination to God
the just Judge of all. No self-respecting magistrate would ever be
guilty of such miscarriages of justice. So it is hardly necessary
for God to declare (as he does in Ex. 23:7 RSV; cf. 1 Kings 8:32),
"I will not justify the wicked." For of course he would never
dream of doing such a thing.

Yet here in Romans 4:5 Paul has the effrontery to write that
God *does* do the very thing he says he will never do, the very
thing which he condemns others for doing, and moreover that
he does it habitually. He makes a practice of doing it. He can
even be designated the God "who justifies the ungodly." Has
Paul lost his reason? How can he possibly describe God like that?
Can God overthrow the moral order and turn it upside down?
I hope that perhaps we can now feel the gasp of incredulity with
which Jewish readers would have reacted.

And they would have been right, had it not been for the cross.
Without the cross the just/justification of the unjust would have
been impossible. The only reason why God can "justify the un-

godly" (4:5) is that "Christ died for the ungodly" (5:6).

Returning to chapter 3, notice that Paul refers to the death of Jesus in terms of his "blood" (v. 25), which C. K. Barrett translates "his bloody sacrificial death."[15] For the death of Jesus was such a perfect sacrifice for sin that God is now able, as I might put it, to "righteous the unrighteous without compromising his righteousness or condoning their unrighteousness." Paul uses three expressions to explain what this is which God did through the cross of Jesus Christ: (1) "through the redemption which is in Christ Jesus" (v. 24); (2) "whom God displayed publicly as a propitiation" (v. 25); (3) "This was to demonstrate His righteousness" (vv. 25-26). Associated with the cross, therefore, there is a "redemption," a "propitiation" and a "demonstration." What do these words mean?

Redemption is a commercial term, borrowed from the marketplace, just as justification is a legal term, borrowed from the law court. In the Old Testament it was specially used of the purchase of slaves. To redeem, writes Professor Bruce, was "the act of buying a slave out of bondage in order to set him free."[16] The verb redeem was also used metaphorically in reference to God's deliverance of Israel from their captivities in Egypt and Babylon.

From this meaning and background of the vocabulary of redemption, we learn: that we were slaves, in bondage to our sin and guilt, and unable to liberate ourselves; that Jesus Christ bought us out of that slavery, shedding his blood as the ransom price to rescue us; and that in consequence of his purchase we now belong to him, although our new slavery is the true freedom. We hear much today about "liberation" and "liberation theology." Let us mark well Paul's teaching that (although we should desire to see human beings liberated from everything that dehumanizes them) nothing dehumanizes and oppresses more than guilt, and therefore nothing liberates more than the gospel.

The second word, propitiation, has been resisted by many scholars in recent years. For to "propitiate" means to "appease" or "placate." Unable to accept that God needs in any way to be "propitiated" (a notion which seemed to them heathen rather than Christian), they have argued both linguistically and theo-

logically that what Jesus did on the cross was not to propitiate
God, but to expiate sin, that is, to cover it or put it away. In the
English-speaking world Professor C. H. Dodd was the main ad-
vocate of this view, and his influence is seen in the NEB which
renders the word in verse 25, "the means of expiating sin."
More recently, however, there has been a greater willingness
among scholars to agree that the Bible speaks much of the wrath
of God, and that therefore this wrath must somehow be averted
if sinners are ever to be forgiven.

Another way to understand verse 25, which has been favored
by some commentators ever since Origen, is based on the fact
that the Greek word for "propitiation" (hilastērion) is the regular word in the Septuagint, and is once used in the New Testament (Heb. 9:5), for the "mercy seat," that is, the golden lid of the
ark or covenant box. Here the blood of sacrifice was sprinkled
on the annual Day of Atonement, and here God promised to
manifest his presence. It was, therefore, the place of propitiation. Perhaps then, it has been suggested, the Lord Jesus is represented as the true mercy seat, the reality behind the symbol,
and his cross as the place where God and sinners are reconciled.
Perhaps too this new and real mercy seat (Jesus Christ) "God
displayed publicly," in contrast to the old one which was con-
cealed in the holy of holies behind the veil. F. F. Bruce inclines
to this view.[17] So does Anders Nygren, following Luther.[18]

Other commentators point out the absence of the definite
article in verse 25, and are reluctant to see Jesus Christ likened
to "an inanimate piece of temple furniture."[19] Besides, writes
F. L. Godet, "The Epistle to the Romans is not a book which
moves, like the Epistle to the Hebrews, in the sphere of Levitical
symbolism."[20] These scholars prefer to render the word either
"a means of propitiation" or, more specifically, "a propitiatory
sacrifice." The latter certainly seems to be correct, since Paul
goes on immediately to speak of Christ's "blood," that is, of his
life laid down in a violent or sacrificial death.

If we want to grasp in what sense the death of Jesus on the
cross was a propitiatory sacrifice, we will have to remember that
throughout the Bible, literally from its beginning to its end,
"sin" and "death" are bracketed as rebellion against God and its

just reward. Death (whether physical, spiritual or eternal) is always presented in Scripture as the penalty for sin. Paul himself has already written in 1:32, "Those who practice such things are worthy of death," and in 6:23 he will shortly write, "The wages of sin is death."

So whenever the apostles say, quite simply, "Christ died," even without any further elaboration, there is a wealth of meaning in what they say. For if death is always the penalty for sin, and if Jesus Christ died, and if he was himself sinless, then there is only one possible explanation of his death: he died for our sins. He identified himself with us and substituted himself for us, so that the death he died was our death, in order that we might never have to die it, but instead receive eternal life.

Now perhaps we begin to understand how his death could have been a propitiatory sacrifice. If on the cross, as Paul writes elsewhere, Christ was "made . . . sin on our behalf" and even became "a curse for us" (2 Cor. 5:21; Gal. 3:13), that is to say, if he identified himself with our guilt and bore in his innocent person our judgment, then there is now a righteous basis on which we may be forgiven. Since the penalty for sin has been paid, God can turn from his wrath and justify us. Here are the bold, outspoken words which Charles Cranfield uses to explain "Paul's statement that God purposed Christ as a propitiatory victim." He writes, "God, because in His mercy He willed to forgive sinful men and, being truly merciful, willed to forgive them righteously, that is, without in any way condoning their sin, purposed to direct against His own very Self in the person of His Son the full weight of that righteous wrath which they deserved."[21] That God should thus give full and perfect expression to both his love and his wrath, by bearing himself the fearful condemnation which our sins had deserved, is the very heart of the Christian gospel. It is enough to stretch the largest mind, enough to bend the proudest will, enough to break the hardest heart.

Yet, whenever we talk about Christ as a "means of propitiation" or a "propitiatory victim," we must hedge our words with every possible safeguard, lest we be misunderstood. For this Christian propitiation is fundamentally different from the unworthy notions which are found in some "heathen" or "animistic" or "traditional" religions. The need for propitiation, its author and its nature are all distinct.

Take the need first. Pagan gods have always been irritable and unpredictable. They are subject to moods and fits, and you never know when they are going to fly off the handle. Hence the need to appease them. The holy wrath of the God of the Bible, on the other hand, is entirely predictable. It is never capricious or arbitrary. The only thing which arouses God's anger is evil, and evil always does.

The second difference lies in the author of the propitiation. In pagan religion both ancient and modern it is human beings who, fearful of having offended their gods, determine to bring offerings to placate them. But the gospel begins by declaring it impossible for us ever to win God's favor, for it declares us sinful, guilty and helpless. Then it goes on to say that God himself supplied the propitiatory victim. God so loved the world that he gave his only Son. "In this is love, not that we loved God, but that He loved us and sent His Son to be the propitiation for our sins" (1 Jn. 4:10). Similarly, we are told by Paul in verse 25 that God either "designed" (NEB) or "presented" (NIV) or "displayed publicly" (NASB) the Lord Jesus Christ as a propitiation. The love, the idea, the purpose, the initiative, the action, the gift —all were God's, not ours.

Third, the nature of the propitiation is different. In animistic religions the worshiper brings material gifts, perhaps an animal or fruits or candies, hoping by these to avert the anger of the spirits. In the Old Testament too there were material offerings, but these were prescribed by God himself, and it was recognized that "it is impossible for the blood of bulls and goats to take away sins" (Heb. 10:4). These offerings prefigured a greater offering, the self-giving of the Son of God himself, who bore our sin and died our death.

So then, in summary, the Christian propitiation is not human beings bringing a bribe to appease a bad-tempered deity, but God's grace giving God's Son to avert God's wrath. It is this God-centeredness of the gospel which we must at all costs preserve. It tells of God acting in his own mercy through his own Son to save us from his own judgment. One might dare to state the matter even more simply and say that God himself gave himself to save us from himself.

So far we have considered the two words, redemption and propitiation, which Paul uses to explain the purpose of Christ's death. His third word, used in verse 25 and repeated in verse 26, is demonstration. The cross was a demonstration or revelation as well as an achievement. It not only accomplished the propitiation of God and the redemption of man; it also vindicated the righteousness of God. Here is how Paul put it: "This was to demonstrate His righteousness, because in the forbearance of God He passed over the sins previously committed; for the demonstration, I say, of His righteousness at the present time, that He might be just and the justifier of the one who has faith in Jesus."

Notice at once the contrast between "the sins previously committed," which God in his forbearance "passed over," and "the present time" in which he has acted to "demonstrate" his righteousness. The contrast is between the past and the present, between the divine forbearance and the divine righteousness, and between the "passing over" of sins (which seemed unjust) and their judgment on the cross (which set forth and vindicated his justice). God passed over the sins of previous generations, forbearing to judge them as they deserved, only because he intended that the full penalty for these sins would in due time be borne by his Son. This was the only way in which God could be both righteous himself and simultaneously the "righteouser" or "justifier" of the sinner who believes in Jesus (v. 26). The sin-bearing, substitutionary death of Jesus is the uniquely righteous ground on which God both passed over the sins of former generations and can now in the present righteously bestow a righteous standing on the unrighteous.

Bringing together Paul's three technical terms, we can now summarize what God has done by the death of Jesus. He has redeemed his people, propitiated his wrath and demonstrated his justice. Or better, for this relates the words to one another, he has propitiated his wrath in such a way as to redeem and justify his people and at the same time demonstrate his justice. We can only marvel at his wisdom and his mercy and fall down before him in humble worship.

3. *The means of our justification is faith.* There can be no question about this paragraph's emphasis on faith. Justification is "through faith in Jesus Christ for all those who believe" (v. 22). It is "through faith" that God purposed Christ to be a propitiation (v. 25). And God is "the justifier of the one who has faith in Jesus" (v. 26). Indeed, justification is by faith *alone.* Although this word does not appear in Paul's text, it was a true instinct of Luther (following Origen and other older commentators) to add it. Far from distorting Paul's meaning, it clarifies and underlines it.

Now it is exceedingly important to understand that there is nothing meritorious about faith. When we affirm that sinners are justified "by faith" and not "by works," we are not substituting one work (called "faith") for another (called "obedience to the law"). Nor are we suggesting that in saving us God does a part of the work (sending Jesus Christ to die for us), while we do the other part (believing in Jesus). Salvation is not a kind of cooperative enterprise between God and us, his share being the cross and our share being faith.

Anders Nygren insists on this point with eloquent emphasis. He even rejects the popular description of faith as the "condition" of salvation. When Paul asserts that the gospel is "the power of God for salvation to every one who has faith," he writes, "he has no thought of apportioning to God and man respective contributions to salvation." Again, "it is not man's faith that gives the gospel its power; quite the contrary, it is the power of the gospel that makes it possible for one to believe."[22]

Another way to put this is to say that faith's value is not at all in itself, but solely in its object, Christ crucified. Faith is the hand which grasps Christ, the eye which beholds him, even the mouth which eats his flesh and drinks his blood (Jn. 6:53-56). Yet what saves us is neither the hand nor the eye nor the mouth of faith, but only Christ who is grasped, gazed upon and received, and the vision of whom evokes our responsible faith. As Richard Hooker, that judicious Anglican theologian in the sixteenth century, wrote in *Definition of Justification,* "God doth justify the believing man, yet not for the worthiness of his belief, but for His worthiness who is believed."

Gresham Machen, the lucid Presbyterian writer of this century, also put it plainly: "The faith of man, rightly conceived, can never stand in opposition to the completeness with which salvation depends upon God; it can never mean that man does part, while God merely does the rest, for the simple reason that faith consists not in doing something but in receiving something. To say that we are justified by faith is just another way of saying that we are justified not in the slightest measure by ourselves, but simply and solely by the One in whom our faith is reposed."[23]

Such is Paul's exposition of "the righteousness of God" which is revealed in Christ and the gospel, that is, his righteous way of bestowing righteousness upon the unrighteous. Its source is God and his grace, its ground is Christ and his cross, and its means is faith alone, apart altogether from any human merit.

And in all this Christianity is unique. No other religion proclaims the good news of a free forgiveness to undeserving sinners, as Christianity does. On the contrary, all the religions of the world teach some form of self-salvation, whether by religious devotion or by prescribed ceremonies or by good works or by correct belief, or by a combination of these, sometimes with the mercy of God thrown in, though only for the meritorious. In contrast to these, Christianity is not primarily "a religion" at all. It is "the gospel," the good news that God has had mercy on the undeserving, that his wrath has been turned away by his grace, that his Son has died our death and borne our judgment, and that there is nothing left for us to do except to put our trust in him and call upon him to save us.

Nothing in my hand I bring;
Simply to Thy cross I cling;
Naked, come to Thee for dress;
Helpless, look to Thee for grace;
Foul, I to the fountain fly;
Wash me, Savior, or I die!
    (Augustus M. Toplady, 1776)

The Implications of God's Justifying Grace (3:27-31)

Paul's exposition (in vv. 21-26) of "the righteousness of God through faith in Jesus Christ" will have raised important questions in his readers' minds, especially in the minds of Jewish critics. So in verses 27-31 he anticipates three of them and answers them.

Question 1: "Where then is boasting?" (vv. 27-28). The Jews were inveterate boasters, as indeed are all fallen human beings. They were proud of their unique privileges. In 2:23 Paul has described them as those who "boast in the Law." They imagined that they were heaven's darlings, eternally secure in the favor of God.

But the gospel excludes all boasting, on account of the "law" or "principle" of faith. If we could say, "I have been justified by the law," meaning "by my own obedience and merit," we would have something to boast about. But since we can say only, "I have been justified by faith," meaning "by the merit and work of Christ alone," we have nothing to boast about (v. 28). There is something essentially obscene about arrogance in Christian people and something essentially authentic about humility. We shall not be able to strut round heaven like peacocks, flattering ourselves as if we have got there by our own achievement. Instead, we shall spend eternity ascribing salvation to God and to the Lamb. Praising, not boasting, is the characteristic activity of justified Christians, both on earth and in heaven. Or rather, the only boasting we are free to indulge in is boasting of Jesus Christ our Savior. As Paul put it to the Corinthians, quoting Jeremiah, "Let him who boasts, boast in the Lord" (Jer. 9:23-24; 1 Cor. 1:31).

Question 2: "Is God the God of the Jews only?" (vv. 29-30). The Jews were fiercely nationalistic. They prided themselves on their special relationship to God and despised Gentiles as outsiders.

But the gospel excludes discrimination as much as boasting. God is One and he justifies all sinners in the same way, whether they are circumcised or uncircumcised, namely "through faith." At the foot of the cross of Jesus, when we find this justification and forgiveness, there is total equality—between male and female, black and white, Jew and Gentile. All discrimination is excluded. This doesn't mean that our differences are obliterated. Our skin pigmentation, our cultural inheritances, our sexuality still remain. But these things are rendered of no account before God. The gospel abolishes the barriers to fellowship.

Question 3: "Do we then nullify the Law through faith?" (v. 31). The law, as the revelation of God, was the Jews' most treasured possession. One of their reasons for rejecting the gospel was that they perceived it as a threat to the law, undermining and contradicting it. The law and the gospel seemed to them irreconcilable.

And so they are irreconcilable if by "the law" we mean self-salvation, salvation by obeying the law. But that was never the intended function of the law. If we understand the law correctly, Paul insists that the gospel does not nullify it; "on the contrary, we establish the Law." From his instruction elsewhere we can guess what he means.

First, the gospel establishes the law by emphasizing its true function, which is to give us "the knowledge of sin" (v. 20). It is in this sense that the law is our "schoolmaster" or "tutor" to bring us to Christ (Gal. 3:23-24). It is only those whom the law condemns that the gospel can justify.

Second, the gospel establishes the law by enabling people to obey it. God sent his Son and gives his Spirit "that the requirement of the Law might be fulfilled in us" (8:4). Both Reformers and Puritans used to explain that first the law sends us to the gospel to be justified, and then the gospel sends us back to the law to be sanctified, though of course by the Holy Spirit's power.

The third way in which the gospel establishes the law is by confirming and elaborating its teaching. The truth of the gospel, the apostle has written in verse 21, is "witnessed by the Law and the Prophets." Perhaps this is the most likely explanation of his statement because he immediately proceeds in chapter 4 to refer to Abraham and David as outstanding examples in the Old Testament of the gospel of justification by faith. By these models of gospel truth the law is established.

Here then are the three implications of justification by faith alone, which Paul draws out. First, faith humbles the sinner and excludes boasting. Second, faith unites the church and excludes discrimination. Third, faith establishes the Scripture and excludes every facile attempt to represent Old and New Testament, law and gospel, as incompatible. The Jewish objections, which Paul's answers imply, have no substance.

An Illustration of God's Justifying Grace (4)

Perhaps we should regard 4:1 as a fourth question in the series of Jewish objections: "What then shall we say that Abraham, our forefather according to the flesh, has found?" How did he come to be accepted by God? It was an extremely important question, partly because Abraham was universally revered as the progenitor of the people of God, partly because the Jews regarded him as the epitome of righteousness and were convinced that he was righteous before God because he had fulfilled the law. Was this not written in Scripture? Did not God say to him, "I will greatly bless you . . . because you have obeyed My voice," and later say to Isaac, "I will . . . bless you . . . because Abraham obeyed me" (Gen. 22:17-18; 26:3, 5)?

Of course it was recognized that Abraham believed God as well as obeying him, but his faith was regarded as meritorious too. God's promised blessing was understood as a reward for his faith and obedience. Charles Cranfield cites examples from Rabbinic Judaism in which the expression "the merit of faith" was used in relation to Abraham. Was Paul wrong then? "For if Abraham was justified by works, he has something to boast about" (v. 2), whereas Paul has declared boasting excluded.

Paul allows his imaginary objector to get so far, but no further. The very concept of human boasting is so distasteful to him that he interjects indignantly at the end of verse 2, "but not before God." Let boasters boast, if they will, but they cannot sustain their boasting before God. So the argument is joined. Paul's Jewish contemporaries taught that Abraham was justified by works, Paul that he was justified by faith. He asks, therefore, "What does the Scripture say?" Who is interpreting it correctly?

In the rest of the chapter Paul mentions a number of details in

Abraham's life story. He refers to God's promise to him and Sarah that they will have a son and then a posterity. He refers to God's further promises that he will become the "father of many nations" and that through his descendants the world will be blessed. He refers to Abraham's faith in believing these promises through thick and thin, in spite of his great age and Sarah's barrenness, and to the statement of Genesis 15:6 that when he believed God, his faith was reckoned to him as righteousness. As Paul recalls this story of Abraham's faith, he emphasizes two particular features of it, its priority (that it preceded his works, his circumcision and the law) and its reasonableness (the solid rational grounds on which it rested). These points must now occupy our attention.

1. *The priority of Abraham's faith* (3-16). First, Abraham was justified by faith *before he did any good works*. In verse 3 Paul quotes Genesis 15:6: "Abraham believed God, and it was reckoned to him as righteousness." The context in Genesis is Abraham's childlessness. "O Lord God," he cried, "what wilt Thou give me, since I am childless?" (Gen. 15:2). In reply God took him one night outside his tent. Above him thousands of stars twinkled from a clear oriental sky. "Count the stars," God said to Abraham,"if you are able to count them." I have sometimes imagined that Abraham began: "1, 2, 3, 4, 5, 10, 20, 30, 40, 50." If so, we may be sure that he soon gave up. And God said to him, "So shall your descendants be," that is, as countless as the stars. Then the Scripture goes on: "Abraham believed God," and God reckoned his faith to him as righteousness. That is, God accepted him not because he had done any righteous works which merited acceptance, but because he believed God. He had no righteousness of his own which could be reckoned to him; his faith was reckoned to him instead.

Paul goes on to develop the implications of the verb to reckon. To reckon means to put something to somebody's account. Now money can be credited to a bank account either as a wage or as a gift. Which of these two was the "reckoning" in Abraham's case? Did God reckon righteousness to him as a wage (a reward) or as a gift? The text tells us. Not "Abraham *worked*, and his work was reckoned to him as righteousness," but "Abraham *believed*, and his faith was reckoned to him as righteousness." Paul makes the alternative clear in verses 4 and 5: "Now to the one who works, his wage is not reckoned as a favor but as what is due. But to the one who does not work, but believes in Him who justifies the ungodly, his faith is reckoned as righteousness."

Exactly the same was true of David, to whom Paul now refers in verses 6-8. He quotes from the first two verses of Psalm 32, which declare the blessedness of the person whose iniquities have been forgiven, whose sins have been covered, and "whose sin the Lord will not take into account" or (margin) "reckon." This, Paul explains, is the blessedness of the person "to whom God reckons righteousness apart from works" (v. 6). For here is God refusing to reckon a person's sin against him (which is what he deserves), and instead "forgiving" or "covering" his sin (which he does not deserve). This is God's free and unmerited favor. It is justification by grace without works.

The key to these verses is the verb to *reckon*. It occurs five times in six verses (3-8), and although Paul varies his expressions, they must be taken as identical in meaning. Thus, the justified sinner is a person against whom God refuses to reckon his sin (v. 8), to whom God reckons righteousness apart from works (v. 6) and to whom God reckons his faith as righteousness (vv. 3-5). Putting these three together, we may say that, instead of reckoning his *sin* against him, God reckons *righteousness* to him apart from works, by reckoning his *faith* as righteousness. This person, justified by God's grace through faith, is truly blessed. Abraham was such a man. So was David. And so today is every Christian believer.

Second, Abraham was justified by faith *before he was circumcised* (vv. 9-12). Paul continues to argue his case with imaginary Jews. Granted that God's blessing is pronounced on believers, is it pronounced only upon circumcised believers (Jews), or upon uncircumcised believers (Gentiles) too (v. 9)? To this question also Abraham supplies the answer. The plain fact is that Abraham was justified before he was circumcised (v. 10). His justification is recorded in Genesis 15, his circumcision in Genesis 17, and at least fourteen years (Rabbis calculated a period twice as long) separated these two events. Yet they were related to each other. For Abraham received circumcision as a sign and a seal "of the righteousness of the faith which he had while uncircumcised" (v. 11). Thus Abraham received two distinct gifts from God, first, justification by faith while uncircumcised and, second, circumcision as a visible sign and seal of his justification. But his justification (which was an "inward and spiritual gift" of God) came first; his circumcision (also a gift of God) came later, as an "outward and visible sign." Moreover, this order of events (faith—justification—circumcision) had a purpose (v. 11). It was to make Abraham "the father of all who believe," on the one hand the father of all uncircumcised (Gentile) believers, who by faith have righteousness reckoned to them, and on the other hand (v. 12) the father of circumcised (Jewish) believers, who are not only circumcised like Abraham but also believe like Abraham, and so follow in his footsteps.

Third, Abraham was justified by faith *before the law was given* (vv. 13-16). Paul now reminds his readers that the faith by which Abraham was justified was faith in a promise of God. He calls it God's promise that he would be "heir of the world" (v. 13), a remarkable expression which presumably alludes to the fact that through his posterity all the earth's families would be blessed. Anyway, Paul's point is that God's *promise* and God's *law* are two completely different things. God did not make his promise to Abraham "through the Law," but "through the righteousness of faith." That is, God's word to Abraham was not "obey this law and I will bless you" but "I will bless you; believe my promise." Laws are to be obeyed, while promises are to be believed. They are two distinct realms, which have two distinct vocabularies (vv. 14-16). On the one hand the law requires obedience and (because we disobey) brings us under God's wrath, while on the other the promise requires faith and issues from God's grace. So law, works and wrath go together, as do promise, faith and grace. These sets of words cannot be mixed. The heirs of the promise are not lawkeepers, but believers who are Abraham's spiritual descendants.

If we share his faith, he is "the father of us all," in fulfillment of God's word to him "a father of many nations have I made you" (v. 17) which was the meaning of his new name "Abraham."

Thus, the true descendants of Abraham are not Jews who can
trace their *physical* descent from Abraham and call him "our
forefather according to the flesh" (v. 1), but Christians who
(whether Jews or Gentiles) belong to the *spiritual* lineage of faith
and can call Abraham "the father of us all" (v. 16).

Looking back over the first half of chapter 4, Paul has hammered home his insistence that Abraham was justified by faith.
He was not justified by *works*, for it is written that he "believed
God, and it was reckoned to him as righteousness." He was not
justified by *circumcision*, for he was justified first and circumcised later. And he was not justified by *law*, because his believing response was to God's promise, not God's law, and in any
case God's law was given centuries later. We modern men and
women need to have the same message hammered home to us,
for our fallen nature is inherently proud, anxious to establish a
claim on God, and deeply hostile to the concept of grace,
whereas a Christian is precisely a self-condemned sinner who
despairs of self-salvation, trusts only in God and thus becomes a
child of Abraham.

2. *The reasonableness of Abraham's faith* (17-25). The
apostle has established that Abraham was justified by faith,
and that Christians are those who share "the faith of Abraham"
(v. 16). But what was this faith of his? How did it arise? How did
it grow! What was its rationale? Such questions come as a surprise to many people. They have never thought that faith could
be "reasonable." On the contrary, they have always supposed
that faith and reason were mutually exclusive, and that faith was
a synonym for superstition.

This is not so. Faith goes *beyond* reason, but not *against* it.
True faith always has a rational basis, and its reasonableness is
well illustrated in the story of Abraham. The principle is this.
Faith means believing somebody's word or promise. Now behind every word is the person who speaks it. Behind every
promise is the person who makes it. Whether it is reasonable to
believe a person's word or promise depends entirely on his or
her character. Is he or she trustworthy? That is the question. It is
always reasonable to trust the trustworthy.

Now Paul refers in verse 17 to "Him whom he [Abraham] believed, even God." Who was this God whom Abraham trusted? What was he like? How did Abraham assess his credibility? Well, according to Paul, Abraham believed two fundamental truths about God, which led him to trust his promises. The first was his power, and the second his faithfulness.

Take power first. This is obviously relevant, because when anybody makes a promise, we have to know whether he has the ability, the power, to do what he has promised. What about God's power, then? Has he the power to keep his promises? You bet! See how Paul describes him at the end of verse 17. He is the God "who gives life to the dead" (that's resurrection) and who "calls into being that which does not exist" (that's creation). We human beings are entirely baffled by nothingness and by death. The "angst" of the existentialist is his dread of the abyss of nothingness, and death is the one event none of us can forever escape. But God is not baffled by either. He creates out of nothing and he raises from death. And this God of creation and resurrection is the God Abraham believed in, as is evident from his story, especially the promise of the birth of Isaac and the command to sacrifice Isaac.

God promised Abraham a son when he was an old man of "about a hundred years old" (v. 19), whose body was "as good as dead," and when Sarah was an old woman far beyond the age of childbearing. It would therefore take a supernatural act, a special creative act, for a child to be born to them. But Abraham believed God could do it, for he was the Creator who had called the universe into existence out of nothing.

Then, some years after Isaac's birth, God commanded Abraham to sacrifice him. The agony of this test was not just that Isaac was the son of his old age, his only son, precious and beloved, but that Isaac was also the child of promise, through whom alone God could fulfill his further promise to bless the world by Abraham's posterity. How could God keep this promise if Isaac were to die? The only possible answer to this question is given in the Letter to the Hebrews. Abraham "considered that God is able to raise men even from the dead; from which he also received him back, figuratively speaking" (11:19 margin). After all, Isaac's birth had seemed like life from the dead. Romans 4:19 refers both to Abraham's body which was "as good as dead" and to "the deadness of Sarah's womb." Yet out of that double death a new life had been born. If Isaac were to die, why should God not bring life out of death a second time?

The kind of God Abraham believed in, then, was the God of creation and the God of resurrection. This too is our God, except that we know far more than Abraham, for we live this side of the resurrection of Jesus, and we have a completed Bible in which both the creation of the world and the resurrection of Jesus are recorded for our instruction. They are, in fact, set before us in Scripture as the supreme exhibitions of the power of God. Jeremiah said: "Ah, Lord God! Behold, Thou hast made the heavens and the earth by Thy great power and by Thine outstretched arm! Nothing is too difficult for Thee" (32:17). And Paul prayed that the eyes of our hearts might be enlightened so that we might know "what is the surpassing greatness of His power toward us who believe . . . in accordance with the working of the strength of His might which He brought about in Christ, when He raised Him from the dead" (Eph. 1:19-20). If God has thus exhibited his almighty power, by creating the universe and by resurrecting the Lord Jesus, would it not be reasonable to believe that he is able to keep his promises?

But Abraham was convinced of the faithfulness, as well as of the power, of God. This too was vital for his faith. For there are two main reasons why we human beings break our promises. One is that we lack the ability or power to do what we promise; the other is that we lack the will, being fickle and unreliable creatures. But God has both the ability and the will, for he is faithful as well as powerful. Abraham believed this. Therefore, "In hope against hope he believed . . . according to that which had been spoken." The expression "in hope against hope" is a remarkable one, isn't it? Although there was no hope, yet he went on hoping.

These two hopes seem to reflect the two possibilities, human and divine. Humanly speaking, his faith was "beyond hope," "a defiance of all human calculations."[24] Yet he still believed, "in hope," because he clung to the promise of God. Charles Wesley expressed this admirably in one of his well-known hymns:

In hope, against all human hope,
   Self-desperate, I believe. . . .
Faith, mighty faith, the promise sees,
   And looks to that alone;
Laughs at impossibilities,
   And cries: It shall be done!

Yes, clinging to the promise of God was Abraham's secret. Verse 19 describes him as not "becoming weak in faith," while verse 20 says that he "grew strong in faith." Scripture often indicates that there are different degrees of faith. Some people's faith is "weak"; others' is "strong." Similarly, Jesus could complain of the "little faith" of his own disciples and marvel at the "great faith" of a Gentile centurion.

How then can a little faith increase, and a weak faith grow strong like Abraham's? Well, Abraham's faith grew as he used his mind. "He contemplated" both his senile body and Sarah's barren womb (for he did not close his eyes to the problems). But he also considered God's promise, for it was "with respect to the promise of God" that "he did not waver in unbelief, but grew strong in faith, giving glory to God" (that is, acknowledging the truth about God's faithfulness). Thus, he set the problems in the light of the promise. And as his mind played on the promise, the problems were eclipsed by it. For he was "fully assured that what He had promised, He was able also to perform" (v. 21), and therefore his faith was "reckoned to him as righteousness" (v. 22).

Thus faith rests as much on the faithfulness of God as on his power. There is a fine phrase in Hebrews 11:11 that Sarah "considered Him faithful who had promised." So central is this to the biblical meaning of faith that Hudson Taylor, the great founder of the China Inland Mission, used to paraphrase our Lord's command "have faith in God" (Mk. 11:22) with the words "reckon on the faithfulness of God." All human faith reckons and rests on the divine faithfulness.

Paul ends this chapter (vv. 22-25) by applying Abraham's faith to us. The statement of his justification was not written "for his sake only . . . but for our sake also." For just like Abraham we too will be justified by faith if we "believe in Him who raised

Jesus our Lord from the dead, ... who was delivered up because of our transgressions, and was raised because of our justification." Abraham's faith was a response to certain promises relating to Isaac; Christian faith is a response to certain events relating to Jesus, in particular his death and resurrection, and to the promises of salvation which are founded upon them. Behind these promises and these events stands the same living God. He is the God of Abraham, Isaac and Jacob, and he is the God of our Lord and Savior Jesus Christ.

More particularly, both the death and resurrection of Jesus were part of the divine purpose (v. 25). For he was "handed over" to death and then "raised" from it. Both are represented as divine actions. Because of our sins God handed him over to death, to deal with them. Because of our justification (which his death secured), God raised him from death, to prove it. This is the God we believe in, the God who displayed his love, holiness and power in the death and resurrection of Jesus. Is not such a God absolutely trustworthy, worthy of our faith?

H. L. Mencken, the so-called sage of Baltimore, once defined faith as "an illogical belief in the occurrence of the improbable." His definition is witty, but inaccurate. True faith is neither illogical nor irrational, neither superstitious nor credulous. It is neither whistling in the dark to keep our spirits up, nor convincing ourselves to believe something we know isn't true. No, no. The reasonableness of faith is that it rests on the God who has revealed himself in the death and resurrection of Jesus, who promises to save those who believe, and who keeps his promises. What constitutes authentic faith is "not the sheer fact that one believes the improbable, the impossible, the absurd" but that we "hold to God's promise."[25]

So let us stay our minds on this God—on his faithfulness, on his power as he has revealed himself in Christ and in Scripture. Then our faith will grow and ripen, and then we shall prove ourselves to be genuine descendants of our great spiritual forefather, Abraham.

6
God's
People
John R. W. Stott

Let me begin by explaining and defending my choice of the expression "God's People" as the title for Romans 5:1-11. Some explanation is certainly necessary because "the people of God" are not specifically mentioned here. Nevertheless, they appear throughout in the dozen or so "we" sentences. For in these Paul identifies himself with all those who have been "justified by faith," in other words with the new community of the new age.

The changes of pronoun in these early chapters of Romans have not, I think been sufficiently noticed or appreciated by commentators. The characteristic pronoun of the first half of chapter 1 is *I* as Paul asserts his apostolic commission and gospel, relates himself to his Roman readers and declares, "I am under obligation.... I am eager.... I am not ashamed." In the second half of chapter 1, however, the pronoun changes to *they* as the apostle describes the demoralized Gentile world: "Though they knew God, they did not honor Him as God.... They are without excuse."

With chapter 2 the pronoun changes again and now becomes you, as Paul addresses first the critical moralist ("you are without excuse, every man of you who passes judgment," v. 1) and then the self-righteous Jew ("if you bear the name 'Jew,' " v. 17, and "you therefore who teach another, do you not teach yourself?" v. 21).

With chapter 3 Paul reverts to the third person they, as he describes first "all the world" without excuse before God (vv. 1-20) and then "all those who believe" and are justified (vv. 21-31). This descriptive style continues in chapter 4 as he tells the story of Abraham and his descendants.

But suddenly in 4:16 Paul introduces the first person plural by designating Abraham "the father of us all." "The Jews looked upon Abraham as the great dividing point in the history of mankind," comments Anders Nygren. (He is referring to the fact that it was to Abraham that circumcision was given, and from then on humanity was deeply divided between the circumcised and the uncircumcised.) "But according to Paul, Abraham through his faith became the great rallying point for all who believe, whether circumcised or uncircumcised."[26] Thus, circumcision was a divisive, but faith is a unitive, influence. In Christ, as Abraham's true descendants by faith, we are one.

It is, then, this single new believing community whose identity as the people of God Paul is expressing in chapter 5, first by a whole succession of "we" sentences ("we have peace with God," "we exult in hope," etc., vv. 1-11) and then by the great analogy between Adam and Christ as the respective heads of two communities (vv. 12-21), the Adamic community united in sin, condemnation and death, and the Christian community in grace, justification and life. Hence my title for our text, "God's People."

Most commentators seem to be agreed that a new section of Romans begins with 5:1. Paul has been expounding the doctrine of justification by faith (its need, source, basis and means); now he begins to describe its consequences or fruits in the new, justified community. Anders Nygren suggests (followed by C. E. B. Cranfield) that Paul states the theme of the whole letter in 1:17 ("he who through faith is righteous shall live"); that in the letter's first part (1:18—4:25) he "has painted the picture of him 'who through faith is righteous' ''; and that "the task of the next four chapters is to show what it means to say that he who through faith is righteous 'shall live.' '' For the believer has "through Christ . . . been delivered from the age of death and received into the age of *life*. What does it mean to '*live*,' in this pregnant sense?"[27]

To grasp Paul's full answer to this question, we would need to study not the next eleven verses only, but the next twelve chapters. For Paul describes in chapters 5—8 the freedom of those who are in Christ, in chapters 9—11 the unfolding historical purpose of God, and in chapters 12—16 the ethical responsibilities, individual and social, in church and state, of God's redeemed people.

But already in the first half of chapter 5 he utters a series of bold affirmations in the name of all God's people who have been justified by faith. There are six of them. "Therefore, having been justified by faith" (v. 1), (1) "we have peace with God through our Lord Jesus Christ" (v. 1); (2) "we have obtained our introduction by faith into this grace in which we stand" (v. 2); (3) "we . . . exult in hope of the glory of God" (v. 2); (4) "we also exult in our tribulations" (vv. 3-8); (5) "we shall be saved" (v. 9, repeated in v. 10); (6) "we also exult in God through our Lord Jesus Christ" (v. 11).

I think you will agree with me that this is a remarkable series of confident statements. Here is Paul's preliminary picture of the community of justified believers. This is the meaning of the "life" which is enjoyed by those who are "righteous through faith." It includes having peace with God, standing in grace, exulting in hope, exulting in tribulation, being sure of salvation and exulting in God.

We Have Peace with God

The pursuit of peace is a universal obsession, and innumerable remedies have been proposed to those who lack it and seek it. It is of vital importance, therefore, to grasp the biblical teaching that true peace is peace with God. As Luther rightly comments, although we do not yet have peace "with men and the flesh and the world and the devil,"[28] we do have peace with God. For God has turned away from us that wrath which previously rested upon us. He has forgiven and justified us. So "having been justified by faith, we have peace with God."

Another word for this peace is "reconciliation." Justification and reconciliation are not identical, though God never justifies sinners without reconciling them to himself, and never reconciles sinners to himself without justifying them. But justification is the verdict of a judge in a lawcourt; it does not necessarily involve him in any personal relationship with the prisoner he has acquitted. Reconciliation takes place, however, when the father welcomes the prodigal home and reinstates him in the family. There is no peace like peace with God. It is peace *with* God as an objective fact which is the foundation of the peace *of* God as a subjective experience. For our Judge has become our Father, and our Creator our Friend.

Moreover, peace with God is "through our Lord Jesus Christ." For he is "the prince of peace." At his birth the good news of "peace on earth" was proclaimed, and by his death "He made peace" between God and man (Is. 9:6; Lk. 2:14; Eph. 2:15; Col. 1:20). This is the "peace" which the prophets foretold as the supreme blessing of the messianic age, the *shalom* of the kingdom of God. And since Christ's kingdom has already begun, it is possible to say that "we have peace with God" as a present possession.

It is true that there are alternative readings in the Greek, and that the subjunctive *(echōmen)* "let us have" peace is rather better attested than the indicative *(echomen)* "we have" peace. Nevertheless, here is a case when the context must be allowed to override the grammar. Throughout the paragraph Paul is making affirmations, ending in verse 11 with the statement that through Christ "we have now received the reconciliation"; an exhortation in verse 1 would be completely inappropriate.

We rejoice, then, in this first fruit of our justification. "We have peace with God through our Lord Jesus Christ." It is not an exhortation but an affirmation, not a feeling of spiritual euphoria but a fact of reconciliation, not a promise for the future but a possession of the present.

We Are Standing in Grace

Through Jesus we have obtained our introduction by faith into this grace in which we stand (v. 2). Paul moves from peace to grace. At the beginning of the letter, he said, "Grace to you and peace from God our Father and the Lord Jesus Christ" (1:7). Grace and peace always belong together. So now he moves from the peace we "have" to the grace into which "we have obtained our introduction" and in which we continue to "stand." Previously we lived under the wrath of God, but now we stand in his grace.

What can we learn about grace? Grace is God's kindness to the undeserving. Grace is the unsolicited, undeserved, unconditional love of God. Grace is God pursuing us until he has found us and persevering with us after he has. Here, however, in verse 2 the "grace" of which Paul writes is less a quality of God (his graciousness) than a position or state into which he has brought us ("the sphere of God's grace," NEB). The whole Christian life is, in fact, "this grace," into which through our Lord Jesus Christ we have been introduced and in which we stand. Notice these two stages which Paul specifies.

The Greek word *prosagōgē* refers to the "introduction" (NASB) or "access" (AV, RSV, NIV) of somebody into the presence of a superior. It was used in secular contexts of subjects granted an audience of their sovereign and in the Old Testament of worshipers approaching God. Having been justified by faith, it is our privilege to enjoy an audience of the Great King and nearness to the God we worship.

Paul then makes the significant addition that now we "stand in" the grace into which we have been introduced. If we were invited to visit the president in the White House or Queen Elizabeth in Buckingham Palace, we would not move in and take up residence. Even when the Israelites spoke in Old Testament times of drawing near to God, they were referring to set times of worship. But justified believers have a blessing far greater than an occasional audience or a periodic approach. We have been granted access into a state of grace *in which we stand*. We are privileged, as it were, to stay in the palace, to live in the temple.

The perfect tenses of both verbs underline this: "We have obtained access into this grace in which we have come to stand." In other words, the relationship with God into which our justification has brought us is not sporadic but continuous, not precarious but secure. We do not pop in and out of grace as a courtier in olden days might find himself in and out of favor with his sovereign. If we could fall in and out of grace, we would be obliged every time to seek rejustification. But no, having been justified by faith once and for all, we stand firm and sure in the grace into which we have been brought. As Paul writes at the end of chapter 8, nothing can separate us from God's love in Christ Jesus our Lord.

We Exult in Hope of the Glory of God

One of the chief points of divergence between the religions and ideologies of mankind is the different views they take of the future. The old religions of Greece and Rome had little expectation to cheer them; they rather looked back to a golden age in the past. The ancient religions of the East are scarcely interested in historical development. Believing in an endless cycle of reincarnations for the individual, their concept of time is more cyclical than linear. Western existentialists, who say life has no meaning, naturally add that questions about the future are absurd, and they lapse into despair. Evolutionists are imbued with hope, but they project it so many millions of years into the future that it offers little comfort in the present. Ordinary people, deeply apprehensive about the ecological crisis and the nuclear stockpile, are usually very gloomy about the future. Only Marxists have a program for the future and dream their dreams (proud, self-confident dreams) of the utopia which will follow the world revolution.

From this medley of dreams and nightmares it is a relief to turn to the reality which God has revealed. "We exult in hope of the glory of God." The Christian gospel offers hope. Without the familiar trio—"faith, hope and love"—there would be no authentic Christianity. This hope is not uncertain like the human hopes of every day. It is a joyful and confident expectation, which is why we can "exult" in it. Also it is another natural fruit of justification. Justification, as we have seen, is the verdict of the Divine Judge who declares righteous those who take refuge in Jesus. In their case the verdict of the last day has already been declared. In this sense, justification is an "eschatological" event. In the case of those who have been justified, "there is therefore now no condemnation" (8:1), for the sentence of the day of judgment has already been given, and given in their favor. So we rejoice in hope of the glory of God; the God who has justified us is going to glorify us.

But what is "the glory of God"? For too many of us it is a synonym of heaven, meaning, "Oh! that will be glory for me." Which is true, but the New Testament emphasis lies elsewhere, namely, on the glory of God. The glory of God is the manifestation of God, his radiant splendor, the outward shining of his inward being. And already his glory has been partly revealed—in the universe, in human beings and supremely in Jesus Christ. As for the universe, the heavens declare, and the whole earth is full of, his glory. The invisible God is seen in his visible creation—despite its present "groaning"—in its beauty and harmony, in the delicate balance of nature and in the intricate complexities of its design. Yet more of God's glory is seen in human beings, whom he makes in his likeness and who are said to be still his "image and glory," in spite of the fact that "all have sinned and fall short of the glory of God" (3:23). But in Jesus Christ there was a yet brighter manifestation of God's glory. "We beheld His glory," John wrote (Jn. 1:14). In Jesus the glory of God broke through the veil of human flesh—in the perfection of his righteousness and love, in his miracles or "signs" (e.g., Jn. 2:11), at his transfiguration, and above all on the cross which he called his "glorification," and in his resurrection. In these ways already God's glory has been seen.

One day, however, the glory of God will be fully revealed, and "we exult in hope" of this prospect. To comprehend this, we may take the three vehicles of God's glory already mentioned, but in the opposite order. First, Jesus Christ will appear in glory. For we are "looking for the blessed hope and the appearing of the glory or our great God and Savior, Christ Jesus" (Tit. 2:13). We shall see him as he is. At that time we shall also somehow share in his glory. The RSV translation of the second part of verse 2 is "we rejoice in our hope of sharing the glory of God." So his glory will be revealed in us too.

Our destiny, wrote Paul elsewhere, is to be "glorified with Him [Christ]." Everything which now inhibits us from being the human beings God intended will be removed; we shall be conformed to the image of God's Son. Then too the groaning universe which "waits eagerly for the revealing of the sons of God" will itself be set free from its slavery to corruption, futility and pain "into the freedom of the glory of the children of God" (8:17-19, 21). In place of pain there will be joy, in place of bondage freedom, in place of death life, in place of decay glory.

All this is comprehended within our Christian hope. "We exult in hope of the glory of God," of his glory as it will be displayed in Christ, in ourselves and in the universe. Everything will be suffused with his glory. The prospect fills us with what C. K. Barrett calls "a triumphant, rejoicing confidence."[29] Meanwhile, we have to serve. The Christian hope of what God is going to do one day is no excuse for our doing nothing meanwhile. On the contrary, the Christian hope is a spur to both evangelism and responsible social activity. Of course we must spread the gospel while there is still time. But we must care for suffering humanity too, and work for a more just and more compassionate society.

Does the fact that only in heaven "they will hunger no more" hinder us from feeding the hungry today, or the fact that only in heaven disease and death will be destroyed inhibit us from fighting them today? Of course not. Then by the same logic the vision of heaven's perfect society of freedom, justice and love should inspire us to seek at least a nearer approximation to it on earth, and not give us an excuse to fold our arms and do nothing. The vision of the future should be a stimulus to the service of the present. For the vision of what God is going to do is a revelation of what God wants. It shows us therefore what we (for his pleasure) should be seeking today, however partially, in terms of the elimination of disease, hunger, poverty and injustice.

At this moment let us pause a moment and look back at the

great Christian words which Paul has so far used: *justification, faith, peace, grace, hope, joy* and *glory*. Together they indicate four stages of our Christian life, one past, two present and one future. First, we have been justified by faith. Second, we have peace with God. Third, we are standing in grace. Fourth, we exult in hope of God's final glory. Peace and joy, grace and glory. It all sounds idyllic. It would be, if it were not for the next affirmation which Paul now makes.

We Exult in Our Tribulations

These "tribulations" are not what we sometimes call the "trials and tribulations" of everyday existence in the world—frustrations and fears, disappointments, unemployment, aches and pains, sickness and bereavement. No, "tribulation" *(thlipsis)* is an almost technical word for the "pressure" which the world exerts on the church, in opposition to it and in persecution of it. This kind of "tribulation," according to Jesus and his apostles, is inevitable for all believers. "In the world you have tribulation," said Jesus (Jn. 16:33). "Through many tribulations we must enter the kingdom of God," Paul warned the new converts of his first missionary journey (Acts 14:22). "Whoever is unwilling to suffer tribulation," was Luther's comment, "should never think that he is a Christian, but rather . . . an enemy of Christ."[30]

We are not only to *expect* tribulations, however. Nor are we only to *endure* them with the grim fortitude of the Stoic. No, we are actually to *exult* in them. This is not masochism, a sick enjoyment of self-inflicted pain. There is a Christian rationale behind Paul's extraordinary exhortation to rejoice in suffering. The first reason, implied rather than expressed, is that suffering—again according to Jesus and the apostles—is the one and only path to glory. It was so for Christ; it is so for Christians. As Paul is soon to put it in 8:17, "if indeed we suffer with Him in order that we may also be glorified with Him." Here he simply puts side by side his two assertions: "we exult in hope of the glory of God" and "we also exult in our tribulations."

The second reason is articulated clearly. It is because we know that "tribulation brings about perseverance; and perseverance, proven character; and proven character, hope" (vv.

3-4). Of course, as commentators point out, this is not by any means always so. Sometimes, tribulation produces failure, bitterness and rebellion. What Paul means is that, if we remember the inevitability of tribulations and prepare for them, and if when they come we see them as part of our heavenly Father's loving discipline, then they can wonderfully refine and sanctify our character.

Tribulation begins by challenging us to persevere. Next, perseverance will lead to "a mature character" (JBP) or "proven character." The Greek term belongs to a family of words which were used in connection with the "proving" of coins and the "refining" of metals. Peter uses cognate words when he calls the testing of our faith more precious than the testing of gold in the fire (1 Pet. 1:7).

Then there is a third reason for rejoicing in tribulations. It is not just that the end of the line of chain reactions from tribulation to perseverance and perseverance to proven character is a strengthened hope, but that this hope will never let us down by turning out to be an illusion. Why not? What is the ultimate ground of our hope of sharing God's glory? It is the steadfastness of God's love. For certainly, though Luther followed Augustine in understanding "the love of God" in verse 5 as meaning our love for him, Calvin was right to follow Chrysostom in explaining it as God's love for us. The whole context demands this.

How, though, can we be sure of God's love? To be sure of our parents' love is almost indispensable to our healthy emotional development as children. To be sure of the love of spouse or friend is marvelously conducive to human maturity. But even richer blessings are given to those who are sure of the love of God, sure that they are no longer under his wrath, but standing in his grace. Such an assurance brings unspeakable joy, freedom and confidence. So how can we be sure that he loves us? He gives us, because he loves us so much, two strong evidences that he loves us!

The first is explained in verse 5: "Hope does not disappoint; because the love of God has been poured out within our hearts through the Holy Spirit who was given to us." Before this in his

letter, Paul has not mentioned the Holy Spirit in the life of the
Christian. In this first reference he clearly implies, as he states
without equivocation in 8:9, that the Holy Spirit is given to
every believer at the time of his justification. It is not possible
to be justified by faith without also being regenerate by the
Spirit. He "was given to us." And this Spirit, given to us to live
"within our hearts," has poured out God's love there. He has
flooded us with an inward assurance of God's love. It is surely
the same teaching as in 8:16, where it is written that "the Spirit
Himself bears witness with our spirit that we are children of
God." Whenever we have within us a deep awareness of God's
love, whenever we sense our personal filial relationship to God,
whenever our human spirit cries out to God saying, "Abba,
Father," it is the Holy Spirit within us witnessing that we are
God's children and assuring us of God's love.

But God has another and objective way of assuring us of his
love, namely, through the death of his Son Jesus Christ. "For
while we were still helpless, at the right time Christ died for
the ungodly. For one will hardly die for a righteous man; though
perhaps for the good man someone would dare even to die. But
God demonstrates His own love toward us, in that while we
were yet sinners, Christ died for us" (vv. 6-8). We saw in 3:25-26
that God demonstrated his justice in the cross; but now we have
to view the cross also as a demonstration of his love. And "demonstration" may well be too weak a word. The Jerusalem Bible
reads, "What proves that God loves us is that Christ died for
us while we were still sinners." NEB is similar, although it
rather effectively reverses the order of the clauses: "Christ died
for us while we were yet sinners, and that is God's own proof of
his love towards us." We still need to ask just how the cross is a
proof of God's love for us.

The essence of loving is giving. "God so loved the world that
he gave...." "The Son of God loved me and gave himself for
me." Agape-love or the love of God is not like the love of fallen
human beings. Our love is always tainted with self-seeking;
his is the selfless desire to enrich, never the selfish desire to
possess. Further, our love is always aroused by something lovable, admirable or desirable in the person we love, whereas

God's love is uncaused and spontaneous. He loves us not because we are lovable but because he is love. So then, the degree of love can always be measured by the costliness of the gift to the giver and by the worthiness or unworthiness of the beneficiary. The more the gift costs the giver, and the less the beneficiary deserves it, the greater the love is seen to be. Measured by these standards, God's love in Christ is absolutely unique, for in sending his Son to die for us, he was giving everything to those who deserved nothing from him.

The costliness of the gift is clear. Verses 6 and 8 both say that "Christ died," but verse 10 clarifies who Christ is: "we were reconciled to God through the death of His Son." The apostle John emphasizes this even more strongly: "By this the love of God was manifested in us, that God has sent His only begotten Son into the world. ... In this is love, not that we loved God, but that He loved us and sent His Son" (1 Jn. 4:9-10). Previously he had sent many prophets, and the angels had constantly done his bidding. But now he sent his one and only Son.

Moreover, in giving his Son he gave himself. Have you ever asked yourself how the cross could be a demonstration of God's love if Jesus were only a man, as some theologians are urging today, even the greatest man who ever lived? If God had given a man to die for us, one of his own creatures, this would have supplied no solid evidence of his love, but rather of his lack of love, since he would not have been personally involved in the giving. The cross can prove God's love only if God and Jesus were so completely one in being that in giving Jesus God was giving himself. Further, God's gift of his only Son was not a random gesture of generosity, but a thoughtful and purposive act. For he gave his Son to *die.* The significance of this is not just that he died a physical death, nor even that he died a cruel and painful death, but that the death he died was the penalty of our sins and involved him in that awful experience of abandonment which made him cry, "My God, My God, why hast Thou forsaken Me?" (Mk. 15:34). Thus in giving his Son to die for us, God gave himself to taste the horrors of hell because of our sins.

And for whom did he make such a costly sacrifice? For us! For us who are called in verse 8 "sinners" (that is, failures who have had a shot at the target but missed it), in verse 6 "the un-godly" (who have not loved God with all our being, nor kept him in all our thoughts), in verse 10 "enemies" (because our failure and our ungodliness are symptoms not just of an unfor-tunate weakness but of our deep-seated hostility to God, our re-sentment of his authority, cf. 8:7), and again in verse 6 "help-less" (for we cannot reinstate ourselves in God's favor or rescue ourselves from our moral bondage).

"Sinners, ungodly, enemies, helpless": that is Paul's fourfold portrayal of us. Yet it is for people like us that God's Son died. Why "one will hardly die for a righteous man" meaning perhaps somebody whose uprightness is cold and clinical, "though per-haps for the good man [whose goodness is warm and attractive, or who is our benefactor to whom we are personally indebted] someone would dare even to die" (v. 7). "But God [the stark con-trast is emphasized] demonstrates His own love towards us [a love distinct from every other love, a love that is uniquely 'His own'], in that while we were yet sinners [ungodly, hostile and helpless] Christ died for us" (v. 8).

Human beings are often generous in the expressions of their love. A young man will give expensive presents to his fiancé; indeed he sees her as worthy of far more than he can afford to give her. He worships the very ground she treads on. But God does not worship us that he should give to us. It is we who should be worshiping him, who instead have withheld our worship and refused him the homage he deserves. Yet it is for his enemies that he gave his Son to die. I say again: he gave every-thing for those who deserve nothing at his hand. Nothing, that is, except judgment. And instead of exacting it, he himself en-dured it. That is love.

How, then, can we doubt God's love? God has both proved his love towards us in the death of his Son, and poured his love within us, into our hearts, by the indwelling of his Spirit. Ob-jectively in history and subjectively in experience God has given us grounds for believing in his love. How grateful we should be that on the one hand he has not left us to our fluctuating feelings but has given us solid evidence of his love in the cross, and on the other has not just given us an external proof, but has added an internal witness. This combination of the historical ministry of the Son of God and the contemporary ministry of the Spirit of God is one of the most wholesome and satisfying features of the gospel.

This tremendous teaching about God's love for us and about our assurance of it is all given in the context of tribulation. "Who shall separate us from the love of Christ? Shall tribulation ...?" (8:35). Tribulation can be very painful, as we feel—like our Savior—"despised and rejected by men." We may be tempted to doubt God's love. There are other problems too which raise questions in our minds—the vastness of an apparently expanding universe and the minuscule insignificance of human beings within it, the chaos of the world scene, natural disasters, personal calamities and the sufferings of the innocent.

How can we believe that on the throne of time and space, history and universe, there reigns a God of perfect love? Well, we have our answer now. The Son and the Spirit both tell us of the Father's love. The Spirit pours his love into our hearts. And the Son's death on the cross was (and remains) the decisive proof that God loves unworthy sinners like us. We learn, therefore, to view all the tragedies of human experience, in the midst of all our tears, from a vantage ground called Calvary. From that perspective we can confront all evil with defiance, and declare "God is love."

We Shall Be Saved
Look at verses 9 and 10: "Much more then, having now been justified by His blood, we shall be saved from the wrath of God through Him. For if while we were enemies, we were reconciled to God through the death of His Son, much more, having been reconciled, we shall be saved by His life."

Both verses concern our future salvation, for both include the identical words, "we shall be saved." Do these words surprise you? We evangelicals are so accustomed to saying (I hope only with great humility, and with confidence only in Christ), "We have been saved," that it may come as a considerable shock to us to hear Paul saying, "We shall be saved."

"Hey, Paul," we are tempted to expostulate, "where is your

assurance now? How can you say that 'we *will* be saved' when you yourself have told us that we *have been* saved? You have said it in this very passage. In verse 1: 'We have been justified' and 'we have peace with God.' In verse 2: 'We have obtained our introduction . . . into this grace.' In verse 11: 'We have received our reconciliation.' Those are marvellous affirmations, Paul. We agree with them. But now you spoil it all by saying 'we shall be saved.' Haven't you got your theology all mixed up, man?"

I'm sure Paul won't mind our having this little altercation with him. I can see the smile on his face and the twinkle in his eye, as he recognizes that the mixed-up theology is ours rather than his! He is well able to answer us. Indeed, he is glad to remind us (because we so often forget it) that salvation is a big and comprehensive word. It embraces the totality of God's saving work, from beginning to end. In fact, he teaches that salvation has three tenses, past, present and future. I am myself always grateful to the good man who led me to Christ over forty years ago that he taught me, raw and brash young convert that I was, to keep saying: "I have been saved (in the past) from the penalty of sin by a crucified Savior. I am being saved (in the present) from the power of sin by a living Savior. And I shall be saved (in the future) from the very presence of sin by a coming Savior."

So that's it: three tenses, three phases of salvation. If therefore you were to ask me, "Are you saved?" there is only one correct biblical answer which I could give you: "yes and no." Yes, in the sense that by the sheer grace and mercy of God through the death of Jesus Christ my Savior he has forgiven my sins, justified me and reconciled me to himself. But no, in the sense that I still have a fallen nature and live in a fallen world and have a corruptible body, and I am longing for my salvation to be brought to its triumphant completion.

What is the future salvation which Paul has in mind? He uses two expressions, one negative and the other positive. First the negative: "We shall be saved from the wrath of God through Him" (v. 9). Of course we have already been delivered from that wrath of God which rested upon us (1:18), for he himself has turned it away from us on account of the cross where in Christ he bore it, so that now we are standing in his grace (v. 2) and basking in his love (v. 5). Yet in the future, at the end of history, there is going to be a "day of wrath" (2:5), on which his just judgment will be revealed and his wrath poured out on those who have rejected him (2 Thess. 1:7-9; Rev. 6:16-17). From that "wrath to come" Jesus has already rescued us according to 1 Thessalonians 1:10. So we may say with confidence, "we shall be saved" from it.

Positively, he writes, "we shall be saved by His life" (v. 10). For the Jesus who died, rose again and lives, means his people to enjoy the power of his resurrection. For we can share his life now, as he liberates us from the dominion of sin and even (2 Cor. 4:10-11) strengthens our mortal bodies. Then on the last day we shall share the resurrection of Jesus. He will give us new and glorious bodies like the body of his resurrection glory (e.g., Phil. 3:21). And the old universe itself will be refashioned, reborn (Mt. 19:28), almost one might say "resurrected," since it is going to be delivered from its present corruption and share "the freedom of the glory of the children of God" (8:21). Paul is going to write about all this later in his letter, about our personal share in the life and resurrection of Jesus in 6:1-11 and about the transformation of the universe in 8:18-25. But he adumbrates these truths here in his simple statement that "we shall be saved by His life."

So the best is yet to be! In our half-saved condition we are eagerly awaiting our full salvation, when, rid of our fallen, selfish nature, we shall glorify God without distraction, shall be invested with new bodies having wonderful new powers, and we shall inhabit (and I trust explore) the new heaven and the new earth. All that is included in the assertion that "we shall be saved."

But how can we be so sure? It is mainly to answer this question that Paul pens these two verses. Both are *a fortiori* or "much more" arguments. The basic form of both verses is identical, namely, "if one thing has happened, much more then will something else take place." What has happened to us? Well, according to verse 9 we have been "justified by His blood" and, ~~ording to verse 10, "while we were enemies, we were reconciled to God through the death of His Son." That is to say, although we were God's enemies, entrenched in our hostility to him, he gave his Son to die for us, and on account of his sacrificial death we have been both "justified" and "reconciled to God." The Judge has declared us righteous, and the Father has welcomed us home. Now then, if God has accomplished this extremely hard task, if he has given his Son to die for us rebels, and has justified and reconciled us, can we not trust him to do the comparatively simple thing of bringing us safe to heaven? If he has done all that for his enemies, how much more will he look after his friends! That's the ground on which we dare to affirm, "We shall be saved." Our confidence will never "disappoint" or "disillusion" us (v. 5) because we know beyond doubt that God loves us, and his love is the love that refuses to let us go.

We Exult in God

Verse 11 summarizes and concludes the section. It is a final and all-embracing affirmation: "We also exult in God through our Lord Jesus Christ, through whom we have now received the reconciliation."

It is most remarkable that Paul has already used precisely the same expression in 2:17, where he wrote of unbelieving Jews, "You boast in God." It is the same verb, the same noun, the same preposition. Nearly all translators, however, by a true instinct, have rendered the verb differently in English, e.g., by "rejoice" or "exult" rather than "boast." For Christian exultation is something entirely different from the vapid boastings of self-righteous religious people. The latter boast of God as if he were their private property, as if they had him on a leash and could lead him around and exhibit him like a pet dog, and as if their possession of God betokened exceptional merit in them and guaranteed complete immunity to his displeasure. To them God is a thing, a possession, a toy.

But to exult in God is the exact opposite of all that. It begins with the humble acknowledgment of our inexcusable guilt before him. It goes on to wondering astonishment that in spite of this he should have loved us and given his Son to die for us. It continues with gratitude that, when we despaired of ourselves and trusted in Christ, he justified, reconciled and redeemed us. It concludes with the confidence that one day he will save us fully and finally. We exult in this God, not in our righteousness on account of which we once blindly imagined that he accepted us, but in his righteousness, his righteous bestowal of righteousness upon the unrighteous; not in our possession of him, but in his possession of us; not in our merit or works, but in his.

We have seen (3:27) that all boasting is excluded. But that means all boasting except the one and only authentic boasting in God. We exult in the hope of sharing God's glory (v. 2). We exult meanwhile in our tribulations (v. 3) which are the path to and the preparation for glory. But above all, we exult in God himself, not in his gifts but in the Giver.

And we exult in him "through our Lord Jesus Christ," that is to say, as he has revealed himself and taken action through his Son Jesus Christ. For we acknowledge it is "through our Lord Jesus Christ" that we have been justified and given peace with God (v. 1), and that it is "through our Lord Jesus Christ" that we have received our reconciliation (v. 11). What God has shown us he has shown us through Christ. What God has done for us he has done for us through Christ. And what God has given us he has given us through Christ. So when we look back to the past, it is to God's action in giving his Son to die for our sins and in raising him from the dead. When we look up in the present, it is to God's throne where he reigns and Christ reigns with him, "our Lord Jesus Christ," the Lord of the new age and of the new community. And when we look on into the future, it is to the glory of God when he will consummate all things through Christ.

Exulting in God is not a horrid, self-centered triumphalism; it is a humble but joyful, God-centered confidence in the triumph of God through Jesus Christ. This is the essentially distinctive feature of the people of God, who enjoy the new solidarity of life in Christ which has for them replaced the old solidarity of death in Adam. In this very paragraph the people of God are seen to have many characteristics—faith, peace, grace, hope, love and tribulation. But none is more characteristic than joy, a joyful exultation in God.

If, then, by God's utter grace, we belong to the new age, the new community, the new solidarity in Christ, we should be the most positive people in the world. We cannot mooch round the place with a drooping, hang-dog expression. We cannot drag our way through life, moaning and groaning. We cannot always be looking on the dark side of everything, as negative prophets of doom. No, "we exult in God." Then every part of our life becomes suffused with glory. Christian worship becomes a joyful celebration of God and Christian living a joyful service of God. So come, let us exult in God together!

Notes

1. See Anders Nygren, *Commentary on Romans* (Philadelphia: Fortress, 1949), pp. 81-92; F. F. Bruce, *The Epistle of Paul to the Romans* (London: Tyndale, 1963), pp. 79-81; Charles E. B. Cranfield, *A Critical and Exegetical Commentary on the Epistle to the Romans*, I (Edinburgh: T. and T. Clark, 1975), 100-02.
2. *Luther's Works*, LIV Weimar edition.
3. Nygren, p. 97.
4. Cranfield, p. 111.
5. Bruce, pp. 86, 91.
6. Ibid., p. 86.
7. These phrases are echoes of what Emil Brunner wrote in his *Dogmatics*, II (London: Lutterworth Press, 1949-62), 92-93.
8. Cranfield, pp. 196-97.
9. Ibid., p. 197.
10. Martin Luther, *Commentary on the Epistle to the Galatians* (Cambridge: James Clarke, 1953), p. 423.
11. Luther, *Lectures on Romans* (St. Louis: Concordia, 1972), p. 135.
12. Cranfield, p. 199.
13. Luther, *Commentary on the Epistle to the Galatians*, p. 101.
14. Thomas Cranmer, *First Book of Homilies and Canons* (London: SPCK, 1914), pp. 25-26.
15. C. K. Barrett, *A Commentary on the Epistle to the Romans* (London: A. and C. Black, 1957), pp. 72-77.
16. Bruce, p. 104.
17. Ibid., pp. 106-07.
18. Nygren, pp. 156-58.
19. Cranfield, p. 215.
20. F. L. Godet, *Commentary on the Epistle to the Romans* (original, 1879-80) (Grand Rapids, Mich.: Zondervan, 1969), p. 151.
21. Cranfield, p. 217.
22. Nygren, p. 71.
23. Gresham Machen, *What Is Faith?* (Grand Rapids, Mich.: Eerdmans, 1925), p. 172.
24. Cranfield, pp. 245-46.
25. Nygren, pp. 179-80.
26. Ibid., p. 175.
27. Ibid., pp. 187-88.
28. Luther, *Lectures on Romans*, p. 43.
29. Barrett, p. 103.
30. Luther, *Lectures on Romans*, p. 289.

Part III
The Obedience of the Messenger

7
Working
Together
Luis Palau

Four thousand leaders of the church of Jesus Christ made a public confession. They had spent ten days studying world conditions in Lausanne, Switzerland. They then printed their confession and it has been spread around the world under the title, "The Lausanne Covenant." It includes these words:

More than 2,700 million people, which is more than two-thirds of mankind, have yet to be evangelized. We are ashamed that so many have been neglected; it is a standing rebuke to us and to the whole church. . . . Missionaries should flow ever more freely from and to all six continents in a spirit of humble service. The goals should be, by all available means and at the earliest possible time, that every person will have the opportunity to hear, understand, and receive the good news. We cannot hope to attain this goal without sacrifice. All of us are shocked by the poverty of millions and disturbed by the injustices which cause it. Those of us who live in affluent circumstances accept our duty to develop a simple life-style in order to contribute more generously to both relief and evangelism.

"We are ashamed," they say. "All of us are shocked," they confess. Why?

One of history's most unforgettable and notable missionaries was Dr. David Livingstone. He was used in a mighty way to reach thousands for Christ and open up a continent to the good things that the gospel brings. He was moved to become a missionary, to reach the unreached millions, when he heard another missionary to Africa, Robert Moffat, say, "I have sometimes seen, in the morning sun, the smoke of a thousand villages where no missionary has ever been." What a shame it is that a hundred years after that statement, so many people have still not heard the gospel of Jesus Christ. We ought to be shocked!

I ask you, can't we team up with one another to reach the unreached millions? Can't we work together to attain that goal? Yes or no? Can't we promise God that by his grace we shall try to reach those thousand villages and many more where the gospel has never been heard?

We believe this generation could be evangelized thoroughly and biblically, but it will take cooperation, team work, respect and sacrifice.

Recently Dr. Jeffrey J. Wiebe declared, "World War 3 has already begun: It is a battle for the minds of the masses—not the individuals, the masses." I believe he is right. And you and I, as caring Christians, are involved in that battle for the minds of the masses.

Before tackling the biblical call to work together, however, you and I must have certain convictions. First, we must have the conviction that it is God's will and purpose that this generation hear the Word of God clearly.

Second, we must have the conviction that it can be done by the power of the Holy Spirit as a body of believers.

Third, we need the conviction that it must be done in our society and it must be done urgently. Os Guinness stated recently, "Our generation is in a shopping mood for answers." Therefore, it is urgent that we move now.

Fourth, we require the determination that we shall do it by faith. We ought to be able to cry, "It shall be done!" There must also be the determination to *plan* to do it, under God, and the determination to rejoice over any methodology that the creative Holy Spirit of God may lay on anyone's heart to accomplish the job.

Take a look at Romans 12:1-13. You will notice three major emphases: the foundation for working together (vv. 1-2), the functional basis for working together (vv. 3-8) and the fuel to keep us working together (vv. 9-13).

The Foundation for Working Together: The Upward Secret

I appeal to you therefore, brethren, by the mercies of God, to present your bodies as a living sacrifice, holy and acceptable to God, which is your spiritual worship. Do not be conformed to this world but be transformed by the renewal of your mind, that you may prove what is the will of God, what is good and acceptable and perfect. (Rom. 12:1-2 RSV)

Verses 1-2 relate what I call the *upward secret* of working together. This is a personal relationship with God. 1 Corinthians 3:9 calls us God's fellow workers. What an amazing statement that is. Workers with God himself! And this is properly so. For we must first be workers together with God so that next we can be workers with each other. This is the identification of the Christian: with the Father and with his Son, Jesus Christ, and his Holy Spirit. For the rest of your life and mine, if we are to work together to obey Jesus Christ and reach the nations with the good news, we must carry it out, conscious that we are, first and foremost, workers together with God.

A living sacrifice is a glad and lifelong surrender of the body as worship to God (v. 1). The body is a symbol of the total personality. God calls us to "a living sacrifice." What does "a living sacrifice" mean? This is one of the deepest biblical principles revealed in the inerrant Holy Scripture. It is a concept that is not easy to understand in a practical, daily manner. But there are parallel passages. For instance, 2 Corinthians 4:10 says, "always carrying in the body the death of Jesus." And in John 12:24 we read, "unless a grain of wheat falls into the earth and dies, it remains alone; but if it dies, it bears much fruit." And the Lord Jesus said in Matthew 16:24: "If any man would come after me, let him deny himself and take up his cross and follow me." What does that mean? Isn't that also parallel to Romans 12:1?

A living sacrifice, the death of Jesus, the grain of wheat falling into the ground and dying, taking up the cross—all teach the same biblical principle. I like to explain it this way: Every time my will crosses God's revealed will, and I choose his will over against my will, that is the living sacrifice, that is the death of Jesus at work in me, that is the grain of wheat falling to the ground and dying, that is taking up the cross. It is my joyful privilege, as a Christian, to choose God's revealed will in the power of the indwelling Holy Spirit over against my own notions when these contradict God's revealed will.

A missionary who helped me immensely in my youth in South America was Edward F. Murphy. He helped me understand this principle when he taught that the walk of the Christian can be stated in two principles: a crisis and a process. Crisis takes place either at conversion or sometime later, when the Christian realizes that he or she must make a profound and far-reaching decision. Is he going to serve God for the rest of his life or will he lead an egotistical, ego-centered, self-pleasing sort of life? "That is the crisis," Dr. Murphy stated.

"But then comes the process," he went on to say. "The process is this very teaching of Romans 12:1. When you have come to the crisis point and have decided that God shall be first in your life, from then on every day of your life you will be choosing, choosing, choosing."

This daily choosing, which we are free to practice because redemption makes it possible (Rom. 6:12-22), is what the Apostle calls, "your spiritual worship." It can be translated "spiritual" or "rational." It is obviously both. This is what the life of our Lord Jesus so vividly demonstrated during his walk here on earth. Before we speak about working together we must be sure that we are seeking, day by day, to choose God's will over our own. Will you do this? That is a crucial question, and the answer will determine the effectiveness of the rest of your life.

Being a living sacrifice also means reprogramming our minds to God's revealed mind (v. 2). It can hurt deeply to experience this reprogramming, this renewal. It is a pleasure, but surrounded as we are by a world that does not submit to God's law (Rom. 8:6-8) and often by Christians who have not learned this principle, the pain can be deep.

To work together within the body of Christ implies a most provocative and profound identification with Jesus Christ. It implies a measure of suffering that few of us have experienced because of our superficiality. Paul expresses it this way in Colossians 1:24: "Now I rejoice in my sufferings for your sake, and in my flesh I complete what is lacking in Christ's afflictions for the sake of his body, that is, the church, of which I became a minister."

Have you ever thought about the significance of that profound identification? What is lacking in the sufferings of Christ for his church is related to the perfection of a redeemed body—all Christians.

When you determine before God that you will look at the church through the eyes of our Lord Jesus Christ, you will have to enter into depths of suffering *for* the church that other believers may not even be aware of. It can be very comfortable to stay with a group that is 95 per cent like you. It can be very comfortable to not have to debate issues of doctrine that you would rather forget and file away for eternity and for discussion in the presence of the Lord. But if you truly love the body of Christ, all the body of Christ, then you will have to enter into the agony that the Lord Jesus, now glorified, agonizes over while watching his redeemed.

But I assure you, there is a tremendous reward in store for you if you make a decision to work together with the body of Christ, for the sake of the body and for the sake of the world, from now until Jesus calls you to his presence.

Will there be agonies? Yes. In our evangelistic crusades in Latin America and Europe, we run into an enormous amount of cynicism from people we expect support from. We hear sarcasm from the intelligentsia when we expected them to at least thank God that we were giving them a helping hand. And often both cynicism and sarcasm come from people who otherwise claim

that they would love to see the body of believers united worldwide. But the Lord Jesus watches from heaven and is pleased
when we endure and push on for his name's sake.

One principle of a renewed, reprogrammed mindset which is
adapted to God's revealed mind that will affect you is the principle of "duty above pleasure." This kind of principle is not
promoted much today. But Christianity always aims for maturity. Make duty your pleasure and therefore you will put duty
above "pleasure." You and I are responsible to our generation.
If we are to see our generation clearly confronted with the
message, the person and the claims of Christ, certainly duty
must come above pleasure in our lives.

This is why some men and women honor God—others simply
fade away. Some prefer to put God before themselves and bless
others. Look at the lives of Jacob, Esau and Joseph. Esau was
purely pleasure-centered, and he is no example to us today in
Scripture. Jacob was one step higher in that he sought satisfaction by seeking for God's best in the Old Testament days. But
Joseph, his son, went even further and made God the center of
his decisions. Consequently, though he suffered for it, he also
became a national leader to God's glory.

When your life is over and you look back, you will be able
to praise God and have no regrets, if putting duty before pleasure
was one of your basic underlying principles. Never give up, for
you are on the road to maturity and you are following in the
footsteps of those whom God has honored in the past and will
honor in eternity.

Dr. Arthur Glasser tells about the famous missionary, Dr.
Frederick S. Arnot. When Arnot was a teen-ager living on the
outskirts of Glasgow, Scotland, he would go out on weekends
to preach the gospel in the tavern district of his town. One
Saturday, he and his companion stood outside some bars and
began to sing hymns. Some of the alcoholics and drunkards
came out and made fun as they sang. When they stopped their
singing and tried to give a message, the crowd would begin to
hoot and howl and shout insults. They would start singing
again, and the crowd would calm down. Then when they tried to
preach again, the shouting drowned them out. After three or

four tries, Arnot and his companion got discouraged. With tears in their eyes they turned to walk away. Suddenly Arnot felt a hand on his shoulder, and as he turned to look, a tall man gazed down at him and said in his Scottish accent, "Keep at it, laddie, God loves to hear men speak well of his Son." With that encouragement, Fred and his companion went back to the corner, courageously spoke out for Christ and their courage calmed down the drunks who listened to the message. From then on, Arnot "kept at it" for decades, and he became one of the most outstanding missionaries of Jesus Christ to Africa in the past century. When you have made a living sacrifice you are in tune with the father.

Our Lord's prayer in John 17:20-23 was about working together. There we read: "I . . . pray . . . also for those who believe in me through their word, that they may all be one; even as thou, Father, art in me, and I in thee, that they also may be in us, so that the world may believe that thou hast sent me." Our Lord's last prayer was that you and I and all the body of Christ would work together to glorify his name so that the world might believe.

Yet this desire of our Lord has at least two vital implications. First, we are already united. Biblical, godly, Christ-exalting oneness already exists in the body of Christ. We *are* one body. This is not ecumenism. Ecumenism speaks of false union, and this is not at all what we are talking about. There is no compromising of basic truth in the union that our Lord Jesus prayed about. No playing "footsie" under the table with those who are traitors to the message of the cross, the blood of Christ and the resurrection of our Lord. That would be intolerable.

This leads me to mention the second implication of our Lord's prayer, and that is that we work together on the basis of the truth divinely revealed in the inerrant, written Scriptures. The reason that working together can only happen on the basis of truth is that any other unity is sheer illusion. C. S. Lewis states, "The great difficulty is to get modern audiences to realize that you are preaching Christianity solely and simply because you happen to think it is true; they always suppose you are preaching it because you like it or think it is good for society, or something of that sort. . . . "

We must now focus on the fundamentals of this divinely revealed truth, on those basics which make Christianity Christian.
In other words, we must focus on the positive, fundamental
teachings of Scripture and in the process decide who we can
work with in the preaching of Jesus Christ and his call to eternal
life by repentance and faith. Don't compromise Christ's teachings by entertaining traitors to the cross.

This, then, is what I call the big decision: Have you truly
presented your body a living sacrifice to the Lord on behalf of
the church? Are you open to work with those who have a similar faith? Are you willing to work together on this basis for the
sake of a lost world? Will you present your body, even now, as a
living sacrifice to the Lord? If this decision has not been made in
your life, will you do it now? And then are you willing, having
made the big decision, to continue the process of submitting to
God's revealed will? If you have taken this big step, then we can
talk about working together.

Working Together in Intelligent Cooperation:
The Outward Secret

> For by the grace given to me I bid every one among you not to
> think of himself more highly than he ought to think, but to
> think with sober judgment, each according to the measure of
> faith which God has assigned to him. For as in one body we
> have many members, and all the members do not have the
> same function, so we, though many, are one body in Christ,
> and individually members one of another. Having gifts that
> differ according to the grace given to us, let us use them: if
> prophecy, in proportion to our faith; if service, in our serving;
> he who teaches, in his teaching; he who exhorts, in his ex-
> hortation; he who contributes, in liberality; he who gives aid,
> with zeal; he who does acts of mercy, with cheerfulness.
> (Rom. 12:3-8 RSV)

As I said at the beginning, intelligent cooperation is the functional basis for working together. This is what I call the outward
secret. This is our relationship to the church of Jesus Christ, the
local churches, wherever they may be.

Cooperation, not competition, is the teaching of Romans

12:3. There is power in working together. At Lausanne, Henri Blocher called it "diversity without conflict." It is only when we think of ourselves more highly than we ought to think that we create turmoil in the body of Christ. But when we "think with sober judgment" about ourselves, then we can operate by faith and God is glorified. Our heavenly Father looks at you, me and every member of the body, no matter how weak or ignorant we may be in both the Word of God or in secular knowledge, and he loves us alike. God has no favorites. Jesus Christ loves his body, the church. In Acts 20:28 Paul states, "Take heed to yourselves and to all the flock, in which the Holy Spirit has made you overseers, to care for the church of God which he obtained with the blood of his own Son." Every person who is redeemed at that high price is bound to be loved with an eternal love by the living God.

Furthermore, the body of Christ is a marvelous entity. He bought it with his blood and he loved it, and we desperately need each other in the body.

We are members of one another (vv. 4-5). We do not create unity. It already exists. We are called on to maintain that oneness of the body of Christ (Eph. 4:3).

Start experiencing the excitement of the oneness of Christ now. Learn what it means to "work together" with God and with the church. The lessons you will learn will serve you, whether you become a missionary abroad or a servant of Jesus Christ in whatever profession he places you in your home country.

What is the most functional way to experience oneness and working together? How shall we do it? It begins first at your local church. When I was seventeen years of age, in Argentina, I learned this lesson. I thank God that I was brought up in circles that respected the local congregation of believers. There are tremendous weaknesses in every group of people, and the church is no exception. Yet it is God's revealed will that Christians should gather close to home with a group of other Christians to worship him, celebrating the Lord's supper, to build each other up in the faith, to help one another at every possible level and to move out as a unit to reach the world and draw people into the assembly of God.

How can you as a student start working with a local church? It seems hard in the United States, Canada and Western Europe, for young people to have an open door of ministry. But let me suggest some possibilities.

Start with children. There are children everywhere, and children are open to the gentle touch of the Holy Spirit of God coming through the message of the cross, the resurrection and the present power of Christ. The first people that I ever led to Jesus Christ, as I remember it, were six of the ten boys that I taught in a summer Bible club in Child Evangelism Fellowship in Argentina. Once you have led someone to Christ it will get into your blood, and it will never go away. You will love to win people to Christ. The truth of Matthew 4:19, "Follow me, and I will make you fishers of men," will become a marvelous reality for you.

As a student you can also witness to your fellow students or fellow workers at your own age level—the university, the junior college, the high school. These are probably the most difficult places to stand up for Christ. That is why we need the body of believers. When you feel defeated after a time of ministry, the local church can lift you up. You gather with the believers to celebrate the Lord's supper, and there is a renewing and a restoration that takes place.

And as a young person you can work with older people. When I was about nineteen, a missionary put me in touch with a home for the aged in Argentina. There were twelve to fifteen older women in that home. Practically nobody cared for them. I began to visit on Saturdays and continued to do so for years until I left the country. Some of the women came to know the Lord Jesus. Others died. During that time I was working in a British bank. But my greatest joy was when Saturday came around and I became the unofficial minister at that home. Sometimes I helped out by bringing clothing or food. When they died I was there for their burial. And all this time, nobody knew about this nor was it an "official position." Working with those older people was one of the happiest times of my life. You too can find older people to minister to or other situations in which you can work with other believers. One of the goals in working in the local church is to "strengthen those who are weak in the faith" (see Rom. 14:1-12).

You should begin now to work with other believers in a team. In your local church you are bound to find someone that you can team up with and probably several people that you can join. You can serve best in team situations, whether with children, your own peer group at the university, older people or anyone else. I wouldn't think of seeking to serve Jesus Christ all alone, unless I was forced to do so under unusual circumstances. When you work on a team, despite your many weaknesses, you learn to respect the strengths of other people. You learn to fill in where they are weak or when they do not come through as they should. You learn to not despise another person's methods. I challenge you never to despise the methods that any other believer uses to spread the good news. The only exception would be if a methodology were unethical. In that case you deal with the person privately, rather than publicly shunning his methods or heaping on cynicism, sarcasm or criticism.

If you begin in your youth to team up with others to serve Christ, you will have a marvelous, enormous service for Christ.

We noted in Romans 12:4-5 that we are "members" of one another. There is tremendous authority in working in a team situation. In my own crusade ministry when I face a press conference, it gives me tremendous joy to be able to speak well not only of our ministry, mostly centered in big cities, but also to speak well about Wycliffe Bible Translators that work in the jungles or about World Vision, which helps the destitute and victims of earthquakes and political persecution around the world.

There is also great learning in team work. In our crusades we do in-depth family counseling for people who have marriage problems, including guilt, sexual temptations, difficulties disciplining children and so on. One of our team members, Jim Williams, trains local ministers and some of the more educated, mature Christians in the churches to help him in this family counseling during a crusade. This counseling usually results from our television programs in which I answer people's questions on the phone on camera.

In one particular crusade in Paraguay, a simple, humble brother who was illiterate came to take the in-depth family counseling course. Not wanting to hurt his feelings, Jim didn't ask him to leave the class. If there is one advantage that an illiterate person has over most educated people, it is that they have an enormously well-developed memory. They cannot rely on written material or notes, which you and I often do. So he memorized much of the course and had pinned down in his mind the basic answers and biblical responses to problems.

One day when the family counseling center was opened and all the trained counselors were busy dealing with people's problems, a medical doctor came for counsel. He was dressed in quality clothes and the only person available to counsel him was this shoeless, illiterate man! The counselor jumped up from where he had been sitting, patiently waiting, and took the doctor into a private room to speak with him.

The young secretary in charge panicked. She ran to tell Mr. Williams what had happened. They nervously waited for the interview, which lasted one hour, to be over. When they came out, the doctor was thrilled, gave the illiterate brother a big hug and said good-bye. As he was leaving the door, Jim Williams caught up with him and said, "Doctor, if there is anything I can do, please let me know how I can help."

The doctor responded, "No thank you very much, that brother over there helped me a lot—thank you."

Jim said to the young secretary, "If this situation arises again, in which an obviously well-dressed and educated person comes in, make sure the illiterate brother doesn't counsel him. Come and get me, even if you have to draw me away from a counseling session."

The very next day the medical doctor returned with two more men, dressed in an expensive fashion. The secretary ran to call Mr. Williams. Jim came out and said, "Doctor, if there is anything I can do, I would be glad to counsel with you."

The doctor said, "No, thank you. I would like to meet with the brother who helped me yesterday. These two fellow doctors have some of the same problems I had. Mr. _____ helped me so much I want him to help my friends." That was that.

After about an hour, those two medical doctors were converted to Christ. The next day the doctor showed up again, with another medical friend of his. Again, he was led to Christ by the illiterate brother.

When the crusade was over, the four doctors and their wives threw a party in celebration of the transformation they had experienced and the sense of forgiveness of sins that the Lord had given them. Guess who they invited to the party? Not me, certainly. Not even Jim Williams. The illiterate brother was the guest of honor!

When you work within the body of Christ, there is a lot of learning to do. It can never be done in a classroom situation or by being a bookworm. The learning takes place while you work.

Our experience in Latin America, for instance in the Rosario plan crusade in Argentina, demonstrates the impact that the gospel can have in a city, and often in a nation, when Christians work together. In that effort, Pastor Bruno Radi was so lonesome and discouraged in his ministry that he had written to his district superintendent saying he was going to leave the church, and perhaps the ministry, with his wife Perla. But when our team members arrived in the city and had a conference for ministers on seeking God's mind in prayer and in the Word of God and on church growth, his life was revolutionized.

This pastor, who thought he was about to leave the ministry, saw six new Christian congregations begun in a period of eighteen months. Three years later, Pastor Bruno and his wife traveled across the continent and even into the U.S.A. to encourage other ministers and churches to work together to see churches grow, lives changed, and cities touched with the gospel of Jesus Christ.

There is power in working together. Our warfare today is against the spiritual forces of darkness. The Word of God clearly teaches that "we are not contending against flesh and blood, but against the principalities, against the powers, against the world rulers of this present darkness, against the spiritual hosts of wickedness in the heavenly places. Therefore take the whole armor of God, that you may be able to withstand in the evil day" (Eph. 6:12-13). If the enemy of our souls, Satan, is to be put to shame, the body of Christ must work arm in arm to see it happen.

"Two are better than one," the Old Testament states (Eccles. 4:9). Matthew 18:19-20 affirms that, "If two of you agree on earth about anything they ask, it will be done for them by my Father in heaven. For where two or three are gathered in my name, there am I in the midst of them." This is not an idle statement by the Lord Jesus. It is a profound spiritual truth. There is power against the enemy in unity, there is power in prayer when two or more gather together to ask anything of the Father. What a pity that we let this truth go by and we miss out on the blessing. Take advantage of it while you are young, and it will become part of your life for the rest of your years on earth.

Being "members" of one another also means that you are to marry only a true Christian. I want to bring this out in my message for it is vital. 2 Corinthians 6:14-18 strictly prohibits a Christian from marrying someone that is not a true Christian.

"I shall never marry a non-Christian," you must say to yourself before the Lord. Nothing has wrecked more dedicated college and university young people in their youthful goals of glorifying God than disobeying this point.

If you despise this commandment from his revealed will, you will find futility, despair and barrenness is your spiritual life. God will help you find the right partner for your life if it is his will that you get married. In the body of Christ, there is room for single people who live exclusively for the Lord Jesus (see 1 Cor. 7). There is no defense for marrying a non-Christian. Therefore, settle it once and for all, put it out of your mind and never resurrect such a thought again.

God will bless your life for your obedience. He will fulfill Proverbs 3:5-12 forever in your experience. You will know what it is to work together, first in marriage with your partner, then with your children, if God gives you offspring, and then with the rest of the body. I tell you, there is a joy and an excitement to this kind of life.

Marriage is a basic step in learning to work together for the glory of God—two people working with one common goal, the advancement of the kingdom. For some the dreams end as one partner yearns to live a life wholly to the glory of God and the other pulls in different directions. My wife, Pat, and I married with clear commitments to the Lord first, to each other and together to serve him. The verse inscribed in our wedding bands says, "For you shall go out in joy, and be led forth in peace" (Is. 55:12).

There should be a complementary relationship in your marriage and life, not one-upmanship and stealing the show. Marriage is an act of obedience that pleases the heart of God.

In Christ we complete, not compete (vv. 6-8). In the power of the resurrected Christ we can conquer nations for God. Foreigners and nationals can work together arm in arm, not competing for results but complementing each other's work. Theologians and evangelists, local pastors and traveling preachers can work together for the common good and the glory of our living God.

On our team we have sought to bring in various nationalities to demonstrate vividly that Christians can work together. We have six nationalities represented and many cultural backgrounds. We have varying degrees of education and life experiences. There is a tremendous excitement in such a way of life. There is a liberation from manmade shackles. And there is fruit to the glory of God.

Jesus Christ is the great mass strategist. Romans 12:6 says, "having gifts that differ according to the grace given to us." Who gave those gifts? Our Lord Jesus Christ when he ascended into heaven (see Eph. 4). The gifts will syncronize beautifully so that we can work together. Our simple duty is obedience—to do what the Lord has enabled us to do and to function where he has placed us.

It is no use dreaming of other places and other gifts and personality traits that we see in someone else. First of all, that is destructive. Second, it is offensive to our Lord, who created you and placed you where you are *now.* Therefore, work together for Christ. Begin to discover what your gifts from Christ may be *now.* Let him be the great syncronizer of the church worldwide.

Do you remember what the Lord said in Matthew 9:38? "Pray therefore the Lord of the harvest to send out laborers into his harvest." The Lord is looking for *laborers*. The job of a laborer is to do what he is told and to do it to the best of his ability. That is the call of Jesus Christ to you today. Certainly you want to sharpen your gifts, expand your mind, mature your personality, grow. But the main responsibility is obedience, service and labor.

If the church of Jesus Christ had been working, laboring and obeying, it would have continuously evangelized generation after generation. Consider these points:

1. Working together with Jesus Christ as the master strategist, you and I are more productive servants.

2. Working together brings balance into your life—it purifies sectarianism and cultism out of your heart and gives you Scriptural understanding instead.

3. Working together develops responsibility because you use the gifts of the Holy Spirit in your life and you begin to understand and care for the weaker brother.

4. Working together under the master strategist broadens your perspective. You begin to understand the traditions of other Christians, and you get historical equilibrium that keeps you from extremism.

5. Working together puts you in your place. There is a healthy ego-deflation that takes place, not in the sense of discouraging you, but of looking at yourself properly. As Romans 12:3 says, "I bid every one among you not to think of himself more highly than he ought to think, but to think with sober judgment."

6. Working together brings in the harvest. John 4:34-38 is one of the most thrilling passages in relation to our subject today: "one sows and another reaps."

7. Working together builds the house of God in accordance with 1 Corinthians 3:9-11. The reasoning is quite simple and obvious. If you do not work together with another brother or sister or with a team in the fellowship of a local church, how can you receive the building up, the exhortation, the learning by example from the others? In turn, how can they learn from your life example and what the Lord may have taught you about himself?

By working together, we build each other up mutually in the

Lord. We also reach out with far more power and enthusiasm to the world and put to flight the forces of darkness.

There is one last major matter to consider. You could rightly ask me, "Luis, with all our varieties of convictions, sometimes on secondary matters and sometimes closer to the core, with our varied cultural, educational, and social differences, with the ups and downs of life, how can we throughout a lifetime 'work together' with the body of Christ?"

Romans 12 gives us the "fuel" to keep us working together.

An Attitude of Respect: The Inward Secret

Let love be genuine; hate what is evil, hold fast to what is good; love one another with brotherly affection; outdo one another in showing honor. Never flag in zeal, be aglow with the Spirit, serve the Lord. Rejoice in your hope, be patient in tribulation, be constant in prayer. Contribute to the needs of the saints, practice hospitality. (Rom. 12:9-13)

The *inward secret* of working together is the attitude of respect within my inner spirit toward the body of Jesus Christ. Romans 12:9-13 is very clear on this point.

Obviously, working together cannot be based on 100 per cent agreement on every subject, whether it is biblical or functional. I have been married to my wife, Pat, for over eighteen years now. And yet we do not see eye to eye on everything. Do you expect to see eye to eye with me, as well as with everybody else in the body of Christ? Obviously not. Therefore, it is the respect that is born out of love that constitutes the very core of the fuel that keeps us working together. This demands godly attitudes of the inner heart. Start along this path while you are young. 1 Corinthians 3:1-8 will give you guidance as to how to be nonsectarian and yet firmly planted on basic biblical doctrines. This is a delicate balance, indeed, but one that can be achieved and one that the Lord looks for in you and me.

What are some of the characteristics of an active attitude of respect toward others in the body?

An attitude of respect requires a love that is genuine (v. 9). You have heard the old joke, "Oh, I love the world—it is just people I can't stand!" Aren't we all a little bit that way? I sometimes like to sit in a coffee shop in a big crowded city with a cup of coffee and a magazine for cover. Then I just look at people and, if possible, listen to some of them talk. You look at someone's face and try to imagine what is going on in his or her head.

The Holy Spirit can develop in you a loving, tender care for people. As you get involved in the local church you get to know the hurts of other believers and their troubles, problems, failures and sins. You pray about them and your heart begins to melt. There is a key! Pray over people's weaknesses and problems and sins, rather than cutting them down. It will break your heart and give you this kind of sincere love. Paul, at the end of Romans 16, mentions a whole series of individuals by name. He had them on his heart. He loved them and must have prayed for them.

A friend of mine who went to the mission field out of love for people, began to lose the love after about four years. His love for himself outgrew his love for others. "I want a little cottage by the lake and close to a river, where I can fish for trout," he said. "I want to be close to where I can go hunting in the fall. I feel the need to dress better and to dress my wife better," he repeated. Finally he left the field and went back home. But he was miserable.

Not too long ago, he wrote me a very moving letter, which included this paragraph: "To settle down in a comfortable home is a fine thing, and we love our little chalet by the river, but at night I see a world out there and the years go by and I am not a part of any team with a ministry to reach that world with the gospel message." Now he is trying to get back into the Lord's work, having lost the best decade of his life, between his thirties and forties. I believe the Lord will use him again. But how much he missed out on because his love for himself grew greater than his love for the lost and for the church—the body of Christ.

An active attitude of respect requires simple holiness. If you live a truly holy life and have a pure walk with God, you will work with the body, and you will have a humble attitude toward it. Do you cultivate a sensitivity to the indwelling Spirit of God? That is the fuel that keeps you working with others through a lifetime. Do you have a daily devotional life? Do you participate

in the Lord's supper, as he commanded, as often as you can?
Romans 12:9 says, "Hate what is evil, hold fast to what is good."
It was on this theme that Charles Wesley wrote this hymn:

I want a principle within of watchful, godly fear,
A sensibility of sin, a pain to feel it near.
Help me the first approach to feel of pride or wrong desire;
To catch the wandering of my will, and quench the kindling
fire.

From Thee that I no more may stray, no more Thy goodness
grieve,
Grant me the filial awe, I pray, the tender conscience give.
Quick as the apple of an eye, O God, my conscience make!
Awake my soul when sin is nigh, and keep it still awake.

Almighty God of truth and love, to me Thy power impart;
The burden from my soul remove, the hardness from my
heart.
O may the least omission pain my reawakened soul,
And drive me to that grace again, which makes the wounded
whole.

That is holy simplicity and simple holiness, too.

The young nineteenth-century Scottish preacher, Robert
Murray McCheyne, who died at twenty-nine, wrote a letter to a
friend and said, "According to your holiness, so shall be your
success. Mr. Edwards, a holy man, is an awesome weapon in the
hand of God."

Holiness means holy attitudes toward other believers, toward
God and even toward yourself. Hebrews 12:14 states, "Strive for
peace with all men, and for the holiness without which no one
will see the Lord." Do you do that? Colossians 3:15 affirms,
"And let the peace of Christ rule in your hearts, to which indeed
you were called in the one body. And be thankful." Does that
describe you?

An active attitude of respect is a respect that shows (v. 10).
"Love one another with brotherly affection; outdo one another

in showing honor." Again, you see working together requires a certain attitude of your innermost spirit.

We may not always be functioning together, and yet we must stand with each other, pray for each other, praise God for each other, speak well of each other and respect one another.

Whenever possible, however, we are to actually and functionally work and serve together. You cannot keep a distance from your brothers and sisters on purpose. On the other hand, you cannot always be teaming up with every believer in everything that is going on.

When the opportunity to work together arises, the fuel that will keep you working together is a show of respect. First, it is a respect for your brother or sister in the body of Christ.

Second, it is a respect for his or her convictions, even though you may have just as strong opposite convictions in matters not revealed.

Third, it is a respect for the work and for the devotion of the other person to the Lord Jesus. Romans 14 and 15 clearly teach that we may have some sharp disagreements, but we are to build each other up, even then.

Respect shows itself also in an inoffensive, nonthreatening attitude. All forms of intimidation, intellectual threats or, even worse, psychological ostracism of a brother or sister have no place in a person's life who respects the Scripture. "Love one another with brotherly affection," the Scripture says.

Respect that shows must always be watchful of cynicism. The easiest thing for the flesh to do is to make cynical, disparaging remarks of somebody else's ministry. Scripture says that if you want the fuel that keeps you working together, if you want an active attitude of respect, cynicism must go out the window forever. Interestingly enough, cynicism seems to be the domain of the intellectual world. It seems to be so "in" to question things with a smirk. Yet doesn't that grieve the Holy Spirit? Wasn't that the approach that Satan took to make Adam and Eve fall in such a disastrous manner? It certainly was. Let us not walk in our enemy's steps.

The euphoria of working together will strike home in your inner heart when you practice this respect that shows.

An *active attitude of respect is the result of zeal, of dedica-tion.* "Never flag in zeal" (v. 11). I was amazed not long ago by a church in California—the Los Gatos Christian Church. The con-gregation had grown to nearly four thousand. They had a burden to start another church. The pastor, Reverend Marvin Rickard, had been looking forward to it for years. Finally his chance came when the Lord sent a younger preacher by the name of Rich Marshall. They announced to the congregation that anyone who wanted to leave the mother church and go to start a new congregation a few miles away was encouraged to do so. They decided to have a combined budget for a year, to combine their missions outreach for a year and to meet and support one an-other during the whole first year till the daughter church could stand on its own feet.

Great things have happened! Now the mother church in Los Gatos still has four thousand people attending. The daughter church in only five months has grown to almost seven hundred.

That is zeal—to work together for the glory of Jesus Christ. Wouldn't it be great if every new church that is born to preach the gospel were born under those conditions? There is no reason why it shouldn't happen.

An *active attitude of respect, that inward secret that keeps us working together, flows when you are "aglow with the Spirit"* (v. 11). The sooner you start on the road to a life that is on fire with the Holy Spirit, the earlier will come your success and fruitfulness to the glory of God. Start now.

The *fuel that keeps us working together, according to verse 11, is a servant attitude.* "Serve the Lord," it says. Interestingly enough, it is when we serve the Lord that we are most able to work together with the body on behalf of a world that is lost. We are to be servants of the body of Christ as to the Lord. Every-body loves a servant. People will find it easy to work beside you if you have that attitude. The Lord Jesus said of himself, "Even as the Son of man came not to be served but to serve, and to give his life as a ransom for many" (Mt. 20:28). You are honoring a noble heritage when you have a servant's heart.

The *fuel that keeps us working together is your ability to rejoice in the promises of God in the midst of patience and tribu-*

lation. The joy of Christians does not depend so much on cir-cumstances or the love that may or may not come toward them, but on the promises of God. Romans says, "Rejoice in your hope" (v. 12). Christian hope is not, "I hope so, but I'm not sure." Nor is it dreamy, wishful thinking. It is an absolute assur-ance based on the inerrant, written promises of God.

The fuel that keeps us working together is constant prayer for others (v. 12). Prayer for those I work with and prayer for those I cannot physically, practically work with; prayer for their weaknesses, and prayer for what I consider to be their errors or mistaken notions.

The fuel that keeps us working together is that of washing one another's feet (v. 13). Scripture says, "Contribute to the needs of the saints, practice hospitality." In John 13 the Lord Jesus actu-ally said, "You also ought to wash one another's feet" (v. 14). What does that experience teach? First, I have to be on my knees to wash your feet. Second, I have to bow before you to wash your feet. Third, I am taking the attitude of a slave when I wash your feet. And fourth, I am like Jesus when I wash your feet.

Does this sound like too much humbling of yourself and too high a price to pay to work together in the body of Christ to reach a lost world? Remember one thing: if you wish to be a leader among the people of God for the glory of his name, you must be a servant (see Lk. 9—10).

Will your life count for eternity? Fifty years from now as you look back on your life, what will be the sentence you will pass on yourself as a Christian? Will you be able to look back and say to yourself, in the presence of God, "Lord, I obeyed you. I failed many times, but I was dedicated to your body. I sought to work together with other believers in obedience to your commands to reach a lost world in my generation." Will you be able to look into the face of the Lord Jesus at the judgment seat of Christ and say, "Yes, Lord Jesus, I did work with my local church and with your body at large."

If you can say that, fifty years from tonight, your life will not have been lived in vain. It will have glorified God and his reward will be amazing for all eternity.

8
The Messenger's Qualifications

Isabelo Magalit

I was here three years ago at Urbana 76. It was a most moving moment, when the call to commitment was made, to see half of the 17,000 people in this auditorium stand up, signifying their commitment to actively seek God's will concerning world evangelization.

"But the famous Urbana Convention is a joke!" said a veteran Western missionary to me shortly after I returned to Manila. "We have deceived these young people," he continued. "Where will these thousands of missionaries go? Where *can* they go? Who will accept them? When will Western, particularly North American, mission agencies wake up to the fact that their missionaries are simply not welcome in many parts of the world?"

Is my missionary friend, who is an American, right? Is the day of the Western missionary coming to an end? Is it time to say goodbye to the great Urbana missionary conventions? Should the burden of making the gospel known to the ends of the earth now be shifted to the younger churches of the Third World?

No, definitely no. World evangelism is the responsibility of the whole church, no less of the older churches of Europe and America than of the younger churches of Asia, Africa and Latin America. And no more the responsibility of the one group than of the other. In fact, the dimensions of world evangelism are so awesome that only the whole church throughout the world, working in proper partnership, can get the task done. How to work together, as full partners, that is the question. It is a question that deserves plenty of attention, not the least in a missions convention such as Urbana. But no, the day of missions from the West is not over.

The time has certainly come for Western-based missions to give more careful consideration to the kind of missionaries they send. Of course missionaries from elsewhere need the same qualifications. Korean missionaries working in Bangkok need the same qualifications as American missionaries in Manila. But the precise outworking of the qualifications will differ somewhat. Today, I come to you as a Filipino—a brother in Christ—speaking to North Americans who are eager to proclaim the Lord Jesus to all nations.

You must face up to the significance of your distinction—especially you who are Americans—that you come from the world's mightiest nation, which has implications for the missionary enterprise launched from your shores. The drama in Teheran does not detract from the greatness of your power. It illustrates it. The seizure of the U.S. embassy by Iranian students is an act of desperation—the wild swing of a little boy against what he regards as a bully. Yes, your political power has implications.

Your presence and your influence, your interests and your policies, your opinions and your goods—for example, Coke and Superman—are so ubiquitous around the globe that your missionaries cannot help being visible, easily identified as American.

You can affirm that identity unequivocally, without apology, sincerely believing that it stands for what is best in the world. Like one of your television preachers, you may even be convinced that "God loves America above all nations." Yes, you can proudly affirm your American identity.

Or, you can repudiate it in a valiant effort to make sharp the difference between American culture and the eternal gospel. We have all been sensitized to this issue of gospel and culture, particularly as it has been debated since the Lausanne Congress in 1974.

We do not ask you to choose between these two alternatives. The first one—pride in all that's American—happens frequently enough to be worrying, but I trust it is not the majority sentiment in this convention. The second, which is a denial of American culture, is not healthy for your dignity as persons and is probably impossible anyway.

There is a third way. What we are asking of you is to affirm what is positive in your being American and to be sensitive to what is negative. We trust that we are speaking the truth to you in love. Please listen to us because we are your brothers in Christ who greatly desire to be your partners in the worldwide mission of the church. Your mission is our mission, too.

What qualifications do messengers need if all nations are to obey and believe Jesus Christ? I suggest three essentials: First is zeal for God's glory. Second is love for needy people. And third is concern for the unity of the body.

Zeal for God's Glory

The first qualification for messengers is zeal for God's glory.

In Acts chapter 17, Dr. Luke tells us about the apostle Paul in Athens. Paul was waiting for Timothy to join him from Berea. While waiting in Athens, he looked around the city and was provoked as he saw that the place was full of idols. Provoked by idolatry! Dr. Luke uses a strong medical word: Paul had a paroxysm—his heart raced wildly within his breast as he saw the city's idols. He was full of righteous indignation from intense jealousy for the honor of the Lord Jesus. Promptly, he preached to the Athenians about Jesus and the resurrection.

Are you and I really convinced that God the Father has given to his Son Jesus the name Lord, the name which is higher than any other name, not only in this age but even in that which is to come (Eph. 1:21; Phil. 2:9-11)? Are we convinced that right now, the same Lord Jesus is seated at the Father's right hand—the place of highest honor and supreme authority? Do we believe that the Lord Jesus whom we serve is indeed the King of the whole universe? If so, like Paul we should be cut to the heart—suffer a paroxysm—whenever we contemplate the vast numbers of people who do not bow the knee to the Lord Jesus today. Think about it: some three billion people out of the world's four billion do not acknowledge Jesus as their Lord. Many of them do so because they have never properly heard of who Jesus is, and of what he has done for them.

Such a vast multitude would rather worship their ancestors or a piece of wood or stone or some godless ideology or even the material goods of this world, rather than the Lord Jesus! This must drive us to greater zeal in sharing the good news.

"Woe is me if I do not preach the gospel" (1 Cor. 9:16)! For I deprive the Lord Jesus of the honor due his name. He alone is worthy of all "blessing and glory and wisdom and thanksgiving and honor and power and might" (Rev. 7:12). Evangelism is persuading men and women to recognize Jesus for who he is in order that they may bow before him and acknowledge him as Lord and Savior. Messengers of the evangel need more zeal for God's glory if all nations are to believe and obey the Lord Jesus.

But how often our zeal comes from mixed motives. Horatius Bonar (1808-1889), Scottish preacher and hymn writer, had a dream. He dreamt that the angels took his zeal and weighed it and told him it was excellent. It weighed up to 100 pounds, all that could be asked. He—in his dream—was very pleased at the result. But then the angels wished to analyze his zeal. They put it in a test tube and analyzed it in various ways, with this result:

14 parts were from selfishness
15 parts were due to sectarianism
22 parts from ambition
23 parts because of love for humanity, and
26 parts from love to God

Bonar woke up humbled at the thought, and dedicated himself anew.

Are we zealous for Christian service? We must be, for we are here. It must be missionary zeal that led us to this convention in the first place. But if our zeal were analyzed by the angels, what would be the results?

How much of our zeal comes simply from the American value system: the pioneering spirit that stakes out unclaimed territory, the rugged individualism that insists on doing one's own thing, the fierce competitiveness that delights in besting the competition? How much of our zeal would come from the party spirit? I am not only a flag-waving Filipino nationalist. I am also a Bible-believing Baptist and an Inter-Varsity partisan to boot! How much of our zeal comes from a desire to build a religious empire with headquarters in America and branches in a hundred nations? How much of our zeal comes from an emotional need to do something in order to feel useful?

What per cent of our zeal truly comes from a burning desire to promote the glory of God?

Genuine zeal for God's glory is costly, but it will cost us only our pride and our selfishness. God grant that we have less and less of both. Genuine zeal for God's glory can stand criticism—such as I have expressed—for criticism only serves to purify it, like fire purifies gold. Let the testing of our zeal produce purer motives, like gold, much fine gold.

My North American brothers and sisters in Christ, I ask you to send missionaries to the ends of the earth who are zealous for the glory of God alone.

Love for Needy People
The second essential qualification for messengers is love for needy people.

We live in a world of incredible human needs. Hundreds of millions of people are poor and hungry, homeless and illiterate, battered by illness and die young. From Vietnam, people are prepared to risk their lives to escape on rickety boats adrift at sea or live in overcrowded refugee camps with no facilities, to search for a better life. In our day we may be seeing the extinction of the people of Kampuchea, as both young and old die off because help that comes is too little and too late. There are many other examples elsewhere in the world of people in great need of the most basic necessities.

You come from the world's richest economy, the largest consumers of the world's goods and of its energy. Does the contrast mean anything to you?

James, the brother of the Lord, wrote these words to the early Christians:

This is pure and undefiled religion in the sight of our God and Father, to visit orphans and widows in their distress, and to keep oneself unstained by the world.... What use is it, my brethren, if a man says he has faith, but he has no works? Can that faith save him? If a brother or sister is without clothing and in need of daily food, and one of you says to them, "Go in peace, be warmed and be filled"; and yet you do not give them what is necessary for their body; what use is that? Even so faith, if it has no works, is dead, being by itself. (Jas. 1:27; 2:14-17)

Please do not send to us missionaries who insist on a dichotomy between evangelism and social concern. Missionaries who teach that evangelism is our main or even sole concern. Missionaries who say that ministry to the temporal needs of people will also be done, but only as we have time, and as our limited resources allow.

Such missionaries make it difficult for us to defend the gospel against the Marxist charge that Christians promise a pie in the sky for the by and by. That Christians who have links with the West are but tools of Western imperialism, perhaps innocent, but helping to perpetuate the pockets of privilege, leaving the wretched of the earth to remain wretched!

We must not simply react to Marxist criticism, even though I realize that for many of you Marxism is a theoretical question, while for us the Communist system is a live and attractive option. If it can feed the hungry millions, why not, why not? But we are not simply reacting to Marxist criticism. Rather, we must come to realize that unless our love is demonstrated in practical terms of helping to meet the need for daily bread, our gospel of love will eventually sound hollow and unconvincing.

Am I pleading for a return to the old social gospel? No, no. I myself trained as a medical doctor but abandoned the profession in order to become a preacher of the gospel. But I do ask you to resist—to fight—every dichotomy between preaching the gospel of love and demonstrating that love for needy men and women through good works. It was General Booth, founder of the Salvation Army, commenting on James 1, who said: "We will wash it [our money] in the tears of the widows and orphans and lay it on the altar of humanity."

I have long admired the Salvation Army and their twin emphases on soup and salvation. They have much to teach us all. They follow the example of the Lord Jesus closely. For he who came to give his life for our redemption also fed the hungry, healed the sick and welcomed the outcasts of society. He is still our model. His mission is our mission.

I know that those who urge us to do evangelism only are fired by the urgency of the evangelistic task. I share their sense of urgency. In the words of the 1974 Lausanne Covenant: "More than 2,700 million people, which is more than two-thirds of mankind, have yet to be evangelized. . . . Missionaries should flow ever more freely from and to all six continents in a spirit of humble service. The goal should be, by all available means and at the earliest possible time, that every person will have the opportunity to hear, understand, and receive the good news."

Nevertheless, this section of the Covenant, entitled "The Urgency of the Evangelistic Task," goes on to say: "We cannot hope to attain this goal [of world evangelization] without sacrifice. All of us are shocked by the poverty of millions and disturbed by the injustices which cause it. Those of us who live in affluent circumstances accept our duty to develop a simple life-style in order to contribute more generously to both relief and evangelism."

Both relief and evangelism. We cannot, we must not divorce the urgency of the evangelistic task from our duty to help those in need of daily bread.

What does this mean for us today, to us gathered here to consider missionary service? It means facing the question: How can I, as a follower of the Lord Jesus, live more simply today in order to give more to help meet both the temporal and eternal needs of so many people on this planet? Today we had the opportunity to skip lunch in order to help feed the hungry. Praise the Lord for such opportunities! However, let our act be more than a token undertaken only in missionary conventions, perhaps under considerable social pressure. Let our act be a sign of a commitment to a simpler lifestyle so that we can be more generous in sharing our goods.

Let me assure you, my brothers and sisters, that the question is no less demanding on me as it is on you. For I know large numbers of people who live on much less of this world's goods than I do.

Concern for the Unity of the Body

The third essential qualification for messengers is concern for the unity of the body.

In his great treatise on the church, Paul appealed to Christians to be "diligent to preserve the unity of the Spirit in the bond of peace" (Eph. 4:3)—not just to be willing to maintain the Spirit-given unity of believers, but to be eager to do so. It is a lovely picture word, *diligent* or *eager* (RSV). It means to spare no effort. The picture it brings to my mind is that of a miler setting the pace, at the head of the pack, doing the last lap. Coming to the last two hundred meters, he will pull out all the stops. It is time to give it all he has got! He will spare no effort.

Sadly, the missionary enterprise has not been noted for great effort in either maintaining or nurturing the unity of the body. R. Pierce Beaver, the well-known missions historian, was quoted in a paper given at the Lausanne Congress on World Evangelization as saying, "More and more I am convinced that exported divisiveness is the greatest hindrance to the spread of the gospel in the non-Christian world."

The church is a reality in nearly every place in the world where we want to send missionaries. We need to come to terms with her. We must be willing to recognize her as our partner. She may be financially poor, theologically unsophisticated and inefficient in her methods, but she is not our inferior. We cannot bypass her without sinning against the body. Paul reminds us that there is only *one* body (Eph. 4:4) with only one head, the Lord Jesus.

Ah, but someone says, some parts of the body are closer to the head. This person says that we have been given a grand vision for fulfilling the Great Commission, and we have the resources of the mightiest nation on earth for carrying it out. It is only sensible to conclude that the most efficient way to finish the job is to ask the rest of you to join us!

Perhaps we do not say these things. We only act this way. Our actions speak louder than our words: *West is best!* Is this simply bad theology or is it American pride?

One day, a Western missionary said to me in church: "Tomorrow we are sponsoring a youth march for Jesus in Plaza Miranda [downtown Manila]. Why don't you come and join us and bring your students along?"

"Well," I said, "I am not sure that that is the best way to demonstrate the reality of the gospel in this season of student demonstrations."

"Listen," she said to me, "can we ever work together? This division between us is diabolical."

I very nearly said to her, "Yankee, go home!" It was a struggle to keep back the words.

My North American brothers and sisters in Christ: Can we ever be partners? *Partners.* Why do you keep saying that you have a master plan for fulfilling the Great Commission and you want us to join you in carrying out your plans? Why can't you come to us and say: "I have come in obedience to the Great Commission. How can you and I fulfill it together?" Partnership means a fellowship of equals.

A true partnership, a fellowship of equals, is not impossible. Sitting down together, discussing a plan of action in mutual respect and confidence is not an idle dream. In June 1980, some 650 Christian leaders from all over the world will meet in Pattaya, Thailand, for the Consultation on World Evangelization (COWE). COWE, which is sponsored by the Lausanne Committee, is a good illustration of a fellowship of equals both in planning and execution. The COWE Director is David Howard from the United States. The Program Chairman is Saphir Athyal of India, and the Lausanne Committee Executive Secretary is Gottfried Osei-Mensah of Ghana.

COWE is by no means the only example. For those of you who are not very familiar with it, let me commend to you the International Fellowship of Evangelical Students (IFES). Fifty autonomous, indigenous national student movements have banded together to spread the gospel in the student world. Examine the IFES structure, its pattern of authority and decision making, its choice of leaders. We are not anti-American in IFES. Last July, we elected as Chairman of the Executive Committee to serve until 1983, Dr. John W. Alexander. The IFES is not perfect, but you will discover a fellowship of equals.

China, that great nation of one billion people—nearly a quarter of mankind—is slowly opening its doors. What will be our plan of action? Is everyone going to jump on the China bandwagon and insist once again on doing his own thing? Or shall we manifest concern for the unity of the body and ask ourselves: "What kind of action by outsiders will be best for the Church in China? How can we enter into partnership with the Church in China in order to advance the spread of the gospel?"

It is for the sake of the unevangelized millions that messengers need to be concerned for the unity of the body.

Have I been harsh to you today? Have I caused you pain? I can only trust that our exercise tonight has been essential surgery. I pray that the Holy Spirit, the skilled surgeon, will apply the needed pain in a therapeutic way to help the body become healthier. So that the one body—you and I and the people of God across the world—may together proclaim to all nations that there is salvation in no one else, that there is no other name under heaven given among people by which we must be saved, except the name Jesus. Amen.

9
That I Might Believe and Obey

Billy Graham

I have sat out there with you at every session except one, and I have sensed on occasion the moving of the Spirit of God in such power that I had hoped that the speaker would give an invitation —sometimes to receive Christ as Lord and Savior, sometimes for assurance, sometimes for total commitment to Jesus not only as Savior, but as Lord.

Tonight is the culmination in your heart of all that you have seen and heard and felt and learned since you have been here at Urbana, and I am speaking tonight for all the speakers and all the people who have planned this program and have worked so hard behind the scenes. I am speaking, too, for the Lord Jesus Christ tonight, and that is an awesome responsibility—so frightening that my hands at this moment are filled with perspiration and my knees are shaking. I am going to ask you to be in prayer, as you have never prayed.

The world stands on the very edge of Armageddon tonight.

Without God's intervention the world is moving toward that climactic moment of human history that will alter our lives forever.

But tonight you, too, stand at a crossroads in your own life just as awesome, just as frightening, just as thrilling, just as challenging. To some of you it will mean the choice between heaven and hell for eternity. For others it will be a choice of what you are going to do with the command of our Lord Jesus Christ.

Paul tells us in Romans 10:9-17:

If thou shalt confess with thy mouth the Lord Jesus, and shalt believe in thine heart that God hath raised him from the dead, thou shalt be saved. For with the heart man believeth unto righteousness; and with the mouth confession is made unto salvation. For the scripture saith, Whosoever believeth on him shall not be ashamed. For there is no difference between the Jew and the Greek: for the same Lord over all is rich unto all that call upon him. For whosoever [educated, uneducated, white or black, brown] shall call upon the name of the Lord shall be saved. [There are two hundred separate ethnic groups living in the United States. I too belong to a minority because only about twenty-three per cent are Anglo-Saxon in background. We are all minorities.]

How then shall they call on him in whom they have not believed? and how shall they believe in him of whom they have not heard? and how shall they hear without a preacher? And how shall they preach, except they be sent? as it is written, How beautiful are the feet of them that preach the gospel of peace, and bring glad tidings of good things! But they have not all obeyed the gospel. For Isaiah saith, Lord, who hath believed our report? So then faith cometh by hearing, and hearing by the word of God. (KJV used throughout.)

Notice also Acts 17:6 where Paul and Silas are ministering in Thessalonica: "These that have turned the world upside down are come hither also."

The famous novelist, Lloyd Douglas, coined the phrase "magnificent obsession." The early apostles had a magnificent obsession to turn the world upside down with their message. The people of Jesus' day accused Paul of being beside himself.

Governor Festus said to the apostle after listening to him speak, "You're out of your mind, Paul. Your great learning is driving you insane." Paul had an obsession.

When young men and women and even adults offer to leave home and go to the hard places of the world to serve Christ, they too are often accused of being out of their minds. In the late 1930s some young people gathered for a prayer meeting at Columbia Bible College and also at Wheaton College and at Keswick in New Jersey at about the same time. Out of these prayer meetings came the Foreign Missions Fellowship, and out of that grew the Inter-Varsity missions emphasis we see here tonight. It wasn't the faculty; it wasn't the theologians; it was students asking God for a new movement.

The apostle Paul said, "Whether we be beside ourselves, it is to God: or whether we be sober, it is for your cause. For the love of Christ constraineth us" (2 Cor. 5:13-14). The love of Christ drove students to their knees in prayer beside a haystack 175 years ago, and that was the beginning of foreign missions in the United States.

Paul also said, "Knowing therefore the terror of the Lord, we persuade men" (2 Cor. 5:11). Paul had the terror of the judgment of God in mind. "We are ambassadors for Christ, as though God did beseech you by us: . . . be ye reconciled to God" (2 Cor. 5:20).

Think of the glorious daring of those early apostles. Little wonder that the world called them mad! Paul was satisfied with nothing less than taking the gospel to the whole world including imperial Rome. Magnificent obsessions indeed, every one of them. Who could understand their zeal? The apostles carried the flaming truths of the gospel far and wide. Reckoning nothing of peril and reproach, they surmounted obstacles, overcame difficulties and endured persecution. That was their answer to Christ's command—the magnificent obsession of obeying Christ.

These men and women of the past have handed a torch to us tonight. We too must have their obsession. We must dare to believe God for even greater things in this decade of the eighties. While some countries are closing to missions, others are opening. The great cities in many parts of the world are now open in ways I have not known in my years of ministry.

The social needs of the world are tremendous. The social injustices are everywhere. But the spiritual needs are there, too, and there is no dichotomy between these. There may be a priority but not a dichotomy.

I think of the holocaust going on at this moment in Cambodia that is almost equal to the Nazi holocaust in World War 2. I think of the suffering in Uganda and other parts of the world this moment, whether in Iran or wherever we turn. The whole human race is suffering from the spiritual disease of sin, and only Christ and his gospel can meet it. And so let us get on with this obsession with a new dedication and fervor that we have never known before. It is my prayer that this magnificent obsession, the love of God in Christ, will so constrain hundreds of you that you will offer this very night to serve his call, to march under his flag, to surrender yourself to the lordship of Christ, to use your gifts for his service. It is my prayer that we will represent Christ with a fervor that will put all wordly enthusiasm to shame. Night after night on the television we see Iranian students with their fists in their hands, shouting their slogans, wearing their white gowns indicating they are ready to be martyrs for their cause. We should put on our gowns tonight and say that we too are willing to be witnesses, willing to be martyrs, as Elisabeth Elliot has reminded us.

There are four things I want you to consider before I ask you publicly to commit your life to the lordship of Christ.

First, our authority, our command, comes from the Lord Jesus Christ. Just before his ascension, he said, "But ye shall receive power, after that the Holy Ghost is come upon you: and ye shall be witnesses unto me both in Jerusalem, and in all Judea, and in Samaria, and unto the uttermost part of the earth" (Acts 1:8). This command was given in various forms five times. Some scholars believe that Jesus gave it over and over again. He said to the maniac of Gadara, "Go home to thy friends, and tell them how great things the Lord has done for thee" (Mk. 5:19). Jesus had done great things for him physically by transforming him. He had done great things for him spiritually by forgiving his sins. All the way through the Scripture, Jesus said, "Go and do, go and do. Go out quickly into the streets and into the lanes, go out into the highways and hedges, go into the vineyard, go into the village, go into the city, go into the town, go to the lost sheep. Go thou and preach the kingdom of God. Go into all the world."

Jesus really had only two verbs—come, go . . . come, go. "Come to me all you that labor and are heavy laden, and I will give you rest. Come to the cross for salvation. Come be reconciled to God. Come repent of your sins. Go into the world and be a witness even unto death."

With his commands ringing in their ears, the disciples set out not only to reach the world, but to turn it upside down. If ever there was a generation that needs turning upside down, it's ours —morally, socially, politically, spiritually. And this crowd here tonight could do it. There was only a handful then. There are sixteen, seventeen thousand of us! What could be done?

The disciples suffered hardship and persecution in floggings and beatings, and in death, but they said, "We cannot but speak the things which we have seen and heard" (Acts 4:20).

Thus, we are a people under authority. We go because we have been sent. I don't go preaching and traveling because I enjoy it anymore. To tell you the truth, I don't. I go because I'm under orders. I would like to sit back in my mountain home in North Carolina with my wife.

You know we have five children and fifteen grandchildren, and they say, "Poor Daddy and Mother, they're all alone." They don't know what a good time we are having! I tell you, the best is yet to be. I have found that out. When your children are happily married, and they all know the Lord, and you're there with your wife—only then will you know what love is!

But you have to face your task squarely. How do your talents and gifts and training prepare you for Christian service in your Samaria, in your Judea, to the uttermost parts of the earth? Is Christ really Lord of your life? Have you submitted your will to him? your future? your vocation? Do you have this obsession? Then what are you going to do about his command? You have to decide tonight.

Second, consider the message we proclaim. We have been

hearing it over and over again. Time after time in church history the message is blunted, watered down, diluted; it has lost its power. But it has been recovered, as we saw in the multimedia presentation on the first night, as we looked at the history of missions and evangelism.

The early apostles had no doubt about their message. They said, "neither is there salvation in any other" (Acts 4:12). Not in Buddhism or Islam or any other. There can be no syncretism. There is only one way, the way of the cross, the way of the resurrection. There is no other way for a person to be saved except through the Lord Jesus Christ. There is some truth in all religions, truth in philosophy, truth in so many areas, but the totality of truth lies in the person of the Lord Jesus Christ.

"I am truth." No one ever said that before. "I am the way ... no man cometh unto the Father, but by me" (Jn. 14:6). Whoever said that? He must have been crazy, or he must have been a liar, or he must have been who he claimed to be. That was the intellectual decision that I had to face some years after I had received Christ. I had to fight it all over again.

My wife went to Wheaton College and lost her faith. She became an agnostic for nearly a year, and she argued with everybody she could find. She had come from a missionary home in China, and she had loved the Lord all her life and had written poetry about Christ and God and had marked her Bible from one end to the other before she ever got to Wheaton. There was nothing at Wheaton that caused her to lose her faith. Still, she began to question her faith for the first time, and a fellow student whom she almost married led her step by step intellectually.

"I fought with him," she said. "I argued with him and debated with him, hoping to lose."

Some of you are arguing and debating tonight in your mind, hoping really down deep to lose the argument.

You know, suicide is the greatest killer of students today. Twenty years ago when we were here at Urbana, the watchword of the world was *hope*. Tonight it's *despair*.

But tonight God has a great message he wants to deliver to the world. A message of hope. Yes, we are sinners, but God says, "I love you. I sent my son to die on the cross for you, to shed his blood. I raised him from the dead. He's coming back. He's the future world ruler. The future belongs to him. I will give you eternal life." That's good news. That's what the gospel means— good news—to a despairing world, to a despairing young person. And God has asked you to be his ambassador.

Third, consider the people we are to reach. Jesus said his disciples were to begin at Jerusalem and go to all nations. They were surprised when he mentioned Jerusalem first. Ronald Mitchell from Sierra Leone on the first night talked about that. Your Jerusalem is where you live—your school, your job, your home, your family, your friends. Jesus said, after transforming the maniac, "Go back home."

You here at Urbana have to go back the day after tomorrow to the same address, the same friends, the same classroom, the same teachers, but you won't be the same. Are you going to slide back into the old routine, the old way, the old sins, the old failures, the old habits? You have come here with a great resolve, and you have seen and heard much, and it has thrilled you. "This is what I want to be with all my heart," you have said. But then you have to go back.

The world that our Lord is talking about includes the geographical, the psychological and the sociological world. It includes the world of the school and business, government and labor. I would challenge you tonight to be a witness for Christ wherever God sends you.

During the past three years since the last Urbana conference, God has sent me throughout India, Africa, the Far East, Latin America, Europe, Australia, Hungary, Poland and Eastern Europe. I am finding a receptivity to the gospel on a scale I have not known in my many years of preaching. I thought by now that I would be finished. I should have been by all human standards. George Whitfield was dead at my age.

But the doors are open more today than ever before. They are open to you with the gospel because the world is searching and grasping desperately for an answer. Answers, answers, answers. Help, help, help, help, help! Homes being broken and torn. Help!

The fields are white unto harvest. But I warn you that harvest time is brief. Jesus said, "The night cometh, when no man can work" (Jn. 9:4). Go now. Do now. Prepare now.

Now does that mean that I leave seminary or Bible school, jump on a DC-10 and get somewhere now? No, it means that you prepare and prepare well.

I remember Dr. Donald Gray Barnhouse used to come to these Urbana conventions, and on two of those occasions he drove me to Indianapolis to catch a plane afterward. Once it was snowing. There was ice on the road. I came closer to losing my life then than at any other time, because he preached all the way. He told me everything that was wrong about me, and he straightened me out on a lot of things. He said that if he knew that Christ was going to come in three years, this is what he would do: "I'd spend two and a half years in preparation. Then I'd go out and preach for six months."

Get your preparation done. I can't emphasize that too much. As John Stott has pointed out, we are out to persuade men with the body of truth, to persuade their minds as well as to touch their hearts and reach to the center of their being which is their will.

Fourth, we need to consider the power we have been promised. In the Bible twenty-three Hebrew and Greek words are translated "power." The one which Jesus used, that I want to mention comes in this verse: "Ye shall receive power, after that the Holy Ghost is come upon you." A few years ago a picture in *Life* magazine showed a straw that had penetrated a light pole during a tornado. I asked myself how such a fragile straw could penetrate a light pole. It is because the power of the wind which was driving it was so tremendous.

Christ has promised a power far greater than that. Our power comes from the Holy Spirit. You are not going home alone. You are not going home without help. You are not going to your Jerusalem or to the uttermost part of the world without God's power. The Spirit prepares the heart. The Spirit guides us. The Spirit gives us boldness. The Spirit has given us the Word of God. The Spirit gives us wisdom. The Spirit alone can bring conviction and faith. Therefore, we are dependent on him.

Every time I get up to witness for Christ, I know that I have some things on my side. I know that somebody is lonely. I know that some people are empty. They have no purpose. They are saying to themselves, "I don't know where I came from or why I'm here or where I'm going." I know that there are some people in the audience who are afraid to die, some people still with guilt. The Holy Spirit has already prepared the way by the very nature of man. And our mission will never be accomplished by organization or methods. It will be accomplished by the power of the Holy Spirit—using us perhaps, but the Holy Spirit will do it.

Christ is asking you tonight to renounce your plans, your goals, your ambitions and your motives, and he asks you to put his plans first, make his goals your top priority. He asks that your ambitions and motives become his. In the New Testament the word Christian is used only three times (Acts 11:26; 26:28; 1 Pet. 4:16). On each of these occasions the idea of suffering and persecution is in the background. To serve Christ will cost you. It may mean that your girl friend is going to drop away because she is not the right one for you. You have to be willing to give her up. It was the first thing that God spoke to me about after I received Christ.

In the latter part of the nineteenth century, there was at Cambridge University a wealthy, highly educated athlete. He was one of the greatest cricket players of his day. His name was C. T. Studd. His father was a friend of Queen Victoria and was one of England's foremost owners of racehorses. Dwight L. Moody went to Cambridge and there was a great spiritual awakening. C. T. Studd was converted. He resigned from the celebrated Cambridge Eleven cricket team and led the Cambridge Seven as a frontier missionary, triggering one of the most momentous movements of modern missions. Reflecting on what made him do it, C. T. Studd said: "If Jesus Christ be God and died for me, no sacrifice can be too great for me to make for him."

Adoniram Judson was born in a Congregational minister's home. When he was five, his father was already teaching him to read Greek. As a young man he went to Brown University. That was the time of the French Revolution, and Brown University was filled with unbelief, agnosticism and skepticism.

His roommate was named Ernest. They went through college

as unbelievers, and when they graduated neither was a Christian.

One day Adoniram Judson was riding horseback through New England. At night he stopped at an inn and asked for a room. The innkeeper said, "There's only one room left, and it's next door to a man who's dying. He's making an awful racket, and I don't think you'll be able to sleep."

Judson said, "It doesn't make any difference to me. Give me the room." So they took care of his horse, and he went up to the room.

During the night he heard a voice in the next room. Sometimes it would ask God for mercy, and sometimes it was swearing and taking the name of God in vain. Then later in the night the voice stopped, and Judson went to sleep.

The next morning he asked the innkeeper, "What happened to the man in the room next to me last night?"

"He died," the innkeeper said.

"What was his name?" Judson asked.

"His name was Ernest." This man had been Judson's roommate through college.

Judson got on his horse, and every time the horse's hooves hit the ground, the words kept running through his mind: "Dead ... lost. Dead ... lost. Dead ... lost. Dead ... lost." And Judson turned around and went home.

He entered Andover Seminary, and there he got converted and came to know Christ as his Savior. As a result of that conversion he got a vision for the world and became the first missionary to leave American shores for the foreign field. He went to India and was baptized by William Carey, and then he went on to Burma and suffered. But today thousands of Christians in Southeast Asia call him blessed.

Throughout this great student conference God is calling you.

"Yes, Lord, I will go where you want me to go. I'll be what you want me to be," or "No, Lord, I'm not going to surrender that much to you. I'll give you fifty per cent or seventy-five per cent, or maybe eighty per cent, but I can't go all the way. The price is too high."

It will take courage for you to make that decision, but that is your terrible, terrible freedom, because God gave you a will of your own. "Whosoever will save his life shall lose it," Jesus said, "and whosoever will lose his life for my sake shall find it" (Mt. 16:25).

God is not calling us to a playground or a sports arena. He is calling us to a battleground. God has promised us his full resources in the battle.

I am sure that you have heard the story many times of that famous organ in the cathedral in Freiburg, Germany. The man who had played it for many years had become quite old. One day a stranger came in and asked if he could play the organ. The man said, "No, I'm the only one allowed to play this organ." The stranger persisted and finally the old man gave in. The stranger began to play music more beautiful than the old organist had ever heard, and his eyes began to fill with tears.

At the end he asked the stranger, "What is your name?"

And the answer came back, "My name is Felix Mendelssohn."

The old man told the story over and over again, and he would always end by shaking his head and saying, "And to think I almost did not allow the world's greatest master to play on this organ!"

Jesus Christ has spoken to you. You could be on the verge of missing God's great call to your life. If you answer yes, you are in obedience to him, and it brings a fulfillment, a joy and a peace in this life, and rewards in the life to come. If you say no, which is your privilege and right, it means to continue to wander and the wandering will get worse, the floundering will get worse, the questions will be harder and the answers will become more difficult. And at the end it will be judgment and eternity without God. It is my prayer that you will believe and obey.

10
Until
He Comes

Gottfried Osei-Mensah

Take a look at Matthew 24:1-14:

Jesus left the temple and was walking away when his disciples came up to him to call his attention to its buildings. "Do you see all these things?" he asked. "I tell you the truth, not one stone here will be left on another; every one will be thrown down."

As Jesus was sitting on the Mount of Olives, the disciples came to him privately. "Tell us," they said, "when will this happen, and what will be the sign of your coming and of the end of the age?"

Jesus answered: "Watch out that no one deceives you. For many will come in my name, claiming, 'I am the Christ,' and will deceive many. You will hear of wars and rumors of wars, but see to it that you are not alarmed. Such things must happen, but the end is still to come. Nation will rise against nation, and kingdom against kingdom. There will be famines

and earthquakes in various places. All these are the begin-
ning of birth pains.

"Then you will be handed over to be persecuted and put to
death, and you will be hated by all nations because of me. At
that time many will turn away from the faith and will betray
and hate each other, and many false prophets will appear and
deceive many people. Because of the increase of wickedness,
the love of most will grow cold, but he who stands firm to the
end will be saved. And this gospel of the kingdom will be
preached in the whole world as a testimony to all nations, and
then the end will come." (NIV used throughout this chapter.)

In the throne room of the universe there hangs God's time-
table, his calendar of events, the "times or dates the Father has
set by his own authority" (Acts 1:7). Two arrow markers on the
calendar point downward. The first marks the critical junction
of history which divides the era "before Christ" (B.C.) and the
"year of our Lord" (A.D.). Scripture calls it "the fulness of time,"
when God sent his Son, born of a woman, born under law, to
redeem those under law, so that we might receive the full rights
of sons; namely, the Spirit of God's Son in our hearts, the Spirit
who calls out, "Abba, Father" (see Gal. 4:4-6). The second arrow
marks "the Day of the Lord" when the Son of God, now en-
throned at the right hand of the Almighty, will come again in
splendor and power and great glory.

How do we know that Christ is coming again?

Christ Is Coming Again

He said so himself. Two instances will suffice to illustrate. In
his private session with the disciples before he went to face the
cross, he said this to comfort them: "In my Father's house are
many rooms; if it were not so, I would have told you. I am going
there to prepare a place for you. And if I go and prepare a place
for you, I will come back and take you to be with me that you also
may be where I am" (Jn. 14:2-3).

At his trial before the Jewish supreme council, there was only
one statement Jesus made, on the basis of which he was sen-
tenced to death. The High Priest, unable to get any voluntary
response from the Lord Jesus at the trial, finally placed him

under oath: "I charge you under oath by the living God: Tell us if you are the Christ, the Son of God." "Yes, it is as you say," Jesus replied. "But I say to all of you: In the future you will see the Son of Man sitting at the right hand of the Mighty One and coming on the clouds of heaven" (see Mt. 26:63-64; Mk. 14:61-62). No doubt, then, throughout the New Testament the return of the Lord, the anticipation of his coming again, permeates all the apostolic writings (see 2 Pet. 3:3ff.; Tit. 2:11-14; 1 Jn. 3:1-3; Rev. 1:7). The Lord is coming again, according to his own promise.

What is the purpose of his second coming? The Scriptures give us at least three purposes for the Lord's second coming.

Christ Is Coming to Judge

Christ is coming to judge the living and dead (see Jn. 5:22, 27-29; Acts 17:31; 2 Tim. 4:1; 1 Pet. 4:5). "He will punish those who do not know God and do not obey the gospel of our Lord Jesus. They will be punished with everlasting destruction and shut out from the presence of the Lord and from the majesty of his power on the day he comes to be glorified in his holy people and to be marveled at among all those who have believed" (2 Thess. 1: 8-10).

The double description of those who will stand condemned before the Lord is worthy of note. The Bible clearly holds every person responsible for his ignorance of God, "since what may be known about God is plain to them, because God has made it plain to them ... his eternal power and divine nature—have been clearly seen, being understood from what has been made, so that men are without excuse" (Rom. 1:19-20). In actual fact, of course, the unbeliever does not know God, because it is of the very essence of man's sinful nature to suppress this general revelation of God in creation and conscience (see Rom. 1:18, 32; 2:14-15). But the real issue at judgment is unbelief and consequent disobedience of the gospel of our Lord Jesus. "Whoever believes in him is not condemned, but whoever does not believe stands condemned already because he has not believed in the name of God's one and only Son" (Jn. 3:18). The solemn implication of all this for our own commitment to world evangelization is clear: How can they believe in One of whom they have not heard? And how can they hear without someone telling them (see Rom. 10:14)?

Paul's evangelistic ministry was motivated both by his overwhelming sense of indebtedness to the love of Christ, his compassion for the perishing, and also by his dread of standing before the Lord with the blood of those he had failed to warn on his hands (see 2 Cor. 5:10-15; Rom. 9:2-3; 2 Tim. 2:10; Acts 20:26-27; cf. Ezek. 3:18-19). We do well to examine our own priorities as those entrusted with a message of life for a dying world. The interim period between Christ's ascension and return is, by his own appointment, to be filled with the mission of his followers. "And this gospel of the kingdom will be preached in the whole world as a testimony to all nations, and then the end will come" (Mt. 24:14).

Christ Is Coming to Save

He is coming to complete the salvation of his people. "Christ was sacrificed once to take away the sins of many people; and he will appear a second time, not to bear sin, but to bring salvation to those who are waiting for him" (Heb. 9:28). There are different aspects to this consummation of our salvation. The first is personal. The transformation of our personalities into the likeness of Christ which began as a process at the new birth will be brought to its glorious conclusion (see 2 Cor. 3:18; cf. Col. 3:4). The vestiges of sin's power and presence in our bodies as well as its influence on our faculties will be purged completely by our Lord Jesus Christ, "who, by the power that enables him to bring everything under his control, will transform our lowly bodies so that they will be like his glorious body" (Phil. 3:21). This will happen to every Christian either by resurrection or by instantaneous transformation at Christ's second coming (see 1 Cor. 15:42-44, 51-53). In every case the result is the same. The Christlike bodies we shall inherit will be imperishable, glorified, powerful and spiritual.

But there is also a corporate aspect to the consummation of our salvation. The church corporately is described as the bride of Christ whom he loved and for whose purification he sacrificed himself. Now the church awaits the joyful day when Christ will present her to himself in splendor, "as a radiant church, without stain or wrinkle or any other blemish, but holy and blameless" (Eph. 5:27; also Jude 24). That will also be the day when the Lord's universal reign is acclaimed with thunderous Hallelujahs! "Blessed are those who are invited to the wedding supper of the Lamb!" (Rev. 19:9).

The consummation of our salvation has a cosmic dimension as well. The reconciliation and cleansing through the blood of Jesus Christ also has implications for God's creation corrupted by man's sin (see Gen. 3:17-18; Col. 1:20; Heb. 9:23). And now, the entire creation "waits in eager expectation for the sons of God to be revealed. For the creation was subjected to frustration, . . . in hope that the creation itself will be liberated from its bondage to decay and brought into the glorious freedom of the children of God" (Rom. 8:19-21).

Peter tells us how this will be done. By God's decree, the present heavens and earth are reserved for fire, kept for the day of judgment and destruction of ungodly people, when the elements will be destroyed by fire and the earth and everything in it will be burned up. But out of the ashes will come up a new heaven and a new earth, the home of righteousness (see 2 Pet. 3:7, 10, 13; cf. Rev. 21:1). Neither Christ nor his apostles ever spoke of his return to satisfy idle curiosity, but always to stimulate practical action. What difference then should the certainty of his coming again make to our lives and lifestyles? Peter answers, "You ought to live holy and godly lives as you look forward to the day of God and speed its coming" (2 Pet. 3:11-12). And John concurs, "We know that when he appears, we shall be like him. . . . Everyone who has this hope in him purifies himself, just as he is pure" (1 Jn. 3:2-3).

The anticipation that we shall reflect, in our individual personalities and in our corporate relationship, the splendor and moral perfection of Christ should spur us on to holiness now. All the needed resources are given us in Christ for this purpose —a new nature, the indwelling Spirit, the purifying Word of God, access to God in prayer in Christ's name and the discipline of Christian fellowship. To submit to Christ our desires, ambitions and moral choices, and to actively pursue God's standards in behavior and relationships are part and parcel of confessing him as Lord.

Christ Is Coming to Reign

The ultimate purpose of Christ's return is to abolish every other authority and rule and to set up his universal kingdom—God's glorious reign of righteousness, justice, peace and prosperity (see 1 Cor. 15:24-28; cf. Is. 9:6-7). Of course, Christ's reign is not relegated to the future. He ascended his throne in heaven, following his decisive victory over sin, death and the ruler of this world (see Eph. 1:20-22; Heb. 1:3). All authority in heaven and on earth has been given to him (Mt. 28:18). His present, self-imposed restraint in the exercise of his sovereign power needs to be clearly understood. It is restraint born out of patience, not weakness. The Lord is patient, not wanting anyone to perish, but to come to repentance (see 2 Pet. 3:9, 15; Rom. 2:4). It is as the reigning Lord that he sends his ambassadors into the world with the message of reconciliation to rebel mankind. The good news is essentially an offer of royal pardon and elevation to positions of honor in Christ's new regime, an offer made to rebel subjects who could otherwise only expect execution. The church is the community of Christ's reconciled people who joyfully submit to his authority and kingship. They constitute the sign of the kingdom of God and of his Christ in this world, enjoying a foretaste of the kingdom's peace and love, exhibiting its righteousness and justice and spreading the same in the midst of an unjust world.

But the Day of the Lord will terminate the present period of God's favor and introduce with power God's glorious reign. Then the usurped powers of Satan (the ruler of this world) and his evil forces will be finally abolished, and the kingdom of the world will become the kingdom of our Lord and of his Christ, and he will reign for ever and ever (Rev. 11:15).

Until He Comes

When we participate in the rich symbolism of the Lord's Supper, we have before us our motivation, our message and our marching orders. It is a missionary meal.

In the broken bread and poured-out wine, we have a powerful reminder of the price God paid for our liberation from the power of sin, and a compelling reason why we must now be totally dedicated to him and his service. "He died for all, that those who live should no longer live for themselves but for him who died for them and was raised again" (2 Cor. 5:15).

The Lord's Supper also eloquently proclaims the vital message entrusted to us for the world. Paul in Corinth resolved to know nothing while he was with them except Jesus Christ and him crucified (1 Cor. 2:2). The "word of the cross" is the only relevant message for a dying world. Whenever we eat the bread and drink of the cup, we proclaim the Lord's death. We express our faith in the complete adequacy of the one sacrifice for sins offered for all time on the cross (Heb. 10:12, 14). And now we are to proclaim this one and only adequate way of salvation to all people, until he comes.

How anticipatory and expectant is the communion table. The Lord Jesus said at the first Supper: "I have eagerly desired to eat this Passover with you before I suffer. For I tell you, I will not eat it again until it finds fulfillment in the kingdom of God" (Lk. 22:15-16; Mt. 26:29). Blessed are those who are invited to the wedding supper of the Lamb! May the certainty of our participation then motivate us for commitment and service to our Lord now.

"Therefore, my dear brothers [and sisters], stand firm. Let nothing move you. Always give yourselves fully to the work of the Lord, because you know that your labor in the Lord is not in vain" (1 Cor. 15:58). "If we endure, we will also reign with him" (2 Tim. 2:12).

Part IV
The Task
of the
Messenger

11
What Can
One Person
Do?

Elisabeth Elliot

Before most of you were born I was living in a small thatch-roofed house in a small jungle clearing on a small river called the Tiwaenu in the small country of Ecuador. An ordinary day would begin anywhere from three o'clock till five or so in the morning. The low crooning of an Auca song would often fit into my dreams for a while before I wakened and then, gradually, I would come to, and hear the Indians, still in their hammocks in the houses around the clearing, singing their strange two or at most three-note songs: "*Waenoni baronki inunae....*"

I have counted as many as seventy repetitions of verse one, but then, before I would lose my mind, they would go on to verse two: "*MiH baronanai aemumae....*"

While they were singing that verse sixty or seventy times I would hear the pat-pat of feather fans as the women fanned the fires and then the soft cracking sound as they tapped manioc with a stick. This was a starchy tuber they cultivated, the principal food of Amazonian people. They peeled and split it and steamed it in big clay pots with leaves for lids. They would push the glowing log-tips together, set the pots on top, and I would hear the pfff-pfff as they blew on the fire. Roosters would crow, the fanning and the songs would go on, and as dawn broke behind the tall trees I would give up pretending to be asleep. I'd open my eyes to see the two teen-age boys who slept in the house next door. Our houses had no walls, and they had built a platform from which they could watch what went on in our house and keep everybody informed. The first announcement of the day would be *"Baru! Nani omaemunamba!"* which means "She's awake!"

I was a freak to these people. They were the Auca Indians of the Ecuadorian rain forest, a people so isolated that most of them had never laid eyes on anybody they didn't know, so primitive they still made fire with two sticks. They wore no clothes at all, only a piece of cotton string around the hips. When I asked what the string was for they looked at me horrified. "Well, you certainly wouldn't expect us to go around naked, would you?"

They had a notion from way back—nobody could tell me where they got it—that everybody in the world who wasn't an Auca was a cannibal; so when they met up with strangers, they usually dispatched them as quickly as possible with eight-foot wooden spears in order to avoid ending up in the stranger's cooking pot.

One day, two years before I lived there, the Aucas had found five strange white men on a little strip of sand on the Curaray River, men who had been dropping gifts to them from a yellow airplane for several months. The Indians called the plane *ibu* meaning "bumblebee" because the sound it made was almost identical. They had argued among themselves for a long time about whether these men might be as friendly as they appeared to be, shouting and gesticulating from the plane, or whether they were just masters of treachery and deception. They couldn't possibly know that they were missionaries bent only on giving them some very good news.

When they finally found themselves face to face on the sand-strip, the Indians hesitated, uncertain as to what to do. At least, the oldest of the six men, a man whom I later got to know as Gikita, said, "Well, I brought my spear—*butu Wati! taenumu waeninani yaeae*—I'm going to spear them to death." With that he lunged across the river that separated them and sank his weapon into the back of one of the missionaries. A long fight ensued, but ended with all five of the Americans dead.

That's a twentieth-century story. Maybe it seems unusual in the twentieth century, maybe it seems strange that the God whom the five served should allow them to be defeated by a handful of utterly misled, totally ignorant Indians to whom spearing was all in a day's work. But in Christian history the story is neither unusual nor strange, for the history of Christianity is a story of witnesses—men and women who have stood up and testified to what they know about God. Sometimes they've done it in words and sometimes in deeds. There's a long list of such people in Hebrews, chapter 11: Noah, Abraham, Moses, David, Samuel and the prophets—even a harlot named Rahab. There were those not named who conquered kingdoms, shut the mouths of lions, quenched the furious blaze of fire and escaped from death. They were the successful ones—the winners, you'd say. But do you remember the list at the end of the chapter? You never saw any pictures of them in your Sunday-school papers. They were the ones who were tortured, mocked, flogged, chained or stoned to death. There were some, the story says, who were sawn in two. They are in the same list, remember, right in there with the winners. We could add the names of the five missionaries in Ecuador—Jim Elliot and his friends, Pete, Nate, Roj and Ed. Some people call them martyrs. You know what the Bible calls them? Witnesses. I'm sure there are some Greek students in the audience this morning who know it's the same word. The word for witness is *marturia*. So in God's categories it really doesn't matter whether, humanly speaking, you win or lose, whether you're a victim or a victor. You're a witness.

And that's what I'm supposed to talk to you about. Witnessing. Specifically, what one man or one woman can do. I started by telling you about my experience of living with people who regarded me as a freak. I haven't time to tell you how I got there, but there I was—some kind of nut. I had hair like palm fiber, they said. Eyes like a jaguar's—blue ones, altogether the wrong color for a person to have. To a people whose skin was the beautiful shade of strong tea mine was pathetically washed-out. I was a head taller than anybody. Before they saw me, they had heard that a very tall foreigner was coming so they built me a house about twenty feet tall. It was an awful letdown for them when I showed up, only five foot nine.

But everything about me was weird. Everything I did was bizarre. I didn't know how to do anything useful like planting manioc or making clay pots or weaving hammocks or catching fish with my hands, and when I tried, they would break up laughing, and my daughter Valerie, who was three and had learned their language almost overnight, would yell, "*hyae akam!*" which means, "Everybody get a load of this!"

Well, the dawn broke in the clearing as I have described. Day after day the women and most of the children would go off to the plantations to work, and the men would go hunting. There I would be sitting in a hammock with my notebooks and file box, scratching the gnat bites, blinking the smoke out of my eyes, trying to figure out a language nobody had ever written down. Suppose you take a piece of paper now and write down, "*Wuru naimae nano kaewuti ani.*" How much did you get? Or how about *MMm wa*—that means, "it stinks."

In the evenings everybody came home, the women from the planting, the men from hunting. They cooked and ate whatever they had brought—manioc, plantains, birds, monkeys, tapirs, whatever. They went to sleep very early and there I'd still be, sitting in the hammock, Valerie asleep in a blanket on a slab of split bamboo beside me. I'd fan my fire, scratch bug bites, study a little bit sometimes, but candles were hard to come by down there, so I would think and pray.

One of the things I thought most about was witnessing. That's why I was there—to witness. It had to mean something besides giving out tracts, speaking to people in gas stations, going from door to door. Those were perfectly valid activities, but the application seemed too limited. One day I found a verse which altered my understanding. " 'My witnesses,' says the Lord, 'are you, my servants, you whom I have chosen' "—for what? To talk about him? To make other people believe? That isn't what this verse says. "I have chosen you to know me and put your trust in me and understand that I am he."

I realized that night in the jungle that I had been chosen to know God. There are two things that make a witness. First of all you have to know something. Then you have to give evidence. God's witnesses know him, put faith in him, understand who he is. In his first letter John says, "We are writing to you about something which has always existed, yet which we ourselves actually saw and heard, something which we had opportunity to observe closely and even to hold in our hands, and yet, as we know now, was something of the very Word of Life himself." John knew what he was talking about.

What are we talking about? Whom are we talking about? We have got to know him. Jesus made it very clear that there is only one route to that knowledge: obedience. "If a man loves me, he obeys me, and I will make myself known to him."

You must know him. You must see him. You must hear his words. That qualifies you as a witness, just as seeing an accident at a street corner makes you a witness. Then what does a witness do? You might be called into court to testify. Leviticus 5 says, "If a person hears a solemn adjuration to give evidence as a witness to something he has seen or heard and does not declare what he knows, he commits a sin and must accept responsibility" (v. 1). John the Baptist came, the Gospel tells us, to witness to the Light. He was not the Light. He came to give evidence. Another faithful witness was Christ himself. By everything he said or did he gave evidence; he was evidence of what the Father was like. He spoke only what he heard the Father say.

Many years ago there were two Inga Indian brothers living on the Putumayo River in Colombia. One day a man came along in a little canoe, stopped, spoke what he said were the words of God and paddled away. A couple of years later the brothers moved on to another river where they could build new houses and find virgin jungle for planting. One day along came the little canoe with the same man who spoke the words of God.

"We know you," they said. "You are Miguel."

"Yes," he said, and told them the same message again, stayed a few days with them and paddled away.

Later they moved back to the Putumayo River and one day, when the new farm was cleared and planted, along came the canoe a third time with the same man in it, an old man by this time, but still faithfully plying the jungle rivers with his message. A witness, simply telling people what he knew. This time, the brothers believed what he said and were baptized.

Katherine Morgan, a widow in her seventies, recently journeyed down that river to a clearing where people were waiting to hear her message. They even had cedar benches with backs to them, a real table and a 500-watt gasoline lantern. Know who they were? The group of believers begun by the two brothers. Miguel, Katherine told me in her letter, knows not one word of Inga, but has won hundreds of these people for Christ.

A witness speaks. His witness is his word. But it is also his life. Witness is action. It makes truth visible. You remember how God instructed Moses to make a particular kind of tent in the wilderness and gave him specific details about dimensions, materials and furnishings, even down to the silver hooks, the bronze pegs and the colors of the embroidery on the waistband of the priests' vestments. Do you know why God did this? It was to make truth visible. It was to give the people tangible evidence of intangible verities. It was a form, designed to hold a special content. The shape of truth. What you do witnesses to what you believe. It gives shape to it. Your life (what people see) is like the tabernacle in the wilderness.

"These very actions which I do," Jesus said, "are my witness that the Father hath sent me. . . . If you cannot believe what I say, believe what I do."

The disciples observed Jesus' actions and saw the manifestation of Truth, the Word made flesh, visible and comprehensible. Then, when it was time for the disciples to take over where he left off, he promised them the one thing that distinguishes God's witnesses from all the rest. He said they would receive power. The process has been the same ever since: we see him, we are given power, we become witnesses. It is our responsibility in that power to make the truth visible, to give form and shape to the message entrusted to us.

Let's look at some of those mentioned in Hebrews who did just that. There was Noah. What an assignment he had—to build that huge boat, of an unheard-of size and shape, on dry land where there wasn't the smallest chance of ever hauling it to any place where it could float. Imagine what the neighbors thought: Poor old Noah. He's gone bananas. But he kept his cool. The account says he built the boat reverently. It also says his action "condemned the unbelief of the rest of the world." That's one of the things a faithful witness does.

What about Abraham? His name is on the list for several reasons, one of them being his willingness to make a human sacrifice. It was the very son through whom God was to fulfill his tremendous promise that God was now asking him to offer up. Imagine the silent journey up the mountain: the old man who had gotten up early in the morning to obey God, the donkey carrying the load of wood, the boy, perhaps ten or twelve years old, and the two servants. When the father and son had left the servants behind, the boy spoke at last.

"Father."

"What is it, my son?"

"Here are the fire and the wood, but where is the animal for sacrifice?"

"God will provide it."

And they went on in silence. In silence too, I imagine, they set about building an alter and arranging the wood. You know what happened next? The Bible says Abraham bound his son and laid him on top of the wood. I wonder if either of them said anything. I try and try to visualize that scene in the lonely spot on the mountain in the wilderness: the father who has known God's leading through so many vicissitudes, in a desperate conflict of desire to be a faithful son to his heavenly Father and a faithful father to his earthly son. I picture not only the life-and-death struggle on the mountaintop but also the throngs of angelic beings, poised, attentive, leaning, as it were, in breathless stillness over that scene. Isaac, helpless and incredulous, looks at his father. The angels wait for the old patriarch's decision. Is his trust in God strong enough to enable him actually to slit the

boy's throat? Will he by his obedience witness to belief or by disobedience to unbelief? The decision matters infinitely—not
only to the old man and the boy, not only to God who gave the
command, not only to the cloud of witnesses who watched, but
to all the world for all time. It matters to you and me.

They wait. Abraham stretches out his hand. His fingers close
around the hilt of the knife. Suddenly the voice of the angel of
the Lord, "Abraham!"

"Here I am."

"Don't touch him. Now I know that you are a God-fearing
man. You have not withheld from me your son. All nations on
earth shall pray to be blessed as your descendants are blessed,
and this because you have obeyed me." Abraham gave un-
equivocal witness to his belief.

Witnessing means obedience. Every time you do what God
says to do or refuse to do what he says not to do you witness—
you give evidence—to the truth. And of course, that's very risky
business. You're likely to be arrested, Jesus predicted, handed
over to prison, brought before governors and kings "for my
name's sake. This will be your chance to witness for me. You
will be betrayed.... Some of you will be killed." Solzhenitsyn,
Dietrich Bonhoeffer, Corrie Ten Boom and thousands of others
know what he meant. They also understood what he said next:
"Hold on, and you will win your souls. In the world you'll have
tribulation, but cheer up, I have overcome the world."

Witnessing conquers the world. But it doesn't exempt you
from suffering.

Daniel was a man who was willing to stand up and be
counted. His witness was so pure that jealous ministers and
satraps knew they would never find any charge against him unless they could find one in his religion. They found it. He was a
praying man, and when he heard the decree that he was to quit
praying, he decided to be judicious and say his prayers on the
golf course with his eyes open. Is that what it says? No. Daniel
knelt by his window facing Jerusalem three times a day, exactly
as he had always done, and of course they got him. The king
gave the order and Daniel was hurled into a pit of hungry lions.

The king had a very bad night—couldn't eat, couldn't sleep,

couldn't even enjoy his harem. But Daniel had a wonderful night. The lions were there, but so was the angel of God. "No trace of injury was found on him," the story says, "because he had put his faith in God." God didn't keep him out of the pit. He went into it with him.

The world says, "What is faith? Show us." Daniel showed us.

Daniel's three friends, Shadrach, Meshach and Abed-nego, were witnesses too. They refused to bow to any heathen image and, when the king asked if they thought their God could save them, they said that he could if he wanted to, but if not, "be it known to your majesty that we will neither serve your God nor worship the golden image which you have set up." The evidence they gave the king was quite simply a matter of life or death. The three men went into the flames, but Somebody was there first. Somebody who, according to the astonished king, looked like a god. The men came out of the blaze without so much as the smell of fire about them.

What they said hadn't had much effect on Nebuchadnezzar. It was what they did that was irrefutable. "Blessed is the God of Shadrach, Meshach, and Abed-nego," the king said, "who has sent his angel to save his servants who put their trust in him, who disobeyed the royal command and were willing to yield themselves to fire rather than to serve or worship any god other than their own God." That's witness. Even if they had been burned to a cinder, the king would have seen absolute trust in action. As the story goes, it took a lot more than the three witnesses to change his heart, but that was God's business. The men were faithful. Don't forget that when you're tempted to wonder what good it does to speak the word or to pay the price of obedience.

Witness enables others to see what they could not otherwise have seen. It changes the picture. Think of Stephen. He never minced any words. Standing before the highest civil and religious court of the Jewish nation, called the Sanhedrin, he witnessed. He spoke the plain truth about Israel's history: "You obstinate people, heathen in your thinking, heathen in the way you are listening to me now, it's always the same. You never fail to resist the Holy Spirit. You who have received the law of God miraculously by the hand of angels, you are the men who have disobeyed it!"

If miracles didn't persuade them, what would Stephen's defense do? I'll tell you what it did: they ground their teeth at him in a rage and stoned him to death. But while the rocks were flying, Stephen saw something. He saw heaven opened, he saw the glory of God and Jesus himself standing at his right hand. That's witness. It conquers the world. It makes truth visible. It changes the picture. When we see Stephen, we see not the fury of the religious Jews, not the rain of stones falling on his head, but a man beholding the Lord. Faith stands in the midst of suffering and sees glory. The church is here not to deliver us from suffering—and I believe you young men and women will be called to suffer. The church will not deliver you from it, but will make witnesses, those who see beyond things like an ark, a sacrifice, a lion's den, a furnace, those who see the promises of God, the angel in the lion's den, the Son of man in the flames, Jesus standing up to welcome his beloved Stephen.

A witness clarifies alternatives. Last October Pope John Paul II, pressed to slacken the rule against the ordination of women, beleaguered by women who preach a spurious doctrine of freedom, clarified the alternatives. Faithful to the gospel, he replied simply that the issue was not one of human rights but of the will of God.

In a suburb of Moscow lives a priest named Dmitri Dudko who holds dialogues every Sunday in his church. It is a very dangerous thing to speak out for Christ in Russia today, and people come and put to him all kinds of hard questions—Is it all right, for example, to emigrate to the West? "When you run away from difficulties," Father Dudko replied, "you run away from Christ's cross." Somebody asked why God had to be crucified, when God should be all-powerful. "You have a modern understanding of power, force, the thunder of artillery. But our God is a God of love, and he chose the cross as the weapon of our salvation," the priest said. "One must choose either the kingdom of God or absurdity." It's a contemporary Russian who says this. Hear his witness. He clarifies the issue for us.

A witness also forces people to face the truth about themselves. George MacDonald told the story of a great red stag that lived in The Highlands of Scotland. He was the pride of every man in the glen, the mascot of the clan and no one dreamed of killing him. But one night when the moon, the snow and the mountains all lay dreaming awake, a visitor from the city, bent on carrying back some trophy to prove his hunting skill to his friends, came upon the beautiful animal silhouetted in the moonlight against the mountain and shot him through the heart. The stag leaped high in the air, fell with his head under him and broke his neck.

When the chief of the clan, named Alistair, heard the shot, rage filled his heart, and he came down the ridge like an avalanche. He gazed speechless at the slaughtered creature, then confronted the city man with the charge of illegal poaching and killing an animal greatly loved and revered by his clan.

"Why the deuce didn't you keep the precious monster in a paddock and let people know him for a tame animal?" the city man sneered.

"He was no tame animal," answered the chief. "He as well as I would have preferred the death you have given him to such a fate."

Alistair went to his brother Ian, his heart bursting with indignation. When he had told the story, his brother said, "You must send him the head, Alistair."

Send the antlers of the great stag to that vile enemy who sent out into the deep the joyous soul of the fierce bare mountains? Alistair fought with himself all night till morning broke. Could this thing be his duty? How frightfully would such an action be misunderstood by such a man! Why should he move to please him?

Suddenly Alistair remembered questioning Ian one day about the meaning of Jesus' words, "Whosoever shall smite thee on thy right cheek, turn to him the other also."

"There are many things—arithmetic is one of them," Ian had said, "which can be understood only in the doing of them."

"But how can I do a thing without understanding it?"

"When you have an opportunity of doing this very thing, do it and see what will follow."

Alistair saw that there lay at his door a thing calling out to be done. "Even if I be in the right," he thought, "I have a right to yield my right and to Jesus Christ I yield it. It cannot hurt the stag. It only hurts my pride, and I owe my pride nothing. The man shall have the head."

Thereupon rushed into his heart the joy of giving up, of deliverance from self. That's witness.

The theme of Urbana 79 is "that all nations might believe and obey Jesus Christ." How can they believe? Somebody has to make the truth visible to them. Somebody has to give evidence.

Is there anybody here who knows God? You'd be glad to raise your hands this morning and be counted. But suppose your answer would send you off to the Gulag Archipelago? Suppose it meant the sacrifice of the most precious thing in your life? or a lion's den? a blazing furnace? a shower of rocks? an Auca spear in your back?

There's an amazing word at the end of the chapter in Hebrews. "It was not God's plan that they should reach perfection without us." Noah, Abraham, Daniel and his friends, Stephen, the five missionaries in Ecuador—they won't reach perfection *without us*? That's what it says. So what are we supposed to do? The book tells us.

"Surrounded then as we are by these serried ranks of witnesses, let us strip off everything that hinders us as well as the sin that dogs our feet and let us run the race that we have to run with patience, our eyes fixed on Jesus, the source and the goal of our faith."

The race *we* have to run. Not Noah's or Abraham's. You're a student, God isn't asking you to build an ark or tie your son down on an altar. He chooses different tests. He writes different exams for each of us, exactly suited to prove the quality of our faith. If to be his witness means for you flunking a course because you refuse to cheat the way everybody else is doing, if it means losing money because you're conscientious about paying your income tax when you know nobody's going to know about that job you did or those tips you collected, if it means refusing any and all sexual activity until you're married and looking like a freak or a square or a nerd—will you do it for Christ's sake?

Strip off what hinders you, the verse says. You know what it is that hinders—fear, perhaps? of what? suffering? embarrassment? missing out on the fun? What is the "sin that dogs our feet"? gluttony? irresponsibility? procrastination? plain old selfishness? Make your own list, then start stripping it off. Get rid of it. Run your race, eyes fixed on the source and goal, Jesus, who endured a cross.

Remember these serried ranks of witnesses that surround us. Remember that they're cheering for you. Remember the word that was made so powerful to me back there in that thatched house: "My witnesses," says the Lord, "are you, my servants, you whom I have chosen to know me and put your faith in me and understand that I am he."

I would not be truthful if I did not admit that the price of knowing him, of putting faith in him and of understanding who he is has sometimes seemed high to me. I've often felt like St. Theresa who said to God, "If this is the way you treat your friends, no wonder you have so few!" But neither would I be a faithful witness if I did not also say that it's worth the price— it's infinitely worth the price—and that God will never fail you.

Jim Elliot once prayed, "God, light these idle sticks of my life and let me burn out for thee." He got the idea from a poem in *Toward Jerusalem* by Amy Carmichael, given to us on my graduation from college. It has been my prayer for myself. I give it to you this morning so that you can make it your prayer:

From prayer that asks that I may be
Sheltered from winds that beat on Thee,
From fearing when I should aspire,
From faltering when I should climb higher,
From silken self, O Captain, free
Thy soldier who would follow Thee.

From subtle love of softening things,
From easy choices, weakening,
Not thus are spirits fortified,
Not this way went the Crucified,
From all that dims Thy calvary,

O Lamb of God, deliver me.

Give me the love that leads the way,
The Faith that nothing can dismay
The hope no disappointments tire,
The passion that will burn like fire,
Let me not sink to be a clod.
Make me Thy fuel, Flame of God.[1]

Notes
[1]Taken from copyrighted material used by permission of the Christian Literature Crusade, Fort Washington, Pa. 19034.

12
That City Dwellers Might Believe and Obey

Michael E. Haynes

It is a privilege and challenge for me to be invited to share and participate in Urbana 79. This is my third Urbana in four vital, world-changing decades.

You, undoubtedly, like I, have come here to this vast community of academia—strategically located in the symbolic center of this great country—hopefully to hear, consider and respond to "thus saith the Lord God" for your life in these changing and precarious times.

My assignment in this hour is to present the message and the burden which almighty God has laid on my heart for the cities of America and even, yes, the cities of the world.

I come before you in humility and love—grateful and rejoicing that the God of creation, in his infinite wisdom, grace and providence did, one day, confront, captivate, conquer, change and, ultimately, consecrate my life to his service—as an Afro-American, born to a welfare family in the heart of the Roxbury district of Boston, a low income, urban metropolis of Northeast America, USA.

I pray that our Lord will use me to challenge not only individual students to an understanding of the urgency of the urban call, but also the corporate body of Christ and those who have been given the grave responsibility to be its leaders in this age of the eighties.

Because a small, very significant and spiritually powerful Bible college was located in metropolitan Boston, and because this school granted an opportunity for academic training to this somewhat academically inadequate (thanks to the negligence of the city of Boston public school system) city lad, the Christ who had called me to himself for the blessings of redemption, made me a prince, gave me a further and distinct call to go forth and proclaim his salvation even to the ends of the earth.

Berkshire Christian College was my Arabia of contemplation, orientation, preparation and consecration.

It was while a student in college that my mind was led by God to respond to an opportunity for God's worldwide mission —yes, even in the Orient. So, in 1948 I took my longest trip in the United States—hitchhiking from Boston to Chicago to Urbana.

I can recall the stirring congregational singing of Urbana 48 led by Homer Hammontree. I was lifted and moved as I heard the key address given by the young leader of Youth for Christ, Billy Graham.

I came to Urbana as a black city lad, wrestling to clearly ascertain God's will for my individual life. I had an urgent, overpowering sense that he was leading me to a foreign mission field. God seemed to confirm that at Urbana 48 through messages and Bible studies here on this campus.

I did not know as clearly then, but I know so well now, that God brought me to Urbana 48 to receive a special, person-to-person, highly confidential, direction-changing message just for Michael E. Haynes. Today God may well have a highly confidential, direction-changing message just for you.

I left Urbana with many serious ethnic, political and philosophical problems nagging my mind. But, praise God, I left

Urbana convinced that this streetwise, hep lad from the city had been called of God to go out, like Abraham, to a place I could not adequately then perceive nor comprehend. At Urbana 48 God gave me an inner peace which assured me that he could and would use even me in his worldwide mission. Today, I humbly testify that I think he has. So, in fear and trepidation, overcome by love, faith and assurance, I said, "Yes, Lord, I'll go where you want me to go." That is an awesome commitment to make to the God of the universe!

Very soon after this 1948 commitment to the Lord's service, the scenario drastically changed. The international scene changed. Revolution struck China. Its mission doors shut quickly, dramatically and very tightly.

My dilemma was then, "Lord, where are you leading me?!"

After a further period of seminary study, I became engaged in a mission of youth evangelism. I served and supplied in mostly white evangelical churches, some urban, but mostly suburban and rural.

I spent most of my time in the towns, hamlets and villages of New England, upstate New York and the Canadian Northeast.

Personally, I was somewhat glad to escape the noise, tension, clutter, racism, deterioration and pressure of my natural urban habitat for the small quiet towns where I became seemingly comfortable and seemingly well accepted.

But then, unknown to me, in the words of the black spiritual, "my Lord [was] getting me ready for that great day!"

I soon received a very direct, distinct, challenging call in the early fifties—to "come on home to Roxbury!" Come on home! Come home to rapid physical deterioration, to "teeming masses yearning to breathe free," to rampant poverty, "to multitudes in the valley of decision." God knew that there was precious gold in the Roxbury hills!

Friends in Christ, I come to you this day as a living example in dazzling beautiful color to proclaim that God revealed distinctly to me that he has a special love and a very special concern and plan for the cities of America which when implemented can ripple over to the key cities and suburbs and rural areas of this world, making many souls ready and qualified for eternal citizenship in an everlasting just, equitable and harmonious society!

Urbana 79! I declare to you on the authority of God's Word, that at this time in history, God has placed *urban America*—the city dwellers of this nation—as priority number one on his agenda. This gospel must again be proclaimed not only in rhetoric but in courageous deeds of love in urban America showing forth a living, redeeming Christ!

I declare to you loud and clear, that the *cities* of America *are pivotal! They must be given priority*—priority number one!

Jesus Christ, who in his earthly ministry had spent so much time loving, studying, watching, preaching, healing and proclaiming the way to new life in Jerusalem, sent this city dweller on a very circuitous path in order to call me and prepare me for my Jerusalem—yea, even my Nazareth—a ministry in Megalopolis, USA.

Beyond my wildest dreams, desires or expectations, the Lord picked me up, turned me around and placed me smack-dab right in the middle of my own home town, the place of my birth, urban America, USA, the heart of Roxbury, the megalopolis of which Boston—the Athens of America—is the core.

Right in the middle of this so very troubled and tense city, the Lord has placed me, his child, his prince, his servant to become a part of "Caesar's household," and stand deep in the political hub, even in elected office; to become a vital part of the social and human welfare authority; and top level part of the criminal justice system. God placed me dead in the center, at the raw nerves and fiber of the religious world. In so doing the Lord has said, show my love to these my people! Hear the cry of these my people and try to help them! See the political and economic bondage of these my people, and help set them free! And above all, see the spiritual death of these my people and proclaim to them "the acceptable year of the Lord!" Tell them that Jesus is mighty to save!

God, in his infinite wisdom, called me to urban America because it is locked in bondage and sin at high exclusive places of the social aristocracy and down to the often inarticulate and sometimes understandably rebellious and revolutionary masses.

When God assigned me to pivotal Roxbury, USA, the white upper and middle class had just about completely deserted the city. Even Bible-believing institutions had gone, leaving behind tired sanctuaries and buildings which poor but determined groups of newcomers would purchase through exorbitant mortgages.

Poor minority brothers and sisters in Jesus Christ bearing such urbanistic names as African Methodist Episcopal, AME Zion, Apostolic Faith, Church of God in Christ, Missionary Baptist and a host of others became the new religious urban vanguard. They were to be followed by waves of Spanish-speaking Pentecostal assemblies, French-speaking Haitian believers and other similar modern immigrant groups.

While the established church and religious institutions—portfolios, endowments and property-sale-profits in their hands—fled the so-called urban blight to find open space, build colossal, expansive modern structures, rehab Victorian mansions amidst lakes, streams, hills, trees and the beauty of nature, God called me to come home and lift up a blood-bought standard in the name of the divine, resurrected and living Jesus Christ who loved and prioritized the city!

The cities were left to die! Masses of hopeless people had come! Good people had to flee, so they said.

The word *city* became synonymous with poverty, racism, violence, welfare, unwed mothers, abortions, prostitution, hookers, pimps and drugs.

The familiar language and behavior of the city was expressed in such words and terms as: "dime bags," "coke," "shooting galleries," muggings, stolen cars, rent supplement, pocketbook snatching and rapes.

The city became identified with demonstrations, sit-ins, pray-ins, police clubs, courts, vicious attack dogs, abandoned houses street after street and block after block, and complex, inadequate, crime-breeding, unmanageable housing projects. The city became security guards, metal window grills, storefronts and busing, high prices, poor quality goods, red-lining, religious charlatans, racketeering faith healers, prisons and more prisons, murders and more murders, violence and more violence amidst dirt, decay, congestion and exploitation of humans by other humans.

The city was dying! It was just about dead.

God seemingly had "removed his hand" from the city. No good thing could come out of Nazareth! No good thing could come out of Roxbury! No good thing could come out of the city!

Sin had cursed the city! It was dark, evil and hopeless. It was dangerous, demented and volatile. Was there any hope for the city? Would my Jesus dare walk the backwaters, the alleys, the marketplace of the high-rise projects of the city? Could Jesus still save in urban America? Could Jesus still save in the cities of America?

How many so-called responsible people declared the city as contagious and dying and off limits? "Call me anywhere Lord— but please don't call me to center city, USA!" That's how many Bible-believing Christians reacted and responded.

How many so-called responsible people declared the city as contagiously dying and off limits? How many Bible-believing Christians called the city dying and off limits?

How very vivid in my mind are the details of the true story of a beautiful Christian brother who happened to be white and from the Southland.

Hank was a student at a local Christian college. He had violated cultural mores as a Christian and an athlete when, against the wishes of his fiancée and family, he had established a deep, genuine and healthy friendship with a black classmate —visiting his home, entering his social world, worshiping in his church and inviting his black friend to do the same. He developed a burden for the city.

One day Hank asked me if he could be allowed to do his senior year Christian service internship in Roxbury at the church I pastored. I joyfully and prayerfully told him, "Sure Hank, if it is the will of God."

A whole negative, carnal chain reaction followed. His girl emphatically opposed him. His parents opposed him and from long distance called his dean to support their opposition.

"Those people are not like you!" "It's dangerous in the city." On and on the weak, rationalistic excuses flowed. But Hank had heard and loved the Lord of the city. He knew and had seen the Lord walking in Roxbury! He had talked with his Lord right in Roxbury. He had seen the Lord—the same Lord who had saved him—emanating from the lives of black people, brown people, elderly and poor whites, even red people right in the old city. So Hank followed his Lord to the city. The Lord used him— white, Southerner, athlete, tactful, consecrated—to work with a team of black-led youth workers. He was not paternalistic. He was not patronizing. He was willing to follow, to be a yoke- fellow in the city for the Lord Jesus Christ. The people in the city didn't see Hank. They didn't see his whiteness. They saw Christ. Through Hank souls were saved, lives lifted, good- will established. Hank discovered that beneath the poverty, customs and decadence of my city there was raw, precious gold —just waiting to be mined. He found out that there were rare diamonds just waiting to be dug out. He discovered that under the stratas of difference and need there were treasures for the eternal kingdom of God, just waiting to be unearthed.

Hank discovered what Jesus knew: that the societal gathering place of the poor masses of this country and other countries was a spot dear to the heart of God! Jesus loved the city for its dwellers' sakes! He even wept for them! And he beheld the city and he wept—for three decades.

For three decades the inner city of urban America has been stricken from a place of top priority on the agenda of evangelical Christianity. It has wrongly been advertised as being less impor- tant on the church's agenda of mission work as compared with so-called foreign or international ministries. In most instances American cities could only gain a minor, incidental, tokenistic, low priority, so-called home missions gesture!

John F. Kennedy, the thirty-fifth president of the United States, touched on a most significant national issue. During his campaign and the transitional period after his election and throughout his short tenure in office, through executive, legis- lative and voter initiative, he sought to bring about a new, most significant cabinet post with first-class political clout! He recog- nized the overwhelming demands of a changing American so- ciety, a shift of focus to the key cities.

He did not live to see this vision fulfilled. His successor, Lyndon B. Johnson, had the historic and significant all-American privilege of instituting the new secretariat of housing and urban development. Further, in an unprecedented, bold action, he appointed a black, Harvard graduate, the grandson of slaves, Robert Weaver, to fill that vital post.

President Kennedy and a host of other perceptive, prophetic, political scholars realized the vital importance of the city to the overall health and future of the nation.

As goes the city—so goes the nation! As goes the city—so goes the world!

It is in the city that most vital operations and institutions of government, finance, business, banks, insurance, education, medicine and communications exist.

It is in the key cities of our nation and the world that we see great cross-sections of God's special human creation gathering and struggling to survive. These cosmopolitan motifs of cross-culture are potentially symbolic of the universal kingdom of our God and of his Christ, for the reign of whom our hearts so deeply yearn.

What is more beautiful than entering any open marketplace of center city, USA, and observing red, yellow, black and white people crisscrossing, intermingling and sharing life together. How much more beautiful it is to see such a body gathered together around the table of Jesus the Christ, then moving out into the world as one body in Christ, lifting his name in this world. How beautiful it is to see the community of believers together. I got a sense of this the Sunday after Thanksgiving when I had the privilege again to attend All Souls Church in Langham Place in London. I was able to sit and sense the universality of the church of Jesus Christ and to see blacks and whites, people of all languages and all colors coming together in the body of Jesus Christ in the middle of London.

Jesus knew the sin of the city. But he also knew that "where sin abounded, grace did much more abound" (Rom. 5:20 KJV).

God assigned me to center city, USA. In a little more than a decade, I have seen God marvelously at work. He took one of the oldest black Baptist congregations in the nation (organized in

1804), steeped in a dying theological liberalism, stifled by a form and fashion of cold traditionalism, bound by a rootless veneer of religious practices, closed for almost a hundred sixty hours a week, dying, empty, impotent, with no testimony of a living Christ. God, through a dynamic, demanding, durable Christ, brought new life to that fellowship in the center of the city, Roxbury, Massachusetts. Twenty-two representatives of that church in the city, assisted by a suburban church, have been able to come to Urbana 79.

God allowed me to see this ministry serve the felt needs of needy people in the inner-city community. I had the responsibility and opportunity to help point them to the divine Christ. This work became a seven-day-a-week, fourteen-hour-a-day center of Christian service and witness to all kinds of people.

Senior citizens, black and white, Muslims, Episcopalians, Catholics and the unchurched are served in a community outreach program ministered by committed Christians.

Karate classes, sewing classes, an inner-city minority ministerial training program sponsored by a leading seminary, an indigenous lay school of the Bible, daily and weekly social, recreational and spiritual programs for all ages, referral services, a vital social-action ministry which commands the attention of government officials and holds them accountable—an innovative array of programs given by the Holy Spirit in Boston, Massachusetts, to be used as a part of God's worldwide mission so that city dwellers can know and receive Jesus as Christ.

Now in key cities of America we witness a new phenomena. Some call it gentrification: the return to the inner city of young, educated, upwardly mobile, aristocratic whites and upper-class types. The politicians and the bankers have supported and joined this trend. They have rethought and re-evaluated. They are a part of a new, fast-moving trend to recapture and reclaim the inner city—almost at whatever means possible, even exploitation and/or oppression of the powerless and poor. They know the unique significance and value of the city.

But the churches of the living Christ should reclaim the city for Jesus Christ!

It was the great Afro-American Booker T. Washington who

said, "Drop your buckets where you are!" I call the Christian
establishment to see and behold our Lord as he walks through
and weeps over the core cities of America. I call upon you students to hear the call of God to this important battleground
against sin and Satan—urban America.

I adjure you, in Jesus' name, to personally confer with the
God of creation! Ask him, through the Holy Spirit, to illuminate
the challenge of central city, USA, and show you what your role
should be!

As Jesus approached and beheld the city he wept over it
(Lk. 19:41)! He saw huddled masses, black, poor white, Hispanic, native Americans, Orientals, refugees, the angry poor, the
disenfranchised, the unloved, the hungry, the hated and the
despised. For them he left his kingly throne, came to earth,
suffered, bled, died and rose again. Now Jesus lives and walks
today through the cities of America and the cities of the world!

Jesus lives today and he walks today, from Boston to Balti-
more, New York to Newark, Philadelphia to Port-of-Spain, Los
Angeles to London, Kinshasa to Kansas City, Nairobi to New
Orleans, Bridgetown to Buenos Aires, Pittsburgh to Paris,
Caracas to Calcutta, Jakarta to Jerusalem.

Where cross the crowded ways of life,
Where sound the cries of race and clan,
Above the noise of selfish strife,
We hear Thy voice, O Son of Man!

O Master, from the mountain side,
Make haste to heal these hearts of pain,
Among these restless throngs abide,
O tread the city's streets again.
    (Frank Mason North)

I submit to you this day that Jesus Christ, the sovereign Lord
of the universe, has declared and willed that city dwellers shall
hear and believe the message of the gospel of eternal life. God
this day may be directly calling you to personally covenant with
him in a partnership to fulfill the most exciting, yet demanding

and critical, mission of the church of Jesus Christ in this age and for the 1980s right in center city, urban America, USA.

Brothers and sisters in Jesus Christ, our Lord is waiting for you to walk and work the city streets with him in a divine mission for redemption. Would you be willing to go to the city?

13
That Rural Peoples Might Believe and Obey

Gregorio Landero

It is a great privilege to be here today. I am aware that I am not here as a professional in some subjects. I have just come as a friend, as a brother who wants to share with you blessings that I have found in God's Word. I know that my presence here is a gift of God to me. It is something that I don't deserve, but we are here this morning for God's glory.

The subject I have been assigned is very important: that the rural peoples might believe and obey God. I want to tell you that there are eleven churches in Colombia that have agreed to pray for this conference. And I am sure God has many people here that he is calling to the mission field.

Let me tell you about the rural people I serve by describing for you a typical scene:

I arrived at a home surrounded by fruit trees and hills; I saw a thatched hut. Five dogs, in bad physical condition, came out to greet me. A barefoot, disheveled woman came out to the patio with a naked baby on her hip. She shouted at the dogs, and said to me, "Sit down, sir." The next moment a hen flew to where the rice had been put out in the sun to dry, spilling it all over the floor. She shouted again to scare the chicken, and tried to pick up the rice.

I said, "Let me help you." Right away I began to pick up rice.

She called out to Fransisco, telling him to come out. I continued my task. When I turned toward her, I saw two children trying to hide under her skirts; she couldn't move. Soon I heard a voice, "Friend, how are you?"

"Fine, thanks, Fransisco, my friend."

"What can I do for you?"

"I was just passing by, and wanted to meet you. When I heard you use the word 'friend' I remembered that Jesus used that word too. He said, 'You are my friends if you do what I command.' I want to be a real friend to you, Fransisco."

He said, "I'm too busy to talk about these things."

"That may be true, but you should hear more about your friend Jesus."

We continued with our talks. Later on he accepted Christ as his Savior. Fransisco represents the rural people that I'm going to talk about.

We are convinced that all anthropology and all sociology depends upon christology.

God created human beings as man and woman in his image. As such, he gave them their characteristically human faculties: rational, moral, social, creative and spiritual. He also ordained that they should bear children, fill the earth and subdue it, and he gave them lordship over all other living things (Gen. 1:26-28).

These divine commandments constitute the origin of the rural people's identity. According to the measure by which we employ our creative faculties to obey God's commandments, we glorify him, serve others and fulfill part of our destiny on earth.

But we are fallen beings, dead in our failings and sin; all of our labors are accompanied by sweat and struggle (Gen. 3:17-19). They are distorted by selfishness. As a result not one single aspect of our humanity is perfect in itself; this is why we need a Savior.

According to the Scriptures, God's commandments are centered around the person of Jesus Christ. After the redemption of man through the death of his beloved Son, God charged the redeemed man with the task of watching over his people, the people redeemed through his blood who are to accomplish his purpose.

This can be done in two ways. First, by announcing the good news to all mankind, proclaiming God's decision to save mankind and forgive him through the person and death of his Son Jesus Christ, inasmuch as in him alone we have eternal life and forgiveness of sins. God has provided us with the means to do this through advanced technology. We could utilize means such as: radio, television, planes, helicopters. The explosion of new land vehicles, the many rural roads that now penetrate areas heretofore once forgotten and other vehicles which provide transportation over rivers, seas, lakes and ravines—all these God has placed within our reach.

There is only one problem: the *human* element, men and women whom our Lord redeemed with his blood and to whom he endowed his Spirit. Sometimes we fail by refusing to accomplish the purpose God has given us. But God offers us another opportunity to obey his command, "Go into all the world and preach the gospel to all creation" (Mk. 16:15). This is what I understand as proclamation.

Second, God charged his disciples, the leadership of his church, with the pastoral ministry which, according to my observations, the apostolic writings, the Bible and the Illustrated Spanish Bible Dictionary, means: *to care for*, *nurture* and *protect*. For this reason the Lord said he would bring "shepherds after My own heart" (Jer. 3:15).

The rural person needs to be cared for, protected, taught about his new life in Christ. The rural person depends on the one who instructs him, and he trusts in what he *hears* and *sees* (Gal. 6:6). These are two of the five senses most highly developed by the rural person. For this reason the Bible is so emphatic, so specific in stating exactly the importance of biblical instruction and education—that the rural person might believe and obey God. According to Numbers 27:17 rural people require much atten-

tion. A flock with no shepherd generally perishes. Jesus felt
compassion for and was moved by the multitudes in the countryside who were forsaken and scattered like sheep without a
shepherd (Mt. 9:36). According to this, then, rural people are
ready to listen to and obey the voice of God, but they lack adequate pastoral care.

Characteristics of Rural People

Since a large portion of the Holy Bible is set in a rural, peasant
culture, it reveals the mentality and characteristics of rural
people. Rural people hunger and thirst for justice. Thus they are
open to the message of justice and peace. Rural people are shy,
unskilled in expressing themselves verbally. Jesus compares
them to restless, stubborn sheep, who are ready to obey and follow instructions and be protected. Rural people feel a need to
gather, to unite with others and experience the warmth of being
in a family with others who are unprotected from the threat of
loneliness. They seek life together, an expression of equality.

Rural people are hungry for something that will give them
hope, that will provide a better future. They are eager to demonstrate the sincerity of their hearts and always wait to discover by
actions who truly loves them. But too often they are deceived
and betrayed by strangers who appear to love them but are
traitors of their consciences; who appear to be pious but by ar-
rogantly desiring to dominate and gain power negate the efficacy
of their love. This confuses the rural man and stands in the way
of his coming to Jesus. It is necessary to apply the teaching of
Christ, "Love ... your neighbor as yourself" (Lk. 10:27).

Three questions come to my heart: Have I loved my rural
brother as myself? Have I desired for him the blessing and abun-
dance that I enjoy? Have I given up anything to live equally with
my brother?

According to my observations in the Bible, our Lord prac-
ticed these things in his daily life. This was Jesus' triumph in the
countryside, in the hills of Jerusalem, in the bays of the Sea of
Galilee, in the hamlets along the Jordan River. He loved his rural
brother as himself, giving himself for the good of others, serving
them as a human and loving them as God.

Characteristics of a Messenger

What characteristics should a messenger have? First: in order that rural people might believe and obey God, it is necessary that they be treated as people, as living beings, not as merely lost souls or spirits who do not need human affection.

Second: the evangelist must be aware that these people have just as much understanding as the more privileged city dwellers; they just have not been able to develop their understanding in the same manner as the others. They are people who delight in living within the world God created, cherishing the hope that next year will be better than the last and entrusting their lives in the providence of God that their future will be bright.

Third, in order that rural people might believe and obey God, it is necessary that his messenger clothe himself with the mind of God. This means stripping himself of all he possesses, leaving off becoming what he selfishly wants to be, becoming all that the Lord desires him to be and identifying with the rural man, though not in every particular. As the proverb goes, "In order to milk a cow you have to be willing to get your feet dirty." If we want to win the rural man to Christ we must identify with him.

Our Lord gave us a living model from his great wisdom and with his mind full of desire to save mankind. The Bible tells us that he stripped himself of his glory and made himself equal to lost man and, being a man, he humbled himself before the nations in order to bring us to our heavenly Father. Alleluia! That is why he could say, "Go to all the nations and make disciples."

Let me illustrate this. In a very small rural village there lived a young man, about nineteen years old, who was very indifferent toward religious matters, even the gospel of Jesus Christ. Often pastors, missionaries and other Christian workers who came by itinerating would stay in his home.

But once a missionary by the name of Reed arrived, carrying on his back a bag full of Bibles, tracts and hymnals for sale. After walking many kilometers through three marshes and over mountains, enduring the tropical sun, he arrived in the late afternoon, sweaty, exhausted and almost dehydrated. Half an hour later he was picking up trash on the patio and lighting a fire to burn it. The young man said, "If only to be like this man, I would become a Christian." Later on that young man was converted and traveled with the missionary learning from him for many years.

Today this man has not lost sight of his teacher's example. And I firmly believe that Mr. Reed in becoming a peasant did not cease to be who he really was. In becoming a peasant, he was able to win a peasant to Christ.

I believe that if God's messengers in entering the Lord's work would leave their earthly glory at Calvary to identify with rural people in the uncertainty of life, the horrible fear of death, the hunger, the terrible bodily sufferings and the enormous threat of social insecurity, they would win the rural people to obedience to God. These messengers should also ask themselves the question, "What would Jesus do in this situation?" It comes to mind that he would talk to them about faith in God and believing in his Word. He would give them confidence and security in the person of Jesus, as he did with Peter in John 14:1-2. But I also believe that he would not leave them in their suffering, he would lay his powerful hand on them to heal them and would lift the heavy burden from their defenseless bodies.

I believe with all my heart that hundreds of thousands of people would hear and obey the voice of God through this type of missionary endeavor.

Those fathers, mothers and orphans who suffer from hunger ... I believe that our Lord would do something to help them, even though the Pharisees should say that the people were seeking for bread and not following him just because they love him. I know that Jesus would do what he had to do, just as he multiplied the loaves and fishes and provided food for thousands. The apostle Paul later found himself in the same dilemma and looked for a solution. He gave instructions and urged believers to attend to their own business and work with their hands (1 Thess. 4:11-12).

I also believe that Jesus would identify with the precarious situation, with the living conditions of this underprivileged people and would provide them with guidance and wise counsel. If we believe this and believe that this is what our Lord would do, it is what we should do as God's messengers, pastors, leaders in the labor of the Lord. I know both from experience and from what I've read that during the past twenty years, the church of our Lord Jesus Christ has been equipped with good preachers, good Bible expositors and many doctors of theology. I thank God for this. But what I do not hear about or see very often, is the pastoral work—that labor of love, that incarnation, that penetration, that getting involved in the life of the rural people to save them, instruct them, equip them for every good work (2 Tim. 3:16).

So that rural people might believe and obey God, we must invest time in them. I believe that the missions agencies, ruling practices, church programs, the automation of life and the so-called communicating by correspondence do not take into account the value of dedicating personal time so that rural people may understand what it means to obey God. The rural man can raise his hand many times and fill out many decision cards, but this only means that he agrees with what I have said or preached. What is more important to him is that he in his personal dialog with God is able to receive answers to the anxieties and fears, that he is able to read the holy Scriptures with his teacher, receiving the message and application to his own life. To do this we must forget our watches, our lunch hours and even our families for a while.

One day the Lord led me to a rural church where I had an invitation to be with them for Saturday and Sunday. I spoke to them till noon about God's Word, and we rejoiced. At 2 p.m. I left to try to catch a bus, to arrive at home that evening and be at the office Monday morning. I came across a brother who was waiting for me. With his head lowered, he said, "Brother Landero, I would like for you to listen to me for a moment. I came here because I didn't have the time or the opportunity to see you either at church or in the house you stayed in."

I asked him, "What's wrong, brother? Tell me about it." I thought I would spend thirty minutes with him and then start home, but it did not happen like that.

He said, "Brother, I don't understand the Bible, and there are many passages that don't seem to make sense. So I've decided to return to my past life, to be condemned like anyone else, because I don't feel any peace." He began to sob.

I said, "Don't worry, there's a lot in the Bible that I don't understand either, but with the things God *has* made me understand, I know enough to serve him."

We sat on a tree trunk on the ground until 6:30 p.m., until God forgave him and the Holy Spirit gave him light and understanding. Praise the Lord! I returned to preach the evening sermon with much joy for what God had done in that man. The rural man needs *time*.

What Is God's Desire?
God desires that the rural people hear him and obey him. When he said, "Go therefore to the main highways, and as many as you find there, invite to the wedding feast" (Mt. 22:9), he showed us his burning desire to involve rural people in the wedding feast.

In these last days of the twentieth century, we need to listen to this command. It is a command, an imperative verb, that God desires to bring to himself all people, created in his image and likeness, to the wedding feast of the Lamb on that final day. To accomplish this, there must be men and women who believe in God, people who have decided to listen to and obey God's call.

14
The Messenger and Mission Societies

Warren W. Webster

Today is Sunday. It probably never occurred to you that while we are meeting here some 200 new Christian churches are being started in various towns, cities and villages around the world. It really has nothing to do with this being Sunday because we expect there will be approximately 200 more new churches started tomorrow, another 200 on Tuesday and again on Wednesday and on into the new year. Every week some 1500-1600 new churches are being started to the glory of God.[1] This is simply the average rate at which the Lord is building his church around the world.

We live in an age when the church of Jesus Christ is more widely planted and more deeply rooted among more people than ever before in history. In the last two hundred years since the rediscovery of mission on the part of evangelical Protestants, the Christian faith has literally exploded around the globe. Missionaries have reached out to virtually every country to make the

Christian faith the largest and the first truly worldwide religion.

The Unfinished Task

But the day of missions is not over! While we are encouraged by the accomplishments of the recent past, there is a great unfinished task that remains. Every country of the world is composed of a vast mosaic of "people groups"—tribes, castes, occupational groupings, language groups, religious groups or combinations of these. One estimate identifies more than 16,000 such people groups within the 230 countries and territories in the world.

While we can find Christians in nearly every politically independent nation on the face of the earth, half of the world's population lives in people groups within which there are no Christians. It is sometimes suggested that if all the Christians of the world could be spiritually renewed and would then reach out in witness to their near neighbors, the whole world would be evangelized. The problem is that half of the people in the world cannot be reached through "near-neighbor" evangelism simply because they have no near Christian neighbors who speak their language and understand their culture so as to communicate the gospel to them. Half of the world's people will be reached with the gospel only if Christians somewhere care enough to cross geographic, ethnic, linguistic and social barriers in order to plant the church throughout the world's vast cultural mosaic. This is the unfinished task of missions, and it challenges Christians on all six continents to be involved.

The Role of Mission Societies

In the process of world evangelization, one means that God has used to spread the gospel and plant churches in nearly every land is that of mission societies.

Before we can talk meaningfully about the role of mission societies in world evangelization, we need to feel comfortable about their existence. What are "mission societies" anyway, and what do they do? Have they arisen primarily because of the failure of local churches and local believers to evangelize, or do they have a special strategic role in God's purposes?

Mission societies are people who have banded together in a commitment to the Lord and to one another to make special efforts to cross cultural frontiers in order to evangelize and disciple those who would not otherwise be reached with the gospel in the normal movements of history and commerce.

Some mission societies are quite small, consisting of a few individuals sent out by one or more groups of believers. Others are quite large, serving as a vehicle for sending and supporting hundreds—even thousands—of missionaries. Some missions are backed by the members of an entire denomination or association of churches; others are church-related but interdenominational. Some missions focus exclusively on one country or continent; others maintain a global outreach. Some specialize in Bible translation, student work, literature or radio evangelism; others are involved in a broad spectrum of ministries needed to establish and develop reproducing churches. Some missions function with a centralized budget or pooled funds; many others utilize some type of personalized support.

But the goal of all is the same: to lead men and women to personal faith in Jesus Christ and then to disciple them as responsible members of the ongoing "church, which is His body" (Eph. 1:22-23).

Sometimes students think that because mission societies don't seem to be mentioned in the Bible maybe we shouldn't have them. Of course, we also find no mention in Scripture of Inter-Varsity chapters, Sunday schools, radio broadcasts, jet planes and many other good things that have proven useful in accomplishing God's purposes. Simply because something cannot be demonstrated in the New Testament does not mean it cannot be justified.

We know from Scripture that it is God's will that people and nations everywhere should be reached with the gospel. And so committed Christians across the centuries have felt free, under the Spirit's guidance, to use their God-given reason and creativity in organizing and using whatever structures are necessary to carry out God's purposes in fulfillment of the Great Commission.

We do have a "model" or "prototype" for the modern missionary movement in the "apostolic bands" of the New Testament. In Acts 13 we read how the first Pauline band was formed in Antioch. A group of spiritual leaders in the Antioch church were led by the Holy Spirit to send missionaries beyond their own community. They obediently released Paul and Barnabas from their local responsibilities and freed them for a ministry that ultimately included other team members and carried the gospel to many parts of the first-century world. In setting Paul and Barnabas free for this work, the Antioch church had a part in launching something new.

While Paul may have thought of Antioch as a home base, "once away from Antioch he seemed very much on his own. The little team he formed was economically self-sufficient when occasion demanded. It was also dependent from time to time not alone upon the Antioch church, but upon other churches that had arisen as a result of evangelistic labors."[2]

In time Paul gathered to himself a band of men that included Silas, Luke, Titus, Timothy and others.

Paul's missionary band increased in numbers as the years went by, and from the data we have it seems that Paul himself functioned as the general director and coordinator. He reported back to Antioch from time to time, just as he reported to Jerusalem and other churches. The church in Philippi most likely was a heavy financial supporter of the mission. But the missionary society was not controlled by Antioch or Jerusalem or Philippi so far as we can determine. The church was the church, and the mission was the mission right from the beginning.[3]

So, early in the New Testament we find embryonic mission structures functioning alongside local church assemblies. The organizational forms of both church and mission were simple, for the New Testament primarily describes first-generation Christianity at a time when the mustard seed of faith had just begun to sprout and spread and had not reached full development. Paul's missionary bands have provided a prototype for subsequent mission organizations through which the Lord's obedient disciples in succeeding generations have endeavored to carry out his Commission.

Lessons from History

Viewed historically, mission societies have contributed significantly to the establishing of churches in virtually every independent nation on the face of the earth. Drawing lessons from the pages of history, Peter Wagner tells us that "the best success in world evangelism has usually come from situations in which the church or churches have permitted, encouraged, and supported the formation of specialized *missionary agencies* to do their missionary work.... Those of our ancestors who inhabited the forests of Northern Europe were largely won to Christ through missionaries working in what is called the monastic movement."[4]

The missionary movement is nothing new. Roman Catholic and Nestorian missionaries were active from around A.D. 500. By the eighth century the Nestorian churches of Mesopotamia were involved in an immense missionary outreach through central Asia as far as India and China. Six hundred years before Protestant missions began, Roman Catholic missionary orders had planted themselves around the globe.

But when Protestant missionary energies were finally unleashed in the eighteenth century, they made great strides toward catching up with earlier mission efforts. Peter Wagner reports: "Once missionary societies gained in strength, wonderful things began to happen. More men and women have been led to Christ and more Christian churches have been planted in the world in the 180 years since William Carey than in the 1800 previous years all put together. Missions are not an afterthought to God. They are an integral part of His plan for 'making disciples of all nations.' "[5]

Christian missions have made an unprecedented impact on history and society. In addition to establishing vigorous churches and Christian communities, missionaries in the past played an important role in the abolition of slavery, cannibalism, infanticide and widow-burning. From the beginning Christian missionaries introduced biblical perspectives on human values, family life and the role of women. They pioneered medical and health services in many lands as their ministries of compassion to orphans, lepers, the sick, the dying and the disadvantaged demonstrated Christian love in action. In India alone missionaries established over 600 hospitals. Missions have led the way in founding schools, colleges, seminaries and universities as well as in promoting adult literacy education. In Korea they established the largest women's university in the world. Missionaries have made important contributions to scholarship in the areas of linguistics, ethnography, comparative religion and many other fields. They have been leaders in translating at least some of the Bible into more than 1600 languages—spoken by more than 97 per cent of the earth's people. This is unquestionably the greatest achievement in language communication which the world has ever known. Missionaries have repeatedly demonstrated the Christian value of human life through administering emergency relief and rehabilitation when war, famine, flood, earthquake, typhoons and other natural disasters have struck. Through agricultural and trade schools missions have been involved in developmental projects to stimulate self-help and self-sufficiency on the part of growing Christian communities.

All this tremendous vitality and diversity has been motivated by the concern that where there are no Christians there should be Christians, and where churches are few in number they should be strengthened and multiplied.

You and Mission Societies

In determining where and how you might go with the gospel to unreached peoples or to another culture, mission societies offer a number of advantages for your consideration:

1. As we have seen, mission societies incorporate basic biblical principles of operation and have proven themselves historically as part of God's plan for this age.

2. Missions are church related. They arise out of churches and, in turn, produce more churches—often where previously there were none. Jesus said, "I will build My church" (Mt. 16:18). This must be our top priority in missions because it was his. It has been said: "The mission of the church is missions; the mission of missions is the church." That is one way of saying that every church and every believer has a missionary

responsibility, and every mission society must be committed to strengthening and multiplying churches. In whatever role or capacity you go abroad, I urge you to be closely and vitally related to at least one church at home for prayerful backing and to some assembly of believers abroad for worship, witness and fellowship.

3. One great advantage of mission organizations is that they free witnesses for full-time ministry and long-term contacts with people. This provides time and opportunity for learning languages and cultures in order to communicate the gospel effectively. It is especially crucial for workers committed to Bible translation or called to witness in primitive and rural areas where self-support is extremely difficult.

4. Missions are able to utilize a broad range of spiritual gifts and abilities committed to the Master's use. Intercristo currently lists some 20,000 openings with mission organizations. There are all the strategic needs you would expect for evangelists and disciplers, for church planters and church development advisers, for Christian education specialists and for teachers in schools, Bible institutes and seminaries. But there are also needs for journalists and printers, agriculturalists and engineers, medical personnel, lab and x-ray technicians, administrators and accountants, secretaries and bookkeepers, youth workers, teachers of English as a second language—and many others.

5. Another advantage of mission agencies is that they assume responsibility for planning, under God and in the light of his Word, as well as for supervising and evaluating progress toward goals set by prayer and faith.

6. Missions supply continuity to the work so it doesn't stop when one person leaves or has to withdraw. They also provide a sense of identity, community and fellowship for witnesses who might otherwise feel very much alone. Spiritual gifts exercised within the body complement one another.

7. Missions have been used of God as a reservoir for revival, keeping truths about the lostness of men, the finality of Christ and the urgency of evangelism uppermost in the life and outreach of the church.

8. Missions place a strong emphasis and dependence upon the power of prayer, the Spirit-filled life, personal evangelism and stewardship of life and resources.

9. Missions are responding with great flexibility and creativity to changing times. They introduced theological education by extension in the past decade and now are experimenting with gospel telecasts via satellites. They are leading the way in short-term programs which make use of the skills and dedication of students and laypeople. Some missions even have programs for liaison with self-supporting workers in secular jobs in order to provide spiritual fellowship and pastoral care where desired.

10. Missions today are instilling in younger churches a vision for developing their own mission structures as sending churches.

One obvious disadvantage of traditional mission societies is that because of their visible profile they are generally prohibited from functioning in so-called closed countries. In such situations the efforts of visiting Christian students, tourists and self-supporting vocational witnesses are especially strategic.

But in view of all the factors involved don't be surprised if the Lord leads many of you to give up what you think is a "normal" means of livelihood in order to follow his direction for your life. Remember Jesus had to leave the carpenter's shop to begin his mission. His earliest disciples left their nets and tax-collecting to follow him. Even Paul left regular tentmaking when he became a missionary. Ralph Winter points out that not all self-supporting roles today are in the same category as the tent-making work which Paul sometimes did.

> First of all, Paul did not go primarily because of the job he had. His secular work was a stop-gap employed only part of the time. Second, he was the absolute owner of his business, an entrepreneur. He was not subject to someone else's office hours, nor to the requirements of an organization in which he had no control. Third, his was a special kind of portable job; he could readily move from one place to another as the work of the gospel required.[6]

Michael Griffiths reminds us that "Paul is more usually called 'the apostle' than 'the tentmaker.' There is little doubt which part of his work has survived the longest."[7]

In assessing the strengths and weaknesses of modern mission agencies, Dr. Ralph Winter of the U. S. Center for World Mission concludes that when it comes to cross-cultural communication of the gospel "no one has invented a better mechanism for penetrating new social units than the traditional mission society, whether it be Western, African or Asian, whether it be denominational or interdenominational."[8]

Dr. George Peters states a similar conclusion in his book, *A Biblical Theology of Missions:* "There is no question in my mind that our times and culture demand mission organization and missionary societies. . . . God has set His seal of approval upon the mission societies thus far."[9] "The advantages of being a member of a respectable mission society are so numerous and so evident that we strongly urge young people to associate themselves with a missionary sending agency."[10]

Just as not every Christian is called to be a missionary in a cross-cultural sense, so mission societies are not for everyone who wants to serve the Lord abroad. The Lord uses many means and methods of sending out messengers with the good news. Since Americans in business overseas outnumber missionaries by 100 to 1, committed Christians should make every effort to infiltrate and utilize this vast reservoir of paid-for talent. The truth is that from this generation of Christian students in every land we need tens of thousands who will seriously commit themselves to world evangelization. And we need them both as full-time missionaries and self-supporting witnesses. Whether you go as an exchange student or lecturer, in commerce, industry or government, as an individual or part of a supportive team, as a full-time missionary or in a self-supporting role—the goal is the same: "that all nations might believe and obey Jesus Christ!"

Tools for the Task

Many centuries before the apostle Paul was sent out from Antioch, there lived in the land of Greece a philosopher-scientist named Archimedes. It was he who enunciated the principle of the lever. He purportedly said that if he was given a fulcrum which was strong enough and a lever which was long enough and a place out in space to stand, he could move the world! Technically he was right, but he lacked the tools. What Archimedes lacked we as Christians have. For in the unshakable promises of the inspired Word of God we have the world's strongest foundation. In prayer we have the world's longest lever, for prayer moves the hand that made the world. If we will go on using the Word of God as our foundation and prayer as our lever—energized by the Holy Spirit—we can go on moving the world until Christ comes.

Notes

[1] World Evangelization Information Service News (Lausanne Committee for World Evangelization, Rexdale, Ont., Canada), 9 March 1979, p. 2.

[2] Ralph D. Winter, "The Two Structures of God's Redemptive Mission," Missiology: An International Review, January 1974, p. 122.

[3] C. Peter Wagner, Stop The World I Want To Get On (Glendale, Calif.: Regal, 1974), p. 48.

[4] Ibid., pp. 46-47.

[5] Ibid., pp. 48-49.

[6] Ralph D. Winter, "The Future of the Church: The Essential Components of World Evangelization," An Evangelical Agenda, 1984 and Beyond (Pasadena: William Carey Library, 1979), p. 157.

[7] Michael Griffiths, Give Up Your Small Ambitions (Chicago: Moody Press, 1974), p. 126.

[8] Ralph D. Winter, Penetrating The Last Frontiers (Pasadena: U.S. Center for World Mission, 1978), p. 14.

[9] George W. Peters, A Biblical Theology of Missions (Chicago: Moody Press, 1972), pp. 228-29.

[10] Ibid., p. 224.

15
The Messenger and New Avenues

Ruth Siemens

I am very thankful to God for mission societies and the remarkable way he has used them in these last one hundred fifty years of amazing missionary advance. After all, it was *God* who invented them!

I wanted very much to go with a mission agency, but God unmistakably led me overseas as a self-supporting, nonprofessional missionary. While I was at Biola College, I became seriously ill, and even after I recovered I knew no mission agency would risk taking me overseas. So, reluctantly, I continued my studies, this time on a secular campus, Chico State in California. With several other Christians we started an Inter-Varsity group. God gave me invaluable training through IVCF in evangelism, discipling, Bible study and leadership. I don't know what I would have done in later years without this preparation. I then taught in an elementary school, and with two other IVCF alums started a teachers' Christian fellowship. It was then that God sur-

prised me with a salaried secular teaching position overseas—
a position I had not sought. Two years after graduation, I was in
Lima, Perú.

I had only one clear idea of what I was supposed to do. It was
this: when Jesus was in Palestine, he could walk anywhere he
wanted to. In John 4 he said, "I must go through Samaria." But
now he has made his home in us, and he depends on us to bring
him face to face with the individuals he longs to reach. That is
why Paul says in Romans 12 that we must present our "bodies
a living and holy sacrifice." In Romans 6 he specifies members
of our bodies, meaning eyes, ears, lips, hands and feet. In Romans 10 God himself says, "How beautiful are the feet of those
who preach good news" (RSV). This made me long to bring Jesus
Christ face to face with Peruvians who had never really understood who he is.

But how was I to begin? This is how God helped me: A few
days after arrival in Peru, the schoolboard gave a reception for
teachers. There I met a Peruvian teacher, Marta. I wasn't listening very hard until I heard her say, "I don't know anything
about the Bible and I wish I did. Would you teach me?" I could
hardly believe my ears! Marta and I met every week for Bible
study, and a month later she invited Jesus Christ into her life.
A short time later, another teacher, also named Marta, committed her life to Jesus Christ. This is how God launched me into
a ministry with fellow teachers. Before the year was up, every
pupil in my sixth-grade class ended up in my Sunday-school
class, and almost every one made a commitment to Jesus Christ.
God also saw to it that I had one high-school class, which enabled me to have Bible studies with some of them. I was invited
into many upper-class Peruvian homes—the homes of students
and teachers, where I was able to share Jesus Christ with people
who had probably never met a missionary.

After three years in Perú, I signed a second three-year contract, in elementary-school administration, this time in Brazil,
and here again God gave me an ample ministry in the secular-
school situation. In both countries I shared Jesus Christ also with
people I met casually and with neighbors. I became very involved in the national churches, training Sunday-school teach-

ers and working with youth groups.

But none of this was the main task God gave me to do. He doesn't always tell us in advance, you know. In Perú I audited classes at the university in order to improve my Spanish. One of the students, Maria, became a good friend. She taught me Spanish three times a week. Soon the language lessons turned into Bible studies. Maria invited Jesus Christ into her life. Then I suspected God wanted an IVCF group in Lima. I found a few Christian university students. There weren't many at that time. But all along the way God led me to his hand-picked people, many of whom had more gifts and potential than I had, and I'm awed as I look back, to see how God has used them through the years. Two of them are here—Samuel Escobar and his wife, Lily. I am so grateful God allowed our paths to cross.

For the next twenty-one years my work was mainly to pioneer student groups, first in Perú, then Brazil, then Portugal and Spain, and to help with training in many other countries. When I fulfilled my school contract in Brazil, I gave all of my time to the university work under the International Fellowship of Evangelical Students. In Brazil, at one point, just before our first leaders graduated, I regularly visited forty-five cities. Some of those early leaders became staff. So I have worked as a nonprofessional missionary in a secular job, and I have worked with a Christian agency. I am sold on both ways of working. Only our Commander-in-Chief can decide which way any one of us should go. But we need to investigate the options.

Why Secular Avenues?

In view of the fact that mission agencies are effectively used by God, why should we bother with secular avenues at all?

These non-traditional avenues are needed because of *the nature of our task*. In spite of the wonderful fact that we are now a universal church, three-fourths of God's world is still enemy-occupied territory. Ever since the great revolt that day in the Garden, human and nonhuman forces have been struggling for control of God's world. At stake is God's reputation, his rule over his own creation and the fate of three billion people still in bondage to the imposter, blinded by the "deceiver of the nations." Missionaries are God's troops, armed only with God's Word. As ex-rebels themselves, they are under orders urgently but lovingly to persuade rebels to change sides, to make an unconditional surrender to Jesus Christ, the only rightful King, to whom the world belongs by right of creation and by right of purchase. Missions is bringing this world under the acknowledged rule of Jesus Christ. It is bringing nations to obedience to him. The outcome is absolutely certain because Jesus' death on the cross was the decisive battle. The victory is already won. But fierce fighting still awaits us. Mission agencies are God's regular army, but we need guerrilla forces that can enter closed countries and infiltrate every structure of society. Only the lay person can do this. Because we are at war, one avenue is not enough, no matter how good. We must make creative use of every possible avenue God puts at our disposal.

Second, the *dimensions of the task* demand new avenues. Even where the church is established, each new generation must be won. "God has no grandchildren!" Much of Western Europe today is less evangelized than Eastern Europe. France has more Muslims than conservative evangelicals.[1] But our main target must be the 2.5 billion people who represent cultural groups in which there is no Christian church.[2] Even though some of these 16,000 cultural groups[3] number several million people, it has been suggested that we send two Christians to each to establish beachhead churches, equipped to multiply and evangelize the rest of their people. We would need at least 32,000 new missionaries! Impossible? Of course not! Half that number attended the Urbana convention. Of course, these new workers should come from many countries, not just North America.

Third, we need new, nontraditional avenues because of the *cost* of supporting a greatly increased missionary force. Staggering inflation abroad (up to 179 per cent in Argentina) and a rapidly diminishing dollar—both aggravated by repeated oil crises—make mission costs exorbitant. We must double and triple our giving to mission agencies so they will not have to cut back. At the same time we can double and triple our whole missionary force. We can multiply it by ten, at no cost to the church, by making use of secular avenues.

Fourth, we need new avenues because of *closed countries.* Of the 35,000 North American missionaries today, about 95 per cent work in only 17 per cent of the world. Only a couple of thousand work in 83 per cent of the world.[4] Some countries are tightly closed. Others greatly restrict missionary activity, and some are slowly closing. Fortunately, a few are slowly opening—like mainland China!

We need to concentrate on the three huge blocks of unevangelized people: the Chinese (a billion of them inside China and millions more elsewhere); the Hindus (India has more people than Africa and South America combined); the Muslim world. There is only one new little church in Arab North Africa, and no known Libyan Christian. Yet most of the Muslims are in Asia. About fifty per cent of the world's cultural groups are off limits to professional missionaries. Yet there is not a single country that cannot be penetrated in some way through secular avenues.

Fifth, *our rapidly changing world* requires new avenues. Decolonization, nationalism, resurgence of non-Western religions, urbanization, secularization, industrialization, education are a few of the factors that give the messenger in a secular position an advantage over the professional missionary. This is especially true in reaching the educated and professional classes.

These trends also provide unprecedented opportunities. There are 120 new countries in the world less than thirty years old, seeking help for their development needs. Several million jobs are available to North Americans in these and in older countries as well. These are positions their own citizens cannot at present fill. Some Western cults and non-Christian religious groups have been quick to use these opportunities. How tragic if Christians, for whatever reasons, ignore these new avenues God puts at our disposal.

What Are These New Avenues?
The first is the *secular position abroad,* whether it is with a firm, a voluntary agency, a U.N., U.S. or national government agency or perhaps an educational or medical institution. IVCF's Overseas Counseling Service now has computerized data on more

than 100,000 secular positions. There are 526 job descriptions—everything from beekeeping and fisheries to urban planning—in 230 countries and territories, including the Middle East, Eastern Europe and a few already in the People's Republic of China.

The best positions require good degrees, marketable skills and experience. Some are for people in mid-career or retired people—often there is no upper age limit. But there are many entry-level jobs as well. Careers most in demand are agriculture, engineering, medicine, business, teaching at every level—especially the sciences, math, industrial arts and English as a foreign language. Salaries may be low in relation to the cost of living, but more often they are excellent, with generous benefits besides. (You can support a missionary while you are one!)

Your secular contract may require a long-term commitment. More likely it will be two to three years, renewable. If your term is short, you will want language and cultural preparation before you go. You will evangelize with more urgency and train others to carry on when you leave. (Did Paul stay anywhere longer than three years? Everywhere, he planted churches!)

The secular position as an avenue for missionary work is new only in the sense that it has been used relatively little in recent years. It is an old and very biblical way to make God known. God surprised Joseph and Daniel with secular jobs in pagan foreign governments in Egypt and Babylon. Such strategic positions exist for qualified Christians today. In the New Testament, Paul and his colleagues are the most prominent examples.

In 1 Corinthians 9, Paul argues in defense of the fully supported Christian worker, and on occasion he received gifts (1 Cor. 9; Phil. 1:5; 4:10ff.). But usually, for himself and his team, Paul insists on the self-supporting avenue, not primarily out of need, but as a deliberate policy (Acts 20:33ff.; 2 Thess. 3:6-15). As a "skilled master builder" he was establishing precedents for new churches in pagan pioneer regions. He insists the pattern be continued by his followers. All of Paul's reasons are relevant today.

First, he works for his own support so he will not be confused with the many Jewish and Gentile itinerant false teachers, who lived off the people (Tit. 1:10-11; 2 Cor. 11:12ff.). *He will not allow his motives or his message to become suspect.* Too much is at stake!

Second, he works to provide a role model for these new Christian laypeople, who then as now must constitute the overwhelming majority in the church. In this way he teaches them *a biblical concept of work,* (1 Thess. 4:11-12; 2 Thess. 3:6ff.; Tit. 3:1) which was necessary for these gentile converts, many of whom came from unsavory backgrounds (pilfering was a way of life). *Their transformation* into honest workers and responsible providers *was to be observable* in the marketplace.

Third, by example, Paul teaches *wholesome involvement in secular life, without compromise.* Christian ethics must be *applied,* if non-Christian societies are to be changed. Christian laypeople must do this.

Fourth, Paul demonstrates that *a secular job, at home or abroad, is no excuse for not being deeply involved in spiritual ministry.* God's people is a holy nation, exclusively made up of "priests," who are individually and collectively "to declare his mighty deeds" (1 Pet. 2:4-10). They must do this in the places where they spend most of their waking hours. While professional missionaries concentrate on their primary task, we need self-supporting role models for balance.

Fifth, Paul works in order to teach new believers to give out of their hard-earned incomes to Christians and non-Christians in need. Generosity is not an optional characteristic of God's people (2 Cor. 8:1ff.; 9:6ff.). Family members are to be provided for. Church members shall care for each other. Far-flung Christian communities in this way are welded into one supra-national family—a miracle! Social concern will make God's love believable to non-Christians (Gal. 6:10; Tit. 2:14; 3:8, 14).

Sixth, and most importantly, *Paul is setting a pattern for the extension of God's kingdom that could never be curtailed by lack of funds.* Missionary work was never to be at the mercy of heads of oil-rich countries. There are now over two hundred Third, Fourth and Fifth-World mission societies, but they are having great difficulty following the patterns our richer Western churches have set. Newsletters from North American agencies indicate they are having to cut back their programs or greatly increase their budgets. The missionary strategist Roland Allen said years ago, "What was a spiritual operation is now largely a financial one," and "Non-Christians are repulsed by the degree to which the work of the church depends on money."[5] Temple Gairdner, missionary to Egypt early in this century, warned against missions by proxy: "You pay someone else to go evangelize and produce churches who then also pay someone else to do it."[6] So Christians everywhere leave the expansion of the church to a few, dedicated, overworked professional Christian workers. A large proportion of Paul's writings have to do with money, because he foresaw problems that would result from its improper use. We should all give *more*, but mission funds should be used selectively for those ministries that require full support, while many others follow Paul's example.

Seventh, Paul's additional personal reason for self-support was his great sense of debt to Jesus Christ. To preach the gospel was an obligation. To do it at his own expense was *Paul's fragrant thank offering to the Lord* (1 Cor. 9:15ff.; Rom. 1:14-15).

The question is not whether self-supporting missionary work is ideal or practical, but whether it is *biblical*. If so, we will not emphasize the disadvantages, but seek ways to solve them.

Not only do secular avenues have biblical warrant, but they have ample *historical precedent*. Throughout history God has used diverse kinds of formal mission structures, but Yale historian Kenneth S. Latourette says, "societies financed by the gifts of many are a recent phenomenon."[7] He says, "The chief agents in the expansion of Christianity appear not to have been those who made it a profession . . . , but men and women who carried on their livelihood in some purely secular manner and spoke of their faith to those they met in this natural fashion."[8] Repeatedly, Christians were scattered in the great displacements of peoples—migrations and dispersions—due to government edicts, wars, floods, famines and commerce. Today the international job market has lured abroad millions of people from many countries. Christians among them must be mobilized for missions after the pattern of the early church. Everywhere they went they preached the Word (Acts 8:4).

It is doubtful whether mission societies could have arisen without self-supporting shock troops to open the way. In the early 1800s Robert Morrison, an interpreter for the East India Company, translated the Bible into Chinese. David Livingstone, who opened Africa to missionary work, was employed for a time as a British consul. William Clark, on sabbatical from the Massachusetts College of Agriculture (now M.I.T.), at the invitation of the Japanese government set up a similar school in Japan, now Hokkaido University. His consistent Christian life and loving interest in the students resulted in the conversion of the entire first class of fifteen students, almost all of whom became outstanding Christian leaders. This was the result of a short, one-year term!

William Carey, who more than any other person should be credited with the rise of mission societies, maintained himself in India managing an indigo factory and later in university language teaching. He said, "We have ever held it to be essential that whenever possible, missionaries should support themselves in whole or in part, through their own efforts."

A second new avenue is the *self-employed missionary*. He sets up his own business overseas. The first missionary ever who moved to a distant land to make God known was a wealthy cattleman named Abraham. Centuries later Priscilla and Aquila moved their tentmaking business from Rome to Corinth to Ephesus and back to Rome, and it maintained them and other missionaries.

A century before mission societies began, Moravian Christians pioneered work in twenty-nine countries in twenty-nine years by sending families to start businesses to support themselves as they evangelized. They also provided vocational training and jobs for new Christians.

A Rhodesian Christian university professor says that today "the majority of missions do not teach nationals to be self-sufficient by showing them ways of getting into the mainstream of economic life and thus generating resources for their own churches" and their missionary efforts.[9] Some Christian businessmen are attempting to make a contribution in this area.

A third avenue, a phenomenon of our jet age, is *study abroad*.

There are scholarships for overseas undergraduate study and post-graduate study, even in closed countries. Students are less suspect and have more liberty to speak out. You can do missionary work while you pursue academic goals. In many developing countries half the population is under twenty-five years of age. They may be more readily reached by young people than by older missionaries. I have seen students effectively win and disciple new Christians in just one year overseas. Marxists in Latin America spend twelve to fifteen years in a university, ostensibly to study, but mainly to gain adherents. Tens of thousands of North American undergraduates and grad students currently study abroad, even in closed countries. You can do medical studies abroad, often at less cost than at home, and witness in that context.

A fourth related avenue is *advanced study and research.* Funded pre- and post-doctoral study abroad is open to people with the right career and language combination. One Christian has been in Romania twice under such grants.

There are *internships, externships and other work-study programs* in most careers at little or no cost. This overseas experience looks great on your résumé later, since 30 per cent of the North Americans employed abroad do not make a satisfactory cultural adjustment, and some firms have a 79 per cent failure rate.[10] You can even do student teaching abroad and earn a credential while you make Jesus Christ known.

Summer service overseas should be seen mainly as exposure to another culture and training for missions, although God can use you even in two or three months. About a hundred mission boards have summer training programs. You may instead want to seek a secular job for an almost expense-free summer working on a fruit farm in Hungary, a youth camp in France, in a hotel in Switzerland, as a governess in Spain, tutoring English in Brazil or Japan, and of course, sharing your faith!

Another new avenue is for parents and older friends—*retirement abroad.* Seven thousand Americans have retired in Poland, where they receive special privileges. Five thousand live in Yugoslavia, 4,000 in France, 6,000 on the sunny coast of Spain, 17,000 in Germany and 50,000 in Italy! Others are in

Latin America. Some have retired in Sri Lanka![11] Sometimes their retirement income will stretch further. And their long experience can be put to good use. Older missionaries are needed in countries where age is held in great respect.

We must not forget the *enormous influx of foreigners* into our country—a phenomenon of our day and therefore another new avenue. At least 235,000 international students, millions of immigrants, refugees and illegal aliens are to be welcomed by us and helped and won to Jesus Christ. Twenty-eight million Americans are of recent non-English language background.[12] This year we have had 20.3 million tourists![13] These people are brought to us as part of God's strategy for winning the world.

The Messenger in These New Avenues

Most of the objections to self-supporting and other nontraditional avenues of missionary work evaporate if we define our terms.

Four million Americans are employed abroad, of whom several hundred thousand are evangelical Christians.[14] Unfortunately, most of them were not effective witnesses at home and are not to be considered missionaries overseas. When does an American Christian employed or studying abroad qualify as a missionary?

First, a genuine missionary, regardless of the context of his work, *makes disciples.* This is the commission Jesus gave us. No matter what other ministries we have, what good we do or what models we provide, we must also evangelize and disciple. The content of the gospel is such that our silence is tacit denial of its truth. Unless we eagerly share the good news with excitement and urgency, people won't believe it, because they won't believe that *we* believe it. This is incumbent on every Christian.

Second, a genuine missionary, professional or nonprofessional, has a *cross-cultural ministry.* He identifies with nationals, lives among them, shares their lives, learns their language. He resists the temptation to spend his time in the American "golden ghettoes," even though these may be spiritually needy also. His base will not be the English language church, unless that is the only way or the best way he can reach the nationals, for example, in Saudi Arabia or Afghanistan. A fine example of this is J. Christy Wilson's new book *Today's Tentmakers*. "Missionary" implies cross-cultural.

Third, even with a secular position, the messenger understands he is a *full-time missionary*. He finds opportunities off the job. But his main ministry is at work. He does his secular work not only for his human employer, but for Jesus Christ. He develops caring relationships with those around him. His genuine concern and the integrity of his life create thirst in his associates. They begin asking the important questions. It is not his fault if the answers are so fantastic they end up believing him! His message is credible because it has already been lived out before their eyes, under pressures, in concrete situations. This is an essential ingredient of good evangelism, and no waste of time. The Person of Jesus Christ within the messenger draws men to himself now as irresistibly as when he walked the dusty roads of Galilee. In free time the Christian sees his colleagues socially. He makes friends with his neighbors. He serves the national church. If there is none, he trusts God to turn his evangelistic Bible study into a house church. It's full-time missionary work!

Fourth, *even before going abroad, the messenger witnesses* to the people already assigned to him on campus, at work, in the neighborhood. Faithfulness is God's prerequisite for further assignments. In a war, inaction is a kind of action. It is helping the other side. Satan could do nothing without human accomplices.

Fifth, the messenger *does not do his own thing*, but is well informed in advance on how God's troops are faring in the country to which he goes, and he seeks their counsel on how he can fit in.

Sixth, the messenger *is sent*. He is convinced God has opened up this new avenue for him. His church and other Christian friends confirm that conviction by committing themselves to pray for him.

Whether an expatriate Christian is a missionary or not, in the full sense of the word, "has nothing to do with his organizational ties, or his means of support, but whether he is there under divine compulsion to communicate the message."[15]

It's the messenger's *motivation* that counts and *the spiritual fruit* God gives him in his work. This is true whether he deliberately seeks employment abroad or circumstances take him there. Recall Jesus' words after he had been seated on God's throne and given all authority in heaven and in earth. He said, "Go, then, to all peoples everywhere [that is, wherever life under God's sovereignty takes you] and make them my disciples" (Mt. 28:18 TEV). He also said, "Look at the fields" (Jn. 4:35 NIV), get information, find ways to go. God guides us largely through data we seek out and prayerfully evaluate.

Peter and other apostles apparently received full support in their travels. Jesus had ordered the fishermen to leave their occupation permanently (Lk. 5:1-11; 1 Cor. 9:5). (The King has totalitarian rights over all we are and have, including our careers, which must be secondary considerations in any case.) But Paul answers charges and reminds his churches several times that he is "no inferior missionary" because he works to pay his way (2 Cor. 12:11-13).

From my own experience, the early years when I was self-supporting were as full-time and as fruitful as the later years with a Christian society. I would love to live all twenty-one years over again, but without the mistakes. It delights me to hear that many of the people who were in those early student groups in Latin America are now pastors, church planters, missionaries, witnesses for Jesus Christ. Most of them are self-supporting in university teaching, medicine and other careers. One was recently elected to the congress of his country.

At present I direct IVCF's Overseas Counseling Service, helping Christians of all ages find these secular openings for missionary work. When a few hundred of you are working overseas, I hope God will let me go again, to a closed country, in a self-supporting capacity.

Jesus Christ has opened new secular avenues for us, to make sure that when we stand before his throne, there will be with us Libyans and Tunisians, Albanians and Bulgarians, Afghans and

Yemenis, Iraqis and Turks, Kurds and Baluchistanis, Malaysians, Nepalis, Mongolians—a large number of Indians and Chinese—no ethnic group left out (Rev. 7:9). We look forward to the time when "The kingdom of the world has become the kingdom of our Lord and of his Christ, and he shall reign forever and ever (Rev. 11:15 RSV).

Notes

[1]Patrick Johnstone, Operation World (Kent, England: Send the Light Trust, 1978), pp. 43, 48-49.

[2]Ralph Winter, The Ground for a New Thrust in World Mission (Pasadena: William Carey Library, 1977).

[3]C. Peter Wagner and Edward R. Dayton, Unreached Peoples 79 (Elgin, Ill.: David C. Cook, 1979), p. 3.

[4]Edward R. Dayton, ed., Missions Handbook, 11th ed. (Monrovia, Calif.: MARC, 1976), pp. 20-22.

[5]Roland Allen, The Case for the Voluntary Clergy (London: Eyre and Spottiswoode, 1930), pp. 58, 105-06.

[6]Ibid., p. 210.

[7]Kenneth S. Latourette, A History of the Expansion of Christianity, vol. 1 (New York: Harper and Brothers, 1944), p. 114.

[8]Ibid., pp. 116, 169, 230, 233ff.

[9]Pius Wakatama, Independence for the Third World Church (Downers Grove, Ill.: InterVarsity Press, 1976), pp. 38, 39-49.

[10]Alison R. Lanier, "Selecting and Preparing Personnel for Overseas Transfers," Personnel Journal, March 1979.

[11]Los Angeles Times, Saturday, 30 July 1977, section 1, p. 10.

[12]TESOL Newsletter (Washington, D.C.: Georgetown Univ.), August 1979.

[13]Nation's Business, November 1979.

[14]Four million is a moderate estimate taken from different sets of incomplete figures from the State Department, the U.S. Census Bureau and so on. If one in five are Christians (a Gallup poll says one in three), then as many as eight hundred thousand could be evangelicals.

[15]Warren Webster, "The Missionary Vocation" in God's Men: From All Nations to All Nations, Urbana 67 Compendium (Chicago: InterVarsity Press, 1968), p. 261.

16
The Messenger in China Today

David Adeney

I came to Urbana with two messages. One was the typewritten script which I fully expected to give. And then something happened. During the last two days I have been thinking of the second message, a message that comes out of China where I was just a few weeks ago. In these last hours I have had a growing conviction, backed by some of my fellow workers on the speakers team, that I ought to speak to you from my experience in China.

I was to have spoken on the missionary's lifestyle, from Acts 20, the words of Paul to the Ephesian elders. After looking at the church in China, we shall come back to Acts 20, and we shall see also a picture of the lifestyle of any servant of God who is seeking to make Christ known in the world today.

When I spoke at Urbana the first time in 1951, I had just come out from China after fifteen months under Communism with the Christian students. This time my visit to China has been very much shorter. But it has been especially memorable because it has given me the opportunity of meeting with friends I have not seen for almost thirty years.

When I arrived at the airport I heard someone call my name. I looked up and there was someone that I had known as a student in this country. I remember meeting him in a lab in Chicago University and speaking to him in Chinese. He was studying for his Ph.D. and had just come to know Christ. We were alone and we knelt down and prayed—in that lab. He told me how lonely he was. He had gone to the nearest church, a Christian Science church, and that hadn't helped much. And then he turned to me and asked how he could get into Bible study and fellowship. He joined the Inter-Varsity Christian Fellowship Bible study at the University of Chicago. He also went to Cedar Campus, and we were together there.

After some time passed, one day he said to me, "I must go back to China. I must go back to my people." On the ship going back, he wrote me a wonderful letter. "It doesn't matter," he said, "whether I live six months or a year or however long. Then he quoted Paul's words to the Ephesian elders: "I do not account my life of any value nor as precious to myself, if only I may accomplish my course and the ministry which I received from the Lord Jesus, to testify to the gospel of the grace of God."

Then there was silence. No news for twenty-three years. I don't know whether you can sense the excitement when I saw a letter on my table in September postmarked from his home town. I knew whom it was from. Here was a letter from this brother, telling me how God had protected him during those twenty-three years.

Now as I was back in China I was to see him again and hear how God had been with him even during the difficult days of the cultural revolution.

One of the most amazing things of this last visit in China has been to see the way the Spirit of God has led me to Christian friends. I was in a church on my last Sunday just seven weeks ago. The tour guide had arranged for us to go to a Roman Catholic cathedral. It was only the third time it had been opened, for the Chinese government has only in the past few months opened churches publicly again. The service was all in Latin.

I was sitting between a Chinese and an African, and to my amazement the African pulled out his Bible with "Church of Uganda" on the cover. As soon as the service ended, I talked with him and his friend from Tanzania. Together we came back to the room I was sharing with Eric Miller in the hotel. For the first time in many months, those medical students, sent over for five years of training, joined other Christians in prayer and in study of the Word of God. I had a letter from him later saying how much that time meant to him. Some of the Chinese Christians are now ministering to him and to his friends. God put me beside that African brother.

A few hours later we went together to the Protestant church where fifteen hundred people worshiped that day. Our African friends had not heard that one was open. Hardly anyone had a Bible, but they had sheets of paper that had been printed with the hymns, Bible passages and the order of service. There was warm participation, and it was a tremendous service. A clear message was given, for which I was thankful. There was a sense that here were people worshiping in public for the first time after many, many years.

At the end I turned round and greeted the three people seated behind me. I spoke to them in Chinese, and at once one of them asked, "Have you any Bibles?" They told me, "We have traveled two days. We come from another province. We heard a church was open. We wanted to see what was happening. We wanted to find out if we could get Bibles."

We spent that afternoon in a Christian home with other local Christians and together listened to a most amazing testimony. I don't know when I have been so moved. They told me that in the area they came from there were 50,000 Christians. They told me that there were more Christians there today than there were before the revolution. They told me of young people coming to know the Lord Jesus. So many young people believed that the officials became concerned and serious persecution followed. They had copied out passages of Scripture because they had no Bible. They often got up for Bible studies at four o'clock in the morning. Now, with greater freedom, they have meetings almost every day of the week, including one for training lay preachers, as they have no pastors now.

During the cultural revolution, rarely was there an opportunity for public witness. When the old pastor died, the Christians said they must witness and hundreds gathered together at
the funeral, the young people dividing into teams and singing
hymns. The person telling me the story, a high-school teacher,
told me how he had written great banners inscribed with such
words as, "I am the resurrection and the life." They carried
those banners in public.

Nothing happened during the service. But at the end, the
brother who had prayed was arrested and imprisoned. Then
when the authorities sought for the one who had written the
banners, in order to take the pressure off others, the school-
teacher came forward and said, "I wrote them." He went to
prison.

His wife was very distressed at home, and then suddenly the
Lord spoke to her, "I am the God of Abraham, I am the God of
Jacob, I am the God of Isaac, I am the God of your husband. Do
not be afraid." In the prison he found himself singing, "The way
of the cross I will follow." Another Christian, who was very
sad and had almost lost faith and courage, heard him sing. It
brought new faith and new strength to him. Yes, it was a time
of suffering. They told me of answers to prayer, of people being
healed, God speaking to them in dreams, of wonderful instances of protection. And that could be true of many, many
parts of China.

Let me tell you some of the lessons which I have learned
from these brothers and sisters. First, I learned to distinguish
that which is essential in a church stripped of all the Western
trappings of the past, no longer identified with Western imperialism—denominations gone, no church buildings, no paid pastors, very few Bibles, no regular Sunday services because people
work at different times in the factories. There was none of what
we associate with the church. There were young people who
have never been to a church service, never possessed a Bible and
yet loved the Lord Jesus Christ.

Here I saw that the church is not, as we so often think, the
outward organization; it is that inner fellowship of men and

women who love Jesus Christ and are faithfully witnessing to him.

The strength of a church is not measured by the numbers who come to the Sunday morning service. The strength of Inter-Varsity is not measured by the 17,000 who come to Urbana. The strength of Inter-Varsity, the strength of a church, is measured by the depth of spiritual fellowship between brothers and sisters joined together in little groups, witnessing and living lives in which the Lord Jesus is glorified.

Second, I saw in that church in China a *reality*. I remember talking to a lady whose Bible had been taken away. She had been questioned again and again, "Have you changed your thinking?"

She replied, "If I said I'd changed my thinking, I wouldn't be true to myself or to you."

"You're too stubborn," they said.

And so she said to me, "I and my husband, we've been the only Christians, and my son who is in his twenties is also a Christian. And we've been alone. You know, in China if you have a Christian you have a real Christian." We are not so sure of that in Hong Kong. But on the mainland there is a reality in faith.

Third, I have learned that the witness of the Chinese church has not been through the pulpit or public witness; it has come through humble and loving service. Paul said to the Ephesians, "I was . . . serving the Lord with all humility and with tears and with trials" (Acts 20:18-19).

In China it has been very difficult indeed to speak publicly about the Lord Jesus right up to about a year ago. Things are rather different now. There is more freedom.

But when I was in China last year, I remember a man saying to me, "I'm a Christian, but I can't talk about it."

I heard about a lady sweeping the floor. There was something so wonderful about her attitude and the smile on her face that my friend went to her when she was alone and asked, "Are you a Christian?"

And she turned and said, "Yes. I can't talk about it, but I seek to show the love of Jesus. When somebody speaks to me, then I share my faith." This is friendship evangelism—making a friend, sharing with somebody whom you can trust. In that way people have come to the Lord Jesus.

I asked a young man who obviously knew the Word of God, "How do you know the Scriptures? Is there a church in your town?"

"I've never been to a church service," he said. "There's lots of Christian families. When I'm in trouble, when I have difficulties, I go into a home. The people there teach me, and thus I've learned the Word of God."

Sharing the gospel in all humility, being humble in our witness—this is what really counts. Yet it is not easy in China.

When I first arrived in China many years ago, I remember meeting the general director of the China Inland Mission, one of the Cambridge Seven, an old man. I don't remember much of what he said to me. I was very young and enthusiastic, just coming from active student work in England. I only remember one thing. "Beware of national pride," he said. "It shows itself just like a person who has been eating garlic."

Now, I didn't think I had any national pride. But you can be awfully proud of being humble. I had to find out. I had to go, not to the student work that I wanted to go to, but out into the country to live for seven years. I had to live in country homes during the war time, go through the bombings and learn from my Chinese brothers and sisters.

Sometimes I had to receive their rebuke. Sometimes, when I was discouraged, I had to receive their encouragement and be lifted up. I had to stand by the graveside of our second child and hear my Chinese brothers praying for us. My wife, Ruth, and I listened to them as they said, "You've taken their most precious possession to heaven. Draw them nearer to heaven."

I had to share with them when the bombs came and when the Japanese army entered the city, be one with them in the midst of difficulties and learn from them. Then I began to understand the meaning of the words of the Lord Jesus, "Blessed is he that endures to the end. Blessed is he that is not offended in me." Paul said that he served the Lord "with tears and with trials, which came upon me through the plots of the Jews"

(Acts 20:19). And I've seen the suffering of fellow workers resulting in the purifying of the church in China.

One of the most moving experiences came when I was visiting a Christian home a few weeks ago. The door was opened by a man with white hair. At first I didn't recognize him, but he smiled at me and said, "I am Stephen."

I had known him as a young student. I went to his wedding. I had been with him in those days in the Inter-Varsity in China. He had been active for the Lord, so gifted, coming from one of the top universities. Now I saw the marks of suffering on his face.

For twenty years he had been in hard labor. In the early days when he was still a bit free and still at home, he would translate from books and send copies to his friends. But they took him away to a labor camp. All that time he was pulling a cart—doing the lowest forms of labor. Only a few months ago, as a result of the government's new "united front policy" in which everyone is called to take part in the "four modernizations" to help build the new China, he was released and sent to a medical college to teach English. I heard about this just before I left the United States, and I brought him some dictionaries which he needed. He got permission to meet me to receive those dictionaries.

Then, as we prayed together, he told me the story of those twenty years. He likened himself to Job, and I was reminded of the words of James, "You have heard of the endurance of Job and have seen the outcome of the Lord's dealings, that the Lord is full of compassion and is merciful" (5:11). Stephen had had that experience.

I said to myself, "Why should he go into a labor camp? Why should he spend twenty years in that kind of work, while I was free to travel around the world to take part in the IFES work throughout Asia and all the joys of that kind of service? Why did my Lord say to him, 'You shall glorify me through suffering'?"

Brothers and sisters, many of you stood up last night to say you were willing to follow the Lord Jesus. Did you also say to the Lord, "Lord, if you allow suffering to come to me, if you take me into a difficult place, if you allow illness, weakness, failure, whatever it may be, or if the time comes that I have to go to prison, I'll still follow you right to the very end"?

Hudson Taylor, when he had had a very difficult year and his wife had died, said, "We have put to the proof his faithfulness, his power to support in trouble, and to give patience under affliction as well as to deliver from danger. I trust that we are fully satisfied that we are God's servants sent by him to the various places we occupy. We did not come to China because missionary work here was either safe or easy, but because God had called us." I believe that's the basic motivation. God has called. God is to be glorified in my life. And the task he has given me I must finish to the very end.

I have been so impressed this time in China by the zeal for the Word of God. Can you imagine what it would be like if there were no Inter-Varsity Press, if there were no Bibles, if there were no beautiful hymnbooks, and you hadn't had these helps for your Christian life for years? And yet in spite of all that you have got to go on witnessing for the Lord? Paul reminded the Ephesian elders that he "did not shrink from declaring to you anything that was profitable, and teaching you publicly and from house to house" (Acts 20:20).

I said to one of my brothers in China, "What about these house churches? Will they continue? Will they be able to go forward even if there is a change in government policy and renewed persecution? Many of the Christians there are quite cautious. They don't know what changes might take place in the future.

He replied, "I just visited a place in another part of China, a completely different part, where there are thousands of Christians." (In some places there are only twos and threes. The vast majority of China's 970 million people have not heard the gospel.) But he said, "In this place there was a commune where two-thirds of the people were Christians. Some years ago (it wouldn't happen today) a brother there was arrested and taken to prison. Others came to visit him, and they too were taken in. Then others went also and they were taken in until the prison was completely full. There was no room for any more." Then he made his point: "The believers are ready to take every risk to proclaim what they believe." Am I? Are you?

A Chinese sister poured out her heart, "Look, we've no Bibles, we haven't the teachers we need, the church is weak. The brothers and sisters could easily be led astray. Oh, send us Bibles."

The Far Eastern Broadcasting Company has been replying to letters—this year over 10,000 letters from every part of China including one from Tibet. Many include requests for Bibles. One young man who received a New Testament wrote back, "I read it all through in two nights, and now I'm beginning to read it again chapter by chapter."

Somebody else wrote, "Look, you sent us a Bible, but there are three of us. We don't know who can read it first. Please help solve the problem by sending two more."

There's a hunger for the Word of God. What a responsibility we have to seek to help them! What is our responsibility? First, we must seek to identify, seek in prayer to make ourselves one with the church in China. True identification with the people is going to entail deep concern for every area of society, a sympathetic entering into the social, the political and the economic problems, together with a sharing of whatever trials and tests may come. Our task is to understand the physical needs of China, the problems the government faces in feeding almost a billion people, and then try to grasp what it means to be a Christian in a society which is essentially a collective society, where you must go where the government sends you, where the one goal is to serve the people. In that society, how do you live for Christ?

If I went back to China, I would want to share with the people in the house churches. The way is not open for missionaries now. But if I were able to live in China again, I would want to learn from those who have experienced more than I have of what it means to suffer for the sake of Christ. I would want to contribute under the guidance of the Holy Spirit insights given to me from the Word of God. But I trust I wouldn't seek to impose customs and patterns of Western Christianity. I would want a Chinese church led by the Spirit of God, dependent upon the Spirit of the living Lord. I would want them to live as Chinese

Christians and identify with them as closely as possible, to rejoice with those who rejoice, to weep with those who weep, to
learn from the experience of God's people, to give not only the
gospel but my own self. Surely this is the only kind of life-
style that is going to be effective in the world today.

When I left China, I traveled to six or seven different Asian
countries. I visited OMF fellow workers and graduates from the
Discipleship Training Center. I saw them working together in
teams. I saw people from the West and from Japan, from Thailand, Hong Kong and Singapore. I saw them together in fellowship, and I realized that today God still calls men and women
to go and work in that fellowship, that kind of unity, true international cooperation.

If God has given you a burden, a vision to share in the work
of God's kingdom in Africa, in Asia, in Latin America, go forward with courageous faith. Brothers and sisters from every
country, every continent, will welcome you when you go to
share with them in the great unfinished task if you come as a
humble servant of the Lord Jesus.

The task is not finished. May God keep me pressing forward
towards the mark of the high calling of God that I might say
with that brother who is back in China now, who came to know
Christ in this country, "I do not consider my life of any account
as dear to myself, in order that I may finish my course, and
the ministry which I received from the Lord Jesus" (Acts 20:24).

17
Where Do We Go from Here?

John E. Kyle

There is a man in this auditorium today who is a citizen of a Third-World nation and is a missionary serving under a Third-World missionary-sending agency. He could teach all of us a great deal about what it means to be a dedicated follower of the Lord Jesus Christ.

When he was a university student, we were together at a convention much like this one in Asia. The year was 1970, and I had the privilege to be with my friend and several hundred other university students to share my burden for world missions.

This student shared with me one evening what it was like to be told by his father, whom he dearly loved, to never come back to the family home because he had decided to follow Jesus Christ as a true disciple. He shared what he was undergoing as a student with no money and a few friends on a large university campus. Yet, his eyes would light up with joy when he shared how he loved Jesus Christ and wanted to serve him. He was certain that God had called him to go to an isolated tribal group in his country in lieu of accepting a position with an engineering firm with all the prestige and security that would be offered him.

During the convention this man helped me talk with other students, like himself, who were asking the question, "Where do we go from here?" And he already had a lot of the answers concerning the need for dedication to Christ and a goal to be attained.

Today he could share with you how he witnessed for Christ as an undergraduate on his university campus and how after graduation he went on to take training to prepare himself to become a missionary. He joined a missionary society and accepted the responsibility of trusting God with his small salary. Eventually he went to an isolated tribal people and helped to translate the New Testament into their heart language. God used him wonderfully to lead many of those forgotten people to a saving knowledge of Jesus Christ.

Now my friend is a guest in our country, studying at a university so that he can return to his nation and assist his fellow national missionaries to complete their tasks more efficiently and effectively.

Today you are sitting here much like my friend did several years ago. Many of you are asking, "Where do we go from here?" It would seem to be almost too simple for me to say in answer, "into all the world and preach the gospel." And yet ultimately that must be the answer because thousands of you here today are following Jesus Christ in obedience. You truly love Jesus Christ and you are serving him right now, and you want more of what he has for your Christian life. Putting it quite directly, then, Jesus said to his disciples in Mark 16:15, "Go into all the world and preach the gospel to all creation."

I vividly remember how right after I accepted Christ as Savior as a young businessman, I heard a missionary who had just returned home from several months in Asia pour out his heart in a series of meetings. As he shared the great needs of lost people in Korea and India, my heart was not only touched, but I was greatly humbled. I wanted to go right then! I wanted to go immediately! To do something now was my heart's cry! Why couldn't I at least mow the church's lawn for the Lord? I heard how a layman in our church was digging out a room that was needed in the basement of our church, and I wondered why I couldn't do something important like that for Christ. Ever feel like that? Yet deep down in my heart I realized that I still had so much to learn about Jesus Christ from the Bible. So I became a better witness among my business associates and neighbors. Where was I to go from there? First to many Bible study sessions, for a special Navigators study course, to serve as a counselor in the Billy Graham Crusade of San Francisco, to take responsibility as an officer in our local church, to attend seminary and eventually to serve as a home missions pastor. Yes, eventually at the ripe old age of thirty-seven I finally went overseas as a missionary. So I think I understand a bit of where you are today.

Where do you go from here? Do you realize that go is an exciting word? It denotes action and we like that as Christians. The word go is used 1,460 times in the Bible! It is used 1,210 times in the Old Testament and 250 times in the New Testament. The word stop is used, interestingly enough, only seven times in the Bible. When Jesus Christ was physically here on earth, he often used the word go in relating to his friends: "Go and sin no more." "Go therefore into the highways." "Go and proclaim everywhere the kingdom of God." "Go after the one which is lost." "Go into all the world and preach the gospel."

When Urbana 79 was planned, the primary goal was set forth as follows: "To glorify the Lord Jesus Christ by helping students find God's place for them in world missions and thus to serve the church in strengthening her ministry in world missions." Have we attained our goals thus far? First, I trust that we have all glorified our Lord Jesus Christ. How have we helped students to find God's place for them in world missions?

Let us review. The plenary sessions have revealed much to us us from God's Word as Dr. John Stott has opened the Bible to us. The other speakers have also wonderfully opened their hearts and shared their lives with us. The missionaries have shared with us the opportunities overseas today to serve Christ. The workshops and seminar sessions and the speaker sessions have been a means of gathering information. All of these opportunities have opened new avenues of thinking for you, I trust.

Yet you undoubtedly realize that if we are to realize our convention theme, "that all nations might believe and obey Jesus Christ," then we are responsible as followers of Jesus Christ who have believed in him to now assume our responsibilities and obey Jesus Christ ourselves.

Last night a multitude of you made decisions that will change your lives, and therefore our world, during the next decade. Tonight as we leave this auditorium after the communion service, we will step out into the 1980s as a great multitude of Christians who are set to follow Christ in a fresh manner.

As David Howard read from the World Evangelism Decision Card last night before Dr. Billy Graham spoke, I heard his words echo in my ears: "I believe it is God's will for me to serve him abroad and will pray and make inquiry to this end." Many of you made this decision. Then Howard read further: "Convinced that I have a part in God's plan for the world, I will actively seek his will for me by increasing my awareness of an involvement in world missions." And many of you made this decision.

Perhaps you, like the Apostle Paul, have in a sense received a vision from heaven since you arrived here at Urbana 79. In Acts 26:16-20, Paul stood before King Agrippa using his personal testimony as his defense. He said that after he met Jesus Christ on the road to Damascus, Jesus said to him:

"Now get up and stand on your feet. I have appeared to you to appoint you as a servant and as a witness of what you have seen of me and what I will show you. I will rescue you from your own people and from the Gentiles. I am sending you to open their eyes and turn them from darkness to light, and from the power of Satan to God, so that they may receive forgiveness of sins and a place among those who are sanctified by faith in me."

So then, King Agrippa, I was not disobedient to the vision from heaven. First to those in Damascus, then to those in Jerusalem and in all Judea, and to the Gentiles also, I preached

that they should repent and turn to God and prove their re-
pentance by their deeds. *(NIV)*

It sounds like Paul took seriously Jesus Christ's last words to
his disciples in Acts 1:8, "But you shall receive power when
the Holy Spirit comes upon you; and you will be my witnesses
both in Jerusalem, and in all Judea and Samaria, and even to the
remotest part of the earth."

I urge you to be true to the vision from heaven that God may
have revealed to you when you marked your World Evangelism
Decision Card. Begin right away when you return to your campus to do the things you have covenanted to do. You may have
marked some of the following steps of action:

Pray daily for specific mission concerns.

Read one or more books about world missions.

Begin a systematic study about world missions.

Join a missions study or action group.

Subscribe to a missions periodical or bulletin.

Develop a friendship with an international student.

Begin to financially and prayerfully support a missionary or
national worker.

Begin correspondence with one or more mission agencies
about service opportunities.

Make plans to participate in a summer missions program.

Seek further training for preparation to become a missionary.

Begin to immediately get involved in carrying out your decisions. If you are serious you will begin to act now. Sure, you
will make mistakes, you will possibly blunder along, and you
will wonder if you know what you are doing. Satan will throw
up roadblocks along your way. But you must keep on being
obedient to your decisions made here at Urbana 79.

Where do we go from here? Back to the campus to begin to
fulfill our decisions made for Christ here at Urbana 79, all this
in glad obedience to Jesus Christ's penetrating words spoken
almost two thousand years ago to people like ourselves when
he said, "Go into all the world and preach the good news to all
creation."

18
Nine Messengers: Their Own Stories

During the convention, nine people shared briefly how God has heightened their awareness of his calling. Their testimonies are reprinted here in alphabetical order.

Robert Batzinger is a post-doctoral fellow in cancer research at the University of Wisconsin and plans on teaching at a Christian college in Thailand. Linnea Berg is at William Carey International University working on a masters degree in teaching English as a second language. Terry Carmen, whose major is industrial arts, is a senior and former Inter-Varsity chapter president at the University of Maryland.

Sir Frederick Catherwood is a member of the European Parliament and lives in Cambridge, England. Elwyn Davies is the general director of the Bible Christian Union, an international mission organization, and a frequent speaker at Inter-Varsity camps and conferences. Hooi Seng Tai is a Malaysian of Chinese descent who is studying computer science and serving as Inter-

Varsity chapter evangelism coordinator at Duke University in
North Carolina.

Ruth Lichtenberger, former NCF staff in the eastern United
States, is now general director of Nurses Christian Fellowship
International, based in London. Ada Lum, former International
Fellowship of Evangelical Students staffworker in Asia, now
serves out of London as Bible study secretary for IFES. Bernie
Smith, who has worked as a pastor, physical education director
and IVCF staffworker in the past, is now a free-lance preacher,
conference speaker and song leader.

Robert Batzinger

I thank God for missionaries. I was born and raised in a Catholic
family and went to church every Sunday as a child, but in my
undergraduate years I got out of this habit for it meant very little
to me. My first years of graduate school were a time of diminishing motivation and increasing spiritual questioning. Since my
applications to medical school had been rejected, I found myself
pursuing a degree in a field which I did not especially like, and
it was drudgery to go to work each day. At the same time, I had
been corresponding with a girl in Thailand and had begun to
study Buddhism in the hope of becoming a member of her
religion. However, I could never forget nor ignore the few things
I knew about God. In order to resolve this problem, I decided to
read the Bible and find its "flaws."

It was about this time that I met Chong, a student in my
department who was from Malaysia and had been a member of
IFES. He came to me one afternoon looking for some chemicals.
While it only took a few minutes to gather the things he needed,
I noticed that there was something different about him. While
I was pleased to show off my knowledge of chemistry, he was
more interested in me as a person. Before he left, he asked if I
would like to attend a Bible study that evening. That question
caught me off guard, and yet I was curious. So that evening, he
brought me to a home where graduate school and medical students were studying the Bible. By the end of the study, I felt
this group had something I needed, but yet I did not know how
to get it.

From that day on, I really found a friend in Chong. We would often get together for discussions and for the weekly Bible studies. When he found out that I did not go to church, we went together to a local church the very next Sunday. I soon recognized my need to become right with God and accepted the gift of grace that God offers to all who believe in the finished work of Christ on the cross.

Since then, my life has changed. Armed with prayer and a growing faith instead of a quivering self-confidence, each day became an exciting challenge. I began to really appreciate my work. Despite my failings, God continues to love and help me. During the rough times I have learned that the Lord can be trusted and desires us to seek him for help. I have also found that God uses people who will seek to obey him and be used no matter where they are.

Linnea K. Berg: OTC

Overseas Training Camp (OTC) illustrated for me the universality of Jesus Christ. I spent five weeks in Guatemala participating in the training program with fellow students, missionaries and nationals. OTC taught me about missions, cross-cultural communication and living, issues concerning rich and poor, and most of all, about my purpose in the world as a Christian. OTC was the privilege of rubbing shoulders not only with fellow students but with missionaries and nationals who stretched and challenged me, loved and accepted me. I studied God's Word with them and its cross-cultural implications. Once in Guatemala, I found myself face to face with surprising lessons I didn't expect to learn.

I visited two World Vision centers. At first, I didn't want to eat with, associate with or love the kids at the center. They were dirty, dressed in ill-fitting clothes and might have carried diseases I'd somehow catch. Here, Christ brought to mind the verses in 1 Samuel where God said, "Man looks at the outward appearance, but the LORD looks at the heart." My Guatemalan hostess at the World Vision centers, with joy and love radiating from her face, abandoned herself in playing with those kids and worked to fix them a meal. She kept smiling. She was an example to me. She illustrated the passage from Philippians where Paul prays that those Christians might have love so abounding that no matter what culture, place or people they are with they may share the gospel and point to Jesus Christ for God's glory and praise. I was beginning to see cross-culturally the universality of Christ's principles.

OTC presented me the challenge of struggling with starkly contrasting lifestyles. One small girl asked me, "Is this the only pair of shoes you have?" to which she added, "What is your other pair like?" I thought to myself, "Which other pair do I describe?" How could I share with her?

I lived with two Guatemalan families. My first family's home had modest furnishings, cold water and small rooms opening up onto a cement patio. When I moved into the second home, I went into culture shock. I had re-entered a house like mine in Minneapolis. I didn't expect it. I found myself criticizing them. They were not living the simple life I thought they should be with so many poor people right down the street. I did not see and failed to accept the fact that God blesses people—the rich included.

God had to teach me through those two contrasting family homes about my attitude toward what he's given others and me materially. Both families showed me service to those around themselves. The Christlike love and expression of hospitality in the homes and lives of the Guatemalan people far surpassed anything I'd experienced before. They gave me gifts for visiting them! I realized there that affluence can be used to serve others or to isolate oneself from the world. Rich and poor are universal, and God's concern for both is too.

Mainly, OTC was a different environment for God to show me his world from a new perspective. Whether in Guatemala worshiping for two or three hours in Spanish and visiting people in homes, or in the US, studying at a university, Christ desires me —all of us—to get past the appearances and the barriers we put up to reach out in love to those around us. I am to serve others, to learn to understand them and to communicate in a personal way the gospel so "that all nations might believe and obey Jesus Christ."

Terry L. Carmen: STIM

Jeremiah 29:11 says, " 'For I know the plans that I have for you,' declares the LORD, 'plans for welfare and not for calamity to give you a future and a hope.' " After my summer in Kenya, I think that what this verse really means is "such a deal I have for you." It was a really great time, and I'd just like to share with you some of my impressions.

After about four days in Nairobi, another American student and I were loaded on a bus and sent to our assignment in Southwestern Kenya. As we drove farther and farther away from Nairobi, it really hit me that I was alone in the middle of Africa, 8,000 miles away from home. "What in the world are you doing here?" I kept asking myself. I felt like leaning out the window and yelling, "Mother!!"

It was then that God brought to my mind a passage from my quiet time in Joshua 1, "Have I not commanded you? Be strong and courageous! Do not tremble or be dismayed, for the LORD your God is with you wherever you go" (v. 9). This passage encouraged me and reassured me that I was not there on another one of my impulsive escapades, but that the Lord had lead me there to serve, to learn and to bear testimony of him.

During one of the weekends we were out visiting some homes way out in the bush. We had gotten as far as the motorcycles could take us and then started to walk the rest of the way. We were shortly met by two men who would guide us, and one of them offered to carry my pack. Visions of the great white hunter and his African porter flashed in my mind, and I quickly refused. But every quarter mile or so he'd ask again, and I kept refusing. My mind was in a turmoil. I didn't know if he simply wanted to help me out of the kindness of his heart, or if it was expected that Americans would not carry their share. Eventually I let him carry it, but it bothered me nevertheless. I think my own macho self-image was a factor also.

I had some problems getting along with the Christian that I worked with during the summer. I won't go into details, but what I learned from that experience is that when I return overseas I would like to go with two or three others who really trust each other already and can labor together in harmony under stressful situations. (Either that or go with a wife, preferably the latter.) I think the main problem in Kenya was that I was too busy adapting to and enjoying the African culture to care very much about my fellow worker.

Toward the end of my time in Kenya, I went to visit a game reserve with some other summer missionaries. While we were there we had lunch at a tourist lodge. This was my first contact with Westerners in nine weeks, and I really felt uncomfortable around them. Their customs seemed strange; most acted in an unfriendly manner, and all of them appeared to be terribly rich. I felt like I had a small taste of what it was like to view Westerners through African eyes.

In Christian circles there is often a mystique about "the call to missions." Before I went to Kenya, I felt that this was just so much hog slop. I felt that Jesus gave the command; the world is in need, therefore I must go. I saw no sense in waiting around for a little voice to say, "Terry, this is the Lord, I want you to go to outer Mongolia." But as a result of actually experiencing the various challenges of cross-cultural work, I am now convinced that a person really does have to sense and firmly believe God is leading in this matter. Otherwise you will burn out.

These are just a few of my impressions, and I hope that it has given you a brief idea of what God taught me during my summer in Kenya. There is no greater way to learn about missions than to experience it firsthand.

Sir Frederick Catherwood: IFES

Most years at this time my wife, Elizabeth, and I act as house parents to a conference of students from all over the world, normally from twenty to twenty-five different countries—the annual conference of the International Fellowship of Evangelical Students (IFES). This conference has been the most moving Christian experience we have ever had. At the conference, you know in your heart what you have learned in your head: that the power of God is not limited to a few favorite nations or cultures, that the church can grow under anti-Christian tyranny and corrupt military dictatorships and that there is no iron curtain which the love and power of God cannot leap. Nothing has strengthened our Christian faith more than seeing the unity of faith and of experience which crosses all barriers that keep men and women apart in this world. We sing in all our languages to the same Lord. We pray in all our languages to the same Father. We see in each other the same Holy Spirit. And we all know that the Spirit that we have in common is far stronger a bond than all the superficial differences which divide us.

When you are there with people from vastly different backgrounds, and you find at once a unity with them, you know that your faith is true and that the power of God exists and the church throughout all the world is one church. The truth of the church comes home to you.

One member of our family became a Christian because he was so impressed by the unity in evidence at the IFES conference. This is not to say that all those students are perfect saints. Sometimes we tend to put on a pedestal people that come from countries where Christians are persecuted and go back knowing they can never get a good job because they do not belong to the correct political party. But they too have to be reminded that lights are to go out at eleven o'clock. Human differences remain.

God's world is a garden with all kinds of different flowers. Those from rich countries with backpacks six feet high wonder how those from poorer countries can get by with so little. And those from poorer countries can't imagine why their rich brothers and sisters need so much.

The gospel has come to the students of the world in all kinds of ways. The flourishing Spanish movement started with a dedicated American girl, Ruth Siemens, working on her own in Barcelona. The Austrian movement, which now covers I think all the Austrian universities, started with a student team of about twenty people who went to Vienna. A Dutch girl, stayed on in Vienna till the movement was self-supporting and could flourish on its own. The influence of just two or three workers in a country can be absolutely incalculable. Their grain of wheat doesn't bear fruit just tenfold or a hundredfold. It bears fruit a thousand times. Student workers reach right into the heart of a country's culture, and God rewards their faith by helping them to bring that country's future leaders into the church.

The quality of these new student movements is really tremendous. They have a great thirst for knowledge of the faith, and they will not be put off by glib answers. They put the problem that you have avoided straight back at you again. They are going straight into the conflict between their culture and the Christian faith. They have to know what they must do and what they must not do. But God is on their side. God goes back with them.

The movement in Spain started during a dictatorship. Now Spain is a democracy and the church is ripe to evangelize. Greece and Portugal are now democracies too. A former student, a Christian, is now the president of Kenya. And there is a tremendous growth in the Chinese movements, just as mainland China is beginning to open its doors again to evangelism. But even where doors are closing in Iran, Vietnam and in some countries in Africa, the Christians that God has raised up in those countries will go on. They cannot be expelled as foreign missionaries. They are still nationals, still leaders in their old communities, still able to build God's church in their own countries.

I'm involved in a lot of things that seem important in this world—business, government, European unity—but none of the things that I have to do is anything compared to the great student work around the world. Business and governments will rise and fall, but the establishment of Christians in leadership around the world has the power of Almighty God behind it. And nothing, no laws, no international treaties, nothing, will have more influence for good in the improvement of this fallen world or in the salvation of souls for the world to come. And that is why my wife, Elizabeth, and I have dedicated our energies to this work. That is why we give our money first to this work.

We commend today this great student work to you, for your prayers, for your talents, for your money. I am a businessman. I like to see my dollar for the Lord go as far as it can. I think it goes farthest in student work because through it you are evangelizing and building the country's own future leaders, and in a few short years they will take up the work on their own. They don't suffer from culture shock. They already know the language. And as the students graduate they begin to build up their own financial support in their own countries.

In IFES we've always had more projects than we can finance, more superb volunteers than we can take on, and we rely on your generosity. This Urbana offering is the biggest single source of income for all student work overseas. And let me say that whatever complaints people may make about American culture, I have no complaints. You shouldn't deride your culture too much. There are strong Christian strands running through your culture, and you don't want to tear those up. But whatever people may say, they have no right to complain about American generosity, which is rooted in that culture. You are a great and a generous nation, and the rest of the world is grateful to you. You set a standard for the world in your generosity. I'm sure that you will always do so. And may you do so today.

Elwyn Davies: Christians in Russia

Nearly two thousand years ago the Lord Jesus said, "I will build my church and the gates of hell will not overcome it." Search as I will, I find no indication in Scripture, in history or in experience to indicate that he has changed his plans. He is still building and the gates of hell still do not overcome his church.

In May and June of 1979, I sought to fulfill a promise I had made in 1975 to return for another visit to the churches in the Soviet Union. My wife and a member of our team in the Bible Christian Union accompanied me. We took the long journey through six of the Soviet republics: three in European Russia and three along the border of China and Mongolia and then on into Siberia itself.

In all of these areas we ministered to overflowing crowds in churches in city after city. There were tens of thousands of evangelical Russian believers who gathered hungrily to hear the Word of God. I was very encouraged to find everywhere except in Siberia that there were large numbers who listened regularly to our Russian Radio Bible Institute and to other programs that are broadcast from different stations. In nearly all of these churches, some additional meetings were held exclusively for young people.

The main service normally lasted about three hours. They

would have a brief intermission and then stick me in front of 50 to 200 young people, age 18 to 25. For two solid hours these students would pelt me with questions covering all kinds of subjects, including America and China, the Jews and Scripture, questions which revealed a great hunger for the Word of God, questions which showed that after sixty-two years of Communism in the Soviet Union (which means among other things sixty-two years of totally atheistic education), there are tens if not hundreds of thousands of young people in the Soviet Union today who have turned to Jesus Christ and are not ashamed to confess him.

We estimate that for all of our meetings during May and June in six republics and in Siberia, an average of twenty per cent of every congregation was composed of young people of college age. When I told them about Urbana, I found myself in great difficulty because I was talking a language they could not understand. They did not understand a *mission* or *missionaries* or the idea of a *missionary society*. And they were appalled to think that there would be 16,000 or 17,000 young people gathered together without having to have special permission from Washington.

One thing that thrilled me was that every time, without exception, these long question-and-answer periods ended with their standing and saying, "When you get back, give the Christians of the West our love. Tell them we love them, and, as we ask them to pray for us, tell them we pray for them."

After sixty-two years of Communist domination, people continually ask, "What are the Russian believers like?" Russian believers are law-abiding people who take the laws of their country seriously. They passionately love Russia. They are also very hungry for the Word of God.

In Siberia I was amazed to see the number of children and grandchildren of the exiles of Stalin's time, people who had been sent there as punishment for their witness for Christ. I was amazed to find thousands of these people now living for Jesus Christ and leading others to a knowledge of him.

In a pastor's home I talked quietly with the head of the house about his family. He last saw his father when he was a boy of four. He saw him through the barbed wire of a forced labor camp. This quiet man, whom I watched and exalted in sharing with him in a communion service for some eleven hundred believers, showed me his father's Bible. I handled it, looked at it and asked him, "Tell me, did your father drop it in the mud? Half of the Old Testament seems to be stuck together."

And very gently, oh so gently, he said, "That's not mud, that's blood. My father's blood." That is a Russian believer today.

We read in the book of Revelation, "Then one of the elders said to me, 'Do not weep! See, the Lion of the tribe of Judah ... has triumphed. He is able to open the scroll....' Then I saw a Lamb, looking as if it had been slain" (5:5-6 NIV). The mud that some see is really the blood of the martyrs that is producing in Russia today an amazing church filled with the presence and the power of God. Young people, these are the ones who send their love and greetings to you.

Hooi Seng Tai

I come from a typical Chinese family in Malaysia. My parents are not Christians and are not very religious. I never went to Sunday school and never had any kind of religious education when I was young. When I was fifteen, however, I was invited by a friend of mine to join a youth group that met in a church about a mile from my home. There I learned about sin, the Lord Jesus Christ and the way of salvation. At one of those meetings, the counselor of the group, Mr. Amarasingham, gave me a copy of the New Testament. I read the Gospel records in the New Testament every night before I went to bed, and I attended the weekly meetings regularly.

After one year, I was convinced that Jesus is the Son of God. It was just before Christmas, and the youth group had planned to go caroling, to sing the good news of God incarnate. Then one night I realized that I had not yet committed my life to the Lord Jesus. So I knelt down in my room and asked the Lord to save me. I committed my life to him. The following Easter, I was baptized.

My parents did not object to my becoming a Christian as long as it did not interfere with my studies. I even began to take a younger sister of mine to the youth group meetings, and after attending the meetings regularly for about a year, she too became a Christian.

I became involved in the Inter-School Christian Fellowship, and I attended many training programs by the ISCF staffworker, Paul Ponnampalam. Paul was the person who taught me most about the Bible. Soon, I was reading, studying and seeking to obey the Word of God. Paul later joined the International Fellowship of Evangelical Students as a staffworker and was still encouraging me when I left Malaysia.

As I look back on my life, I can see the Lord working in my life and in the lives of others to bring me to know him. Although I could not understand it then, I know now that it was the Holy Spirit who convinced me of the truth of the Scriptures and gave me the conviction to commit my life to Christ. He opened my eyes so that I saw myself as I really was—proud, arrogant, selfish, hateful, sinful and dead—but he gave me a new life. Then he led me to have fellowship with other Christians and to know Paul and many other people through whom he has patiently taught me his way. Some of the people I have benefited from are OMF missionaries and American missionary lecturers at a theological seminary near my home town.

God is faithful, and although I may fail him, he never fails me. I know he shall always remain faithful to his Word.

Ruth E. Lichtenberger: NCFI

I met Sylvia heading toward her first-year microbiology class at University Hospital in Rio de Janeiro. We didn't have much time to talk prior to the class, but I discovered she was the daughter of second-generation English missionaries in Brazil. Sylvia was obviously more comfortable speaking Portuguese than English.

After the microbiology class, Sylvia was eager to have me meet her nursing friends. Through interpretation, I asked them why they had chosen to go into nursing school. A registered nurse in Brazil is expected to be an administrator. These student nurses were keen to be at the bedside and anxious to change the present system. They had gone into nursing to serve people, not to manage them.

Sylvia plans to complete nursing school in Brazil, requalify in England, gain experience in patient care and return to Brazil to influence the nursing profession and patient care.

Her plans are not only for the future. She is sharing her faith with her classmates. Now a group of nursing students meets for Bible study, aiming to bring their Christian faith together with their professional education. Another nurse in Brazil is translating the textbook *Spiritual Care: The Nurse's Role* into Portuguese.

Nurses Christian Fellowship International (NCFI) believes that applying biblical principles can help to raise standards of professional nursing at every level and in every culture.

What would be your answer to comments like these?

"How can I respond to a patient who has just had surgery to change his sex? He became a Christian a few months ago and now wonders if he has disobeyed God."

"I don't think I can work in the Intensive Care Unit any longer. The doctors expect us to pull the plug on the life-support machine, terminating the patient's life."

"The doctors are anti-Christian at the Psychiatric Hospital. We are forbidden to talk with the patients about Jesus."

Students like Sylvia need help in thinking through these issues from a Christian perspective. She and her friends were crying out for men and women they could relate to as examples of practicing their profession according to Christian principles.

Bible study guides, books and other written material could help them do this when older Christians aren't available.

IVP will sell thousands of dollars worth of books in the next few days and your bookshelves are already full. A vast majority of the world, however, has only a handful of books in its homes.

In English, I can offer eleven Bible study guides prepared specifically for nurses. There are none that I know of in Portuguese and very few in other languages.

The faculty at Catholic University in Quito, Ecuador, has decided to use the *Spiritual Care* textbook in the student nurses' English class.

NCFI is concerned to assist faculty to teach, to assist students to learn and to assist RNs to practice Christian principles in

nursing care. To do this we need nurses who are committed to
nursing as a calling from God to share that commitment through
their example of patient care, through the printed page and perhaps by going to another culture and sharing Christ's love in a
caring profession.

Another student nurse, Sölbjørg, left the Faroe Islands to
study nursing in Denmark. She became involved in the NCF
Bible study, learned how to assist patients in spiritual need and
how to have a Christian influence where she worked. Two
months ago, Sölbjørg returned to the Faroe Islands and began
work at her local hospital. A month later I received a letter saying
a prayer group had started, and one of the nurses was ready to
start inductive Bible study. While in Denmark Sölbjørg attended the equivalent of a Level II Bible and Life weekend. We
prayed with her for the opportunity to share what she had
learned. She also wrote, "It's easy to know how to be 'salt' and
'light' here: answer the call bell, put the patient ahead of your
coffee break, don't grumble about the other staff when their
backs are turned." She went on to say, "Many patients have their
Bibles on their bedtables so it is easy to find something to talk
about.... Our country is developing very quickly and often in a
wrong way from a Christian point of view."

NCFI is committed to training nurses to develop Fellowships
in their own countries. These Fellowships will assist nurses to
practice according to biblical principles, raising the standards
of professional nursing in their own countries, which should
have an influence on every aspect of life there.

Ada Lum: IFES

Sometimes I think I'm one of the most privileged of Jesus' missionaries. First, because I'm participating in a ministry that is
strategic for national churches—that of evangelizing and discipling students. Second, because I have the best of friends to
work with. And third, because God is always sending at the right
time just the right kind of horrible problems to keep me from
getting complacent.

One of the first set of horrible problems I found overseas was
how to work with others. In my earliest service there had been

little of the kind of apostolic teamwork one sees in Acts and the New Testament letters. At that time I was a lone staff member in Hawaii, some 2,000 miles from the nearest staff member in California. So I thought it was normal to reach students on all levels —junior high, senior high, university and nursing students. I also assumed that it was normal for one to do all the necessary secretarial work by oneself, all the church and public relations and to look after the rich Christian tourists.

Only later did it dawn on me that staffworkers in Canada and the States concentrated on either university or high-school students. Nevertheless, in God's marvelous wisdom this seemingly abnormal start in the student ministry was part of his preparation for pioneering work overseas; that is, working with local brothers and sisters on any level and being ready to do anything to help establish national evangelical student movements.

And so it was in Asia that I was re-educated. Then I began to know the practical reality of what it means for members to belong to one another in the body of Christ, what it means to exercise our mutual pastoral responsibilities as spelled out in the New Testament, and what it means to pull together in national and international work. In Asia I found that I had much more to learn from brothers and sisters than I could ever teach them. And for that I will be eternally grateful to God. If I taught them how to use their minds in Bible study, they taught me things of the Spirit, things of the heart.

Not that this has come smoothly. I began in Hong Kong mainly to fulfill a teen-age promise to God to serve him overseas. In my parochial outlook I did not know that he was raising up his student witnesses all over Asia—from Korea and Japan in the north, down to the Philippines and Indonesia in the south and westward to India and Pakistan. But my senior colleagues, traveling throughout this region, knew. Once in a while our orbits would coincide, and they would say something like this: "The new student movement in Vietnam is getting off the ground with Paul and Maida Contento. But they must take their regular furlough. (That's once in a decade.) The students want to invite you to train them for a year in Bible study and evangelism. Will you accept?"

Or: "At last we've found a few Christian students in Bangkok meeting for prayer and Bible study. They were amazed to hear that in other Asian universities Christians are doing the same thing and reaching out to non-Christians. These Thai students could be the nucleus we've been looking for so many years. I've suggested that they have a training conference next summer, and they're interested. It would be good if both of us could go."

Or: "The student movement in country X is the fastest growing in Asia, but they have been very cautious about IFES or any overseas link, even though I've assured them that we are not a Western organization. Now they're willing to try you out for three months. They especially want to learn how to prepare and publish their own Bible study materials. They want you to concentrate on the women staff, but leave the men alone. This is the opportunity we've been praying for. How about it?"

At first I wasn't keen about itinerating. I wanted to have a home and a settled ministry. And so when the boss would suggest these opportunities, I would tell him that I thought it was God's will for me to continue in the country where I was at that time. One day David Adeney, who was then my boss, said, "But that's what you said about the last three countries." Well, I'm glad that he persuaded me to see these unique opportunities. Otherwise, I would have missed out on God's expanding work in and through students in a most exciting period of Asian church history. And I would have missed the deep friendships with some of the most practical saints walking this earth today.

So rich were those years that it was hard for me to leave Asia two years ago. But I knew my time was up there. I had little more to contribute to the maturing student movements. I think it is significant that Bel Magalit's present colleague in Asia has a different kind of ministry from what mine had been. These independent student movements asked Ellie Lau (from both Hong Kong and Canada) to be their first regional missionary secretary. Ellie lives and works for a time in a needy country to find out what kind of help they want, and then she returns to inform national student movements which are ready to send out workers and support.

Now I am based in London, a most convenient location for

our intercontinental ministry. I am still basically doing the same kind of work and finding it as exhilarating as ever. It seems that every time we look up there is another request for help from students or young workers in new areas of university Christian witness.

In the nature of Western mission publicity, international staff can become highly visible. Our national brothers and sisters are less visible—but not less important. We are all important in God's world mission. He needs all of us in one way or another. In IFES we try to aim not only for teamwork, but also for team thinking and team planning. We work at complementing each other's contributions to this ministry. We try to bear each other's workload. We substitute for one another in emergencies. But we also get frustrated with one another, impatient, critical. We know we have to pray daily for one another, and sometimes admonish one another. But basically we are concerned with together fulfilling the mission God has assigned to us.

And always I need to check myself that the exhilaration in this work for our Lord Jesus does not overtake my devotion to him.

Bernie Smith

I consider this a tremendous privilege to be leading singing again at this great student missionary convention here at Urbana. And I am very happy I was invited to share a portion of my testimony.

David begins Psalm 103 with the exclamation:

Bless the LORD, O my soul;
And all that is within me, bless His holy name.
Bless the LORD, O my soul,
And forget none of His benefits.

Then David goes on to enumerate the things God has done in his life and the lives of others that bring praise to his lips.

Some time ago I was talking with a friend and I confessed to him that God is so good to me that sometimes it's almost embarassing. Let me hasten through some of the high points of my testimony, and you will see why I'm excited about the Lord.

It was at an Inter-Varsity Christian Fellowship summer camp

in northern Ontario that I became a Christian. This was at the end of my freshman year at Kent State University.

Prior to that time, as a religious non-Christian, I was struggling with the rightness or wrongness of a Christian playing for dances—as I had been doing. I had had my eye fixed on a career in show business and thought that night-club work could be the avenue to lead me into such involvement. But God had other plans. And when in my times of personal devotions I would say to God, "Lord, here's my life, take it and use it as you see fit," the thought would occur to me (and I believe it was the voice of the Lord) "Bern, your bass is standing between you and God."

This thought had plagued me for months, and though I had talked with a number of others about it their comments or counsel gave me no peace or helpful direction. So finally, while lying in my bunk one night there at Campus in the Woods, while others were drifting off to sleep, God was plaguing me with this thought: "Bern, your bass is standing between you and God." So in the quiet of my heart I said, "OK, Lord, if you don't want me in dance work, I won't play for any more dances."

Looking back I consider that at that time I became a member of the family of God, for it was then that I removed the gods of dance work and show business from my life. I made Jesus Christ LORD, first in my life.

Within the same week of my conversion to Christ, I sensed his call to the ministry. This disturbed me since I considered the ministry one of the dullest professions a person could consider. But God's call was definite, and I was afraid to disobey.

I finished Kent State University in 1958 and was invited to join the staff of Inter-Varsity Christian Fellowship to work among high-school students in Ontario, Canada. I did this for five years, then resigned to teach in a kindergarten to grade eight system in Windsor, Ontario.

After five years of teaching, I was invited and returned to Canadian IVCF staff to resume work among high-school students.

In the latter 60s Canadian Inter-Varsity was having its problems. Our general director had resigned, funds weren't coming in well, and there was a lot of concern for our future. In fact, things got so bad that a decision was reached to release three staff members as a means of lightening our financial burden. I was one of the ones chosen to be released.

This turn of events puzzled me greatly. My wife and I looked at each other and asked, "What's God trying to tell us?" Our answer did not come quickly, but before too long it occurred to me that God was saying, "I've called you into youth work, and I haven't called you out. Just continue preaching as calls come your way and I'll look after your salary."

I did continue preaching. And God looked after my salary. In my first year of free-lance itinerant ministries God increased my salary by $4,000. In fact, after just two months of free-lancing, God looked after our needs so generously that I refused to put a price tag on my ministry or even mention money unless persons asking me to speak at a given event insisted on some kind of guideline. My guideline was simply "traveling expenses and a modest day's wage for each day I'm with you." I felt strongly led of God to adopt this financial policy lest any group ever feel they could not afford to have me. And God honored it.

For example, in 1972 our second-hand car simply laid down and died. So my wife and I prayed to God that if he wished to provide us with another second-hand car, as had been done before, we'd be happy to accept it. But if he wished us to buy a new car he would have to provide sufficient money from speaking engagements and unsolicited donations to pay cash for it. Well, the second-hand car did not come, but money sufficient to buy a brand new 1972 Dodge Coronet stationwagon did, and we paid cash for it. Praise God! This was the way things went for us for the next three years until I accepted a position with the Baptist Leadership Training School teaching public speaking and drama, Bible study leadership methods, phys. ed and choir. But while I liked my new job, I missed the freedom to preach on a frequent basis.

One day my wife said to me, "Why don't you resign from BLTS and go back free-lancing? You aren't being fulfilled, are you?"

Her insight amazed me. I taught one more year, making a total of three, and resigned thinking God was calling me to take a church. And calls did come. I agreed to one, then they decided on someone else! In the meantime the other calls ceased coming, and I had no church so I assumed God was leading back into a traveling ministry. But I was a little reluctant to try free-lancing in western Canada since it is so much more sparsely populated than the East. Furthermore, I was not known in the West as a preacher but as a choir leader. Yet I reasoned that financial support was no harder for God in the West than in the East.

So for the past three and a half years we have looked to God alone to supply our needs as I took speaking engagements, song-leading assignments and whatever else the Lord provided.

Let me share a few interesting events showing how God has looked after our needs these past three years.

I was speaking one weekend for a charismatic fellowship in Ottawa. After my final presentation my host said to me, "Bernie, while you were speaking, God spoke to me. I leaned over to my wife and said, 'Bernie needs a preaching suit.' " Because his wife agreed, he handed me a personal check for $200. I'm wearing that suit right now!

If time permitted I could go on and on, telling of the many exciting ways in which God has looked after our needs. But it's not only because of financial sufficiency that I'm excited about God. In many other areas he has met our needs—in the richness of friendships, the opportunities in ministry, conversions, extremely good health and a happy marriage.

To bring my testimony up to date let me share that as of the first of the year—Lord willing—I am to begin pastoring a new community church just over seven miles west of Calgary, Alberta. This move is a very timely one as my children are ages 14, 13 and soon to be 11, and they need a father around much more than free-lancing allows.

So I say with David, "Bless the LORD, O my soul;/And all that is within me, bless His holy name!"

19
Student Messengers around the World
Chua Wee Hian

Over nineteen hundred years ago, the apostle Paul wrote these words about the situation in Ephesus: "There is a real opportunity here for great and worthwhile work, even though there are many opponents" (1 Cor. 16:9 GNB). Tonight I will speak on the opportunities for and the opposition to student work around the world. Paul's perceptive analysis applies today in the IFES family. Let me illustrate.

In the city of Torejon, Mexico, there is a group of medical students. They are eager to witness the grace of God in Jesus Christ, but they find it difficult to meet in a classroom or lecture room. So do you know where they meet for their evangelistic Bible studies? In the university morgue. There amidst hanging corpses which they dissect, the students gather with their non-Christian friends and, as a result many students turn from death and darkness to life and light. Those students use their opportunities to proclaim Jesus Christ even though the setting may be strange to some of us.

In neighboring Guatemala I remember walking to the National University with my colleague, Mardoqueo Carranza. There were only fifteen committed Christian students in that university, and they were going to launch a huge evangelistic campaign. They had the vision to rope in the local churches and students from a local evangelical seminary. Together they sought to proclaim the Lord Jesus Christ in the university for four nights. They prayed, they worked hard. And hundreds of students attended the meetings. The result—over 40 conversions and about 500 people registering for Bible correspondence courses. Now this small Christian fellowship has the delightful task of looking after 40 new converts and keeping in touch with 500 others.

But my colleague, Mardoqueo, also has a heartbreaking job. His parish includes Nicaragua and El Salvador, and his ministry has been to students whose lives have been marred by the tragedies in their countries. Some have lost loved ones. Bitterness has filled their souls. IFES staff workers seek to bind their wounds, help them to think through the difficult issues of their day, help them to relate biblical faith to the changing situation of their country. So opposition sometimes comes in the form of war or civil strife, but the opportunities are there.

Further south in Buenos Aires we have a publishing house called Ediciones Certeza. One of my colleagues, Samuel Escobar, sometimes speaks about a form of Latin American Christianity, "Coca-Cola Christianity"—not necessarily the real thing. We believe in the IFES that we need to provide tools for Bible study. So Bible commentaries and study guides are translated and written to help the church in Latin America grow, to give aids to our student groups, to evangelize, to build up their members. There are great opportunities to distribute this literature in Latin America.

But again there is opposition. This time it comes in the form of spiraling inflation. In Argentina the inflation rate is 180 per cent per annum. From a business viewpoint it would mean that we would have to close down our publishing house, but thank God for the family of IFES. InterVarsity Press in this country has come to our rescue, and they have helped the Argentinian movement of our Latin American work to publish some of the books in this country and to ship them from Downers Grove.

Let me take you now to Asia. Soon after World War 2 a great revival broke out in mainland China. Inter-Varsity groups sprang up in all the universities of that country. Then in 1949 the Communists took over China and the Inter-Varsity had to disband. Some of our workers suffered great loss. Our president, David Adeney, was in China recently. He was able to meet some of these coworkers. One of them had been in prison for over twenty years because he stood firm for the Lord Jesus Christ.

But whereas there was opposition, whereas the gospel was proscribed and restricted in terms of its propagation, there were other Chinese in Southeast Asia who, because of their liberty, were able to proclaim the gospel freely. In Taiwan, every summer hundreds of students go to evangelistic camps and nearly half the non-Christians who go to these camps are converted.

In nearby Hong Kong a group of graduates had the vision to publish a magazine called Breakthrough. This magazine is being published monthly. Some 40,000 copies are distributed and sold on the streets and bookstores of Hong Kong, not in Christian bookstores but on the secular market. And those who are interested in knowing more about their faith can phone counselors who are able to arrange face-to-face meetings with those who want to know more about the Lord Jesus Christ. Many students have been won to Jesus Christ through Breakthrough and the counseling service.

In my home country of Singapore, there are over 6,000 students in the university and the Inter-Varsity chapter has a membership of nearly a thousand students. This vast fellowship is divided into about 160 action groups. These small groups are in fact evangelizing fellowships. They use every opportunity to proclaim Jesus Christ to their contemporaries. These students agree among themselves to attend meetings regularly, to be committed to pray for one another, to work together in the service of the gospel. They even sign a covenant saying that the only excuse for not attending a meeting is when they are fatally ill or dying. This sense of discipline and commitment makes the fellowship grow and grow.

Just a few weeks ago I received an interesting document typed and written on rice paper, telling the delightful story of how Nepali Christian Fellowship had been formed. In the Hindu kingdom of Nepal it takes great courage to stand up as a Christian. As I looked at that document with all the signatures, my heart leapt up in thanksgiving to a mighty God for the courage of these friends. They could be put in prison. They have a price to pay. They are willing to stand up for Jesus Christ. Yes, there are unparalleled opportunities to proclaim the gospel. Every time we seek to present the gospel, there is Satan and his hosts challenging our advance.

Let me take you to Africa. During the dark days of Idi Amin's regime, the Christian students in Makere University continued to witness boldly to Jesus Christ. Hardly a week elapsed without a conversion, and that group is now a mighty force in Uganda.

I think too of some of the men from this country who are helping us in the IFES as staff workers. Hank Pott used to work in UCLA. He went first of all to Zambia to train a national worker. He was able to encourage a young graduate called Derek Mutungu. With others, Hank discipled Derek. Today Derek is the lone staff worker in the Zambian national movement.

Hank meanwhile has moved on to neighboring Zimbabwe/ Rhodesia where he is working himself out of his second job. He is training a local person to take over as traveling secretary. There is a fellowship where blacks and whites can work together to stress their oneness in the Lord Jesus and the power of the gospel.

Then there is Isaac Zokoué, our regional secretary in Francophone Africa, who comes from the Central African Republic. He covers wide distances. At one time he had to travel to nineteen different countries and he had only one other staff worker to assist him. In response to a call, Ann Benninghoff, an American girl, won a Fullbright scholarship to study in the Cameroun. After studying for one year in Yaounde, Cameroun, the students loved her and asked her to remain as their staff worker. Today she is working with the Camerounian movement in fellowship with the IFES.

If you want to know how to work in some of these situations, go to one of these countries, enroll as a student, identify with the Christian students, get to know them. If they love you, and I'm sure they will, you will be invited back as a staff worker.

The greatest need in IFES is the area of Europe. Some years ago I was walking through the University of Roma. I asked a friend, "How many students are there on this university campus?"

She said, "Over a hundred thousand."

Then I asked her, "Jean, how many Christian students are there on this campus who actively witness to Jesus Christ?"

"As far as I know, Wee Hian, only one."

One committed Christian student in that university! You will be glad to know that there are now six committed Christian students. What is that in a university of over 100,000?

The Brazilian movement heard about the situation in Italy. They sent a keen enthusiastic couple, Tacito and Glacy Pinto. And now they are working for the Italian movement in Genoa. They brought with them a zeal and enthusiasm which smashes Italian pessimism, and as a result they were able to get the group going and thriving in the city and university center of Genoa. So we thank God too for this sense of partnership and cooperation.

As we look at Europe there are some countries like Belgium, Greece, Portugal which still need reinforcements. The opposition in these countries does not come from political powers but from apathy—apathy which seems to cripple so much Christian witness and service. We need to pray for revival in those countries so that God's work may speed onward.

Finally, I should mention a new group of witnesses God is raising up in Europe. These are mainly African students. They have been sent by various countries to study in the Soviet Union and in Eastern Europe. I wish you could meet some of these brothers and sisters in Christ. For me they represent a tremendous missionary task force. These students will boldly proclaim Jesus Christ and distribute literature. They will go up to their Russian host and explain the gospel to them in flawless Russian. They will gather together for prayer and Bible study. They will send some of their members to Austria where we hold international conferences. There we seek to equip them and train them so that they will return to these countries to be witnesses of Jesus Christ.

Three years ago we were very excited in the IFES family. We were able to send a Pakistani couple to work in Iran. We praise God for those open doors, for that day of opportunity. But three months ago I had to withdraw this couple from Teheran. Why? Because this colleague was on the assassination list. He was a marked man.

The door seems to be closed, but there are other opportunities. Hundreds of Muslim students are studying in this country and in Europe. Could we not reach them for Jesus Christ? At the moment some of us may be tempted to hate, to discriminate against Iranian students in this country. Isn't God's call to us to love them, befriend them, to win them for Jesus Christ? Let us show the world the meaning of the cross, the love of God.

My dear brothers and sisters, there are unparalleled opportunities to establish student Christian fellowships, to proclaim Christ in the student world. There is also opposition, and that is a call for faithful prayer. Our job is not to retreat or withdraw but to press on, to move forward. Advance must be our watchword as we move into the eighties with God and with one another.

Convention Speakers

David H. Adeney is representative-at-large for Overseas Missionary Fellowship and vice president of the International Fellowship of Evangelical Students. He has also worked with China Inland Mission and Inter-Varsity Christian Fellowship—USA. He is the author of *China: Christian Students Face the Revolution.*

John W. Alexander is president of Inter-Varsity Christian Fellowship—USA and chairman of the International Fellowship of Evangelical Students. He previously served as chairman of the department of geography of the University of Wisconsin and is the author of *Managing Our Work.*

Chua Wee Hian is general secretary of the International Fellowship of Evangelical Students. In the past he has served as associate secretary of IFES in East Asia and as editor of *The Way,* a quarterly magazine for Asian students.

Elisabeth Elliot is visiting professor at Gordon-Conwell Theological Seminary and the author of several books, including *Twelve Baskets of Crumbs, Love Has a Price Tag* and *Shadow of the Almighty.* She served for eleven years as a missionary in Ecuador, where her first husband, Jim Elliot, was martyred.

Billy Graham is perhaps the best-known evangelist in the world. He has held crusades in almost every state in America as well as over fifty other countries. He is the author of several books, including *How to Be Born Again, Angels* and *World Aflame.*

Michael E. Haynes is senior minister of Twelfth Baptist Church in Roxbury, Massachusetts, and a member of the Commonwealth of Massachusetts Parole Board. He also served for five years in the Massachusetts House of Representatives.

John E. Kyle is missions director of Inter-Varsity Christian Fellowship —USA. In the past he has served in the missions program of the Presbyterian Church in America and worked in the Philippines with Wycliffe Bible Translators.

Gregorio Landero is general secretary of Accion Unida (United Action), a program of evangelism and social concern in northern Columbia, South America. He is a former pastor and church coordinator of the Evangelical Churches of the Caribbean.

Isabelo Magalit is associate general director of the East Asian office of the International Fellowship of Evangelical Students. Trained as a medical doctor, he was also the director of the first Asian student missionary conference in the Philippines (1973).

Ronald G. Mitchell is a missionary serving with the United Methodist Church in Sierra Leone. During his present furlough, he is doing degree work at New York Theological Seminary.

Gottfried Osei-Mensah is executive secretary of the Lausanne Committee for World Evangelization. He served for five years as traveling secretary for the Pan-African Fellowship of Evangelical Students before becoming pastor of Nairobi Baptist Church in Kenya.

Luis Palau is best known for his evangelistic crusades held throughout Latin America. He is the former president of Overseas Crusades and the author of several books, including *Heart after God* and *The Schemer and the Dreamer*.

Ruth Siemens serves as staffmember-at-large with Inter-Varsity Christian Fellowship—USA and directs the Overseas Counseling Service. She worked with the International Fellowship of Evangelical Students for many years in Peru, Brazil, Portugal and Spain.

John R. W. Stott is rector emeritus of All Souls Church in London and an honorary chaplain to Her Majesty the Queen of England. He travels worldwide as a speaker and has participated in five Urbana conventions. He is the author of many books, including *Basic Christianity, Baptism and Fullness, Christian Mission to the Modern World* and *Christian Counter-Culture*.

Warren W. Webster is general director of the Conservative Baptist Foreign Mission Society. He served as a missionary in West Pakistan for fifteen years and has traveled extensively on five continents.